2/12

The Making of a
Modern Kingdom

Helbling

The Making of a Modern Kingdom

Globalization and Change in Saudi Arabia

Ann T. Jordan

University of North Texas

WAVELAND
PRESS, INC.
Long Grove, Illinois

For information about this book, contact:
Waveland Press, Inc.
4180 IL Route 83, Suite 101
Long Grove, IL 60047-9580
(847) 634-0081
info@waveland.com
www.waveland.com

Photo credits: Cover © Fedor Selivanov; p. 145 © afaizal; p. 158 © afaizal

10-digit ISBN 1-57766-702-6
13-digit ISBN 978-1-57766-702-5

Printed in the United States of America

7 6 5 4 3 2 1

Contents

Preface   vii
Transliteration   ix

1 **Introducing the Kingdom**   1

2 **The Anthropological Context**   9
   Modernization   9
   Globalization   11
   Complex Adaptive Systems   18
   Orientalism   19
   Rentier State Theory   23
   The Politics of Research   25

3 **The Geography and History of Saudi Arabia**   29
   The Creation of the Land   29
   Modern Climate   33
   The Early Arabians (Paleolithic–CE 600)   34
   The Origin of Islam   37
   Battling for Control of Arabia (1500–1900)   37
   Abdul Aziz al Saud (Ibn Saud)
     and the Rise of the Third Saudi State   40
   Conclusion   49

4 **Traditional Culture of Saudi Arabia**   51
   Personal Experiences   51
   Regional Diversity   53
   The Bedu   55
   Distinguishing the Bedu and the Hadar   68
   The Hadar   70
   Conclusion   73

**5   The Process of Modernization   75
     and Continued Economic Development**
     The Rapid Rate of Change   75
     Complex Adaptive Systems and the Oil Industry   83
     The Continuing Focus on Economic Development   88
     Conclusion   94

**6   The Tertiary Care Hospital of Saudi Arabia: 97
     A Case Study of the Modernization Process at Work**
     The Creation of a Modern Medical System   97

7   Rapid Rate of Change   111
     The Bedu   112
     The Hadar   118
     Saudi Youth: Identity and Change   124
     Conclusion   126

8   Experiencing Life in the Modern Kingdom   127
     Saudi Values and Behavioral Norms   128
     Orientalism and the Western View of the Kingdom   138
     Conclusion   140

9   Saudi Arabia in the Global Spotlight   141
     Religion   141
     Dissent   149
     Women   154
     Conclusion   162

10   Essential Concepts for Reflection   163
     Goals of This Book   163
     "Modern" Reconsidered   168
     Issues and Strengths in the
       Twenty-First-Century Kingdom   168

     References   173
     Index   181

Preface

$\mathcal{T}$his book is the result of a chance occurrence. I never planned to live in the Middle East or write on Saudi Arabia; instead, I was given a unique opportunity to do so. I first came to the Kingdom as the spouse of a high-ranking US State Department Foreign Service officer in 2002. In this position, I met Saudis from a broad range of backgrounds and had opportunities to travel throughout the country. Most of the Saudis I knew best were professionals in academia, business, and medicine. Additionally, I held a Visiting Researcher position at the King Faisal Center for Research and Islamic Studies in 2002 and 2003. There I had access to research facilities and a congenial group of colleagues. I again visited the Kingdom in 2007 and 2009 with students. On these visits we were guests of the Saudi Ministry of Higher Education. Certainly, my positioning in all these contexts impacts my views in this book. It gave me access to places and stories I might never have seen or heard otherwise and probably limited my access to others.

I am an organizational anthropologist. This means I study complex organizations using the methods and theories of anthropology (Jordan 2003). My work focuses on government agencies, for-profit corporations, and nonprofit organizations. In this book I include a study I conducted of a Riyadh hospital as an organization. This book is not an ethnography in that it does not rely solely on my own fieldwork but instead depends additionally on the expertise of many scholars, Saudis and non-Saudis, who have written about the Kingdom.

In anthropology we are always looking for ways to prove to students that what we know is relevant to today's world and not just some exotic and obscure information that may be interesting but has no modern applicability. This is one reason I decided to write this book. As Saudi Arabia is a country frequently in the news but difficult for non-Saudis to comprehend, I felt it would help students to be able to understand the country from an anthropological perspective. The book is a study of culture and change that focuses on modernization and globalization. I hope that it will be used in general, introductory courses in anthropology and in ones on the Peoples and Cultures of the Middle East. It is also relevant to anthropology courses on political economy, religion, organizations, gender, and education.

I am deeply appreciative of the help I received in writing this book. Tom Curtin and Jeni Ogilvie at Waveland Press were supporters of the project from the beginning and supplied crucial advice and assistance in the editing process. They are editors extraordinaire. The review process was rewarding in that I received detailed and useful comments that helped to improve the book and I hope the reviewers will forgive that I did not always follow their advice. I thank Andrew Gardner, University of Puget Sound; Ibrahim Al Beayeyz, King Saud bin Abdulaziz University for Health Sciences; Assad Al Shamlan, Institute of Diplomatic Studies, Riyadh; and Abdullah Al Askar, King Saud University, all of whom took time to read and comment on the manuscript. Their thoughtful reviews were of great value. Additionally, I appreciate Bonnie Lovell's helpful editing of the initial manuscript. I am grateful to the King Faisal Center for Research and Islamic Studies, the Saudi Arabian Ministry of Higher Education, and the US Department of State for providing me with opportunities I would not have had otherwise. My colleagues in the Anthropology Department and the College of Public Affairs and Community Service at the University of North Texas were supportive as always and helped me secure the leave during which I wrote most of this book. I wish to thank Dennis, Mark, Peter, and Andrew for their support and love and to acknowledge Robert Jordan who did the best job possible representing the US in Saudi Arabia. Of course, I take full responsibility for the text that follows and any errors it contains.

Transliteration

*I*n general I have followed the *International Journal of Middle East Studies* (IJMES) protocol and/or the Saudi Arabian Ministry of Information spellings of Arabic words. For place names I have chosen the common English spellings or those used by the Ministry of Information. In situations where these guidelines conflict, I have made decisions based on ease of reading in English and consideration of subject matter. For instance, the Ministry prefers the city in western Arabia holy to Islam be spelled "Mekkah" rather than the IJMES spelling of "Mecca." In this instance, I have used the Ministry spelling. However, with regard to the religious movement begun by Muhammad ibn Abd al-Wahhab, the Ministry states that the use of terms Wahhabi, Wahhabis, (and by extension Wahhabism) are incorrect because Abd al-Wahhab did not found a new branch of Islam but rather was advocating a return to the true Islam. Thus, the movement should not be called by his name. The IJMES, however, suggests the usage of Wahhabism and Wahhabi and those outside the movement do not consider it to be the true Islam but instead a movement begun by Abd al-Wahhab. In this book, I follow the IJMES protocol because it more accurately reflects the modern state of Islam and because readers are likely to be familiar with the term, Wahhabi. For ease of reading in English, I have kept the diacritical marks in Arabic words to a minimum. I have used the left single quotation mark (') for the *'ayn* and the right single quotation mark (') for the *hamzah*.

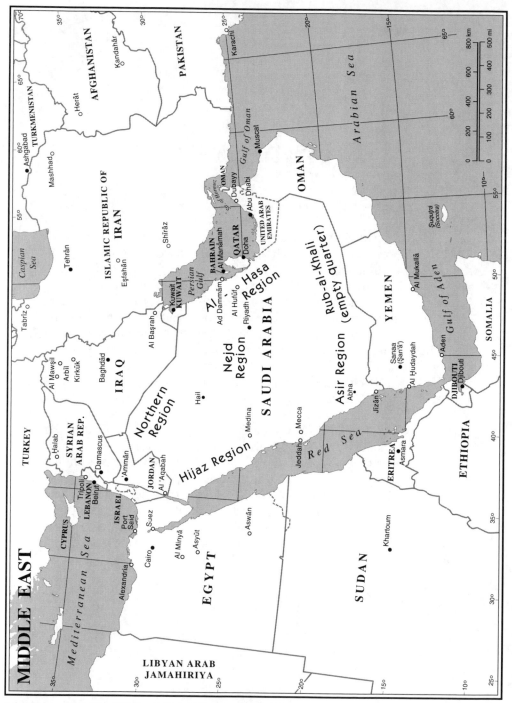

Adapted from Map. No. 4102 Rev. 3, United Nations, August 2004.

Chapter 1

Introducing the Kingdom

The complexity of Saudi state and society is usually understated and stereotyped.

—Fandy 1999:10

*W*e stepped out of the car into the heat of a late afternoon in May and walked up the steps and through the doors of the shopping mall. The marble floors gleamed; the glass storefronts shined. The three-story central lobby of the mall was alive with people. Families and groups of two or three women sauntered along talking and looking at window displays. I was with a group of ten of my students and they wandered and took in the scene. Several of my students spotted a Starbucks and began discussing whether to have a coffee. They strolled over, looked at the merchandise, and ordered lattes. While they drank these, the rest of us made our way slowly down one side of the mall peering at the window displays and discussing the merchandise. This was a high-end shopping center with many expensive shops. We saw Saks Fifth Avenue, Ferragamo, Tiffany, and Gucci. From the center foyer, we could look up and see the railings and walls for floors above us. The mall was enclosed with three stories of aboveground shops and belowground levels of parking and a few more shops. Coming from Texas, we were used to the heat and the upscale shopping center, both of which we could find in any of the larger cities in our state. It all felt right at home to my students and me. However, some unique factors caused the students to realize they were not in Texas any more.

Looking around at the shoppers, it was immediately apparent that this place was different. All the women shoppers, ourselves included, were wearing the *abaya* (a black cloak that covers the body from neck to wrist and ankle) and most wore headscarves to cover their hair. At least half of the women in the mall had their faces covered as well with the *niqab* (a piece of cloth that covers

1

the face and sometimes includes a slit that leaves the eyes exposed). About half of the men were wearing the *thobe* (a long shirt that covers to the ankle) and head coverings while the others had on Western dress. The sales staff in the shops were all male. In addition, as we strolled through the mall, we saw guards at the stair and elevator entrances to the mall's third floor and a sign posted at the stairs stating in both Arabic and English that women should uncover their faces for "security reasons" while a female security guard

Downtown Riyadh. The Kingdom building is in the foreground. Al Faisaliyah building (pyramid shape) is in the center distance.

watched all who entered there. Had the male students in our group attempted to enter the stairs to go up to this floor, they would have been turned away. The top floor of the mall is exclusively for women shoppers. No males are allowed on the floor and women must uncover their faces as they enter to assure that no males are trying to enter by dressing as women. Entering this floor, my female students discovered a different atmosphere. Women were shopping without headscarves and some without abayas. This floor was designed to give women a place to shop in privacy so that they can remove their covering and relax outside the view of men. Shoppers were sitting in small restaurants talking and eating. We passed the Supermodel Café, which was decorated with brightly colored lights and a modeling runway. The salespersons on this floor were all female rather than all male as they had been on the floors below. Where is this shopping center? My students and I are in Riyadh, the capital of the Kingdom of Saudi Arabia (KSA), on a bright afternoon with the temperature reaching 43° Celsius (110° Fahrenheit). It is 4:00 PM and the shops have just reopened for the day after being closed since noon prayers.

The shopping center is Al Mamlaka (The Kingdom), which has 161 shops and covers the lower floors of the Kingdom Center (Burj Al-Mamlaka), a high-rise building in the main business district of Riyadh. In addition to the shopping mall, the building contains a wedding hall that seats 3,000 people, offices, a Four Seasons Hotel, apartments, a restaurant, and finally, some 310 meters (1,020 feet) above the ground, a sky bridge, which is an enclosed, glass-sided walkway with a view of most of Riyadh. We finished our shopping and walked back out onto the street where we were confronted with modern buildings and a snarl of traffic as far as we could see. When completed in 2001, the Kingdom building that we just exited was the 25th tallest building in the world and won the Emporis Skyscraper Award for the world's best skyscraper design. It stands at the opposite end of Olaya Street from another skyscraper, the Al Faisaliyah building, and together they are the visual anchors of the downtown business district, giving Riyadh its signature downtown skyline.

Saudi Arabia is a relatively young state. At the beginning of the twentieth century, there was no Kingdom and no state system in the Arabian Peninsula. The Arabian Peninsula has historically been the home of *bedu* (bedouin), camel pastoralists traversing the deserts, and *hadar* (settled peoples), horticulturalists settled in the oases growing dates and wheat. Politically it was comprised of many independent entities that sometimes fought each other for control of land and material wealth and eked out a living in an environment that remains one of the harshest on earth. The Kingdom of Saudi Arabia was formally declared a nation-state in 1932 after Abul Aziz Al Saud (Ibn Saud) united a previously disparate group of peoples in the Arabian Peninsula through thirty years of conquest and diplomacy.

While Saudi Arabia may seem like a closed society to many in the rest of the world, and indeed it does not issue tourist visas, it is globally connected like other nations and experiences the impact of world events. Twenty-five percent of the population is foreign. The salesman selling me traditional Arab jewelry is likely to be from Yemen; the tailor who sews my clothes is Filipino; the traditional Saudi clothing I buy in the *suq* (market) is made in India; and the prayer rug I see the taxi driver using is made in Japan. This is the face of globalization.

Not all that appears global is new, however. Saudi Arabia is home to a diverse population with connections extending beyond its own borders and beyond the Middle East. The western region of the country, populated primarily by Sunni Muslims, is cosmopolitan, primarily because of its centuries-long, global importance in commerce as trading sites along the spice routes and in the Islamic religion as the home of Makkah and Madinah, the two holiest cities of Islam and the destination of the Hajj, the pilgrimage every Muslim hopes to make in his lifetime. The eastern region of KSA has long been global in a different sense. It is home to Saudi Arabia's large Shi'i Muslim minority population as well as to the very Western oil business. Its Shi'i population is part of a large band of Shi'a that extends through Bahrain, Lebanon, Iraq, and Iran. This region is the area of the oil fields and the home base of Aramco, the state-owned oil company, where half the workforce is likely to be foreign. Aramco first began with an all-U. S. workforce, and the American presence with Aramco still gives the cities of the eastern region of KSA an American feel, even though dress and public behavior are Saudi (Fandy 1999:10). The central region of KSA is the most conservative part of the country and the most isolated, but as the seat of the national government and the home of embassies from around the world, it is equally well connected. Thus, Saudi Arabia is not the closed society that it appears to be on first glance.

The Kingdom is also a country that has changed rapidly, and most of this change occurred in a thirty-year period from the 1970s, when oil money began to enrich the state coffers at an unprecedented pace, until the turn of the century. What changed for Saudi people and what stayed the same? Who was in control of this change and how did it come about? To move from a society with no modern infrastructure, no modern education system, no modern political system, and no modern technology to one of the most modern systems in the world in a few short decades takes more than just oil money. It takes a strategy and an implementation process. It is common knowledge that Saudi Arabia has become a world player in the oil market and that its decisions on oil production impact nation-states around the globe. It is a player on the global stage.

From a Western point of view, the Kingdom of Saudi Arabia is a land of contrasts. There is a seemingly strong contrast between the ultramodern shopping center and the traditional dress of the shoppers, between the twenty-first century quality of the traffic jam and the fact that all the drivers are male because women are not allowed to drive. How did Saudi Arabia get to be this way and what are the people really like who wear those thobes and abayas? Is this a modern country? If so, what does "modern" mean?

When I first arrived in Saudi Arabia in July 2002, I had no idea what the answers were to these questions. During that first visit, I lived in Riyadh for eleven months. I have subsequently returned to the Kingdom twice, most recently in May 2009, for a total of fourteen months spent in KSA. During that time, I have attended many functions, especially ones held by women. These included weddings, dinners, city festivals, and religious events. I walked the streets of major cities like Riyadh, Jiddah, Dammam, and Abha and of smaller cities like Al Jouf and Hofuf. I visited in homes drinking coffee and eating dates in cities and countryside alike. I traveled the desert and talked with local people. As an anthropologist, I am particularly interested in the functioning of organizations, and I conducted a study of the Tertiary Care Hospital of Saudi Arabia[1] in Riyadh where I interviewed hospital staff of varied job descriptions and nationalities. This study informed my work as a whole and led me to conduct research on the process of modernization in KSA and the role of globalization in that process. Additionally, I was fascinated by the women of Saudi, their lives and their thoughts, and so I talked with women to better understand their perspectives and their ways. During my first visit in 2002 and 2003, I was present in Saudi Arabia during a politically charged time period as I arrived less than a year after the September 11, 2001, attacks on the United States and during a particularly tense period of the Israeli–Palestinian conflict. I stayed in Saudi, as it is commonly called, through the buildup to and first stages of the war in Iraq that began in 2003. Everywhere around me, Saudis and foreigners alike were reacting passionately to these events. These reactions, as well as the importance of the media in shaping public opinion, became part of my personal experience and my anthropological analysis.

Today as I write this introduction, however, I still cannot definitively answer the questions I posed above. These questions are too complex for definitive analysis. In this book, however, I provide an anthropologist's thoughts on their answers. I turn my anthropologist's lens on this fascinating country and share with you my understanding of its people and their ways. It is my intention to provide an anthropological perspective on the activities of a nation-state that is of prime importance in today's world but is little understood, especially in the West. To do this, I will weave together three strands of information: (1) my personal reflections, (2) research conducted previously by other, mostly Saudi, anthropologists and social scientists, and (3) my own anthropological analysis of modernization, globalization, and culture change in Saudi Arabia.

My goals in writing this book are fourfold: (1) to describe a process of globalization, specifically how complex organizations (supranational institutions, transnational corporations, national governments, local businesses, and others) join into complex adaptive systems that form, change, dissolve, divide, and recombine to satisfy the goals of the various participating organizations, (2) to provide an example of an emerging economy that was never colonized and also possesses significant resources allowing it to negotiate with world powers from a position of strength, (3) to describe a society undergoing culture change over the last one hundred years and especially rapid change at the end of the twentieth century, and (4) to acquaint readers who have no experience in KSA with the country, its people, and their ways of life through a more complex and nuanced understanding than the understanding that is available through the popular press. Most anthropological studies of emerging economies are of countries with little economic wealth and few bargaining chips with which to negotiate with the global power brokers. Thus, this study of an economy emerging with the political and economic advantage of oil and with involvement in little researched processes of globalization is a valuable contribution to the anthropological literature.

Here is my plan for achieving this: chapter 2 situates this book in anthropological theory. It provides the definitions for key terms, concepts, and theories used throughout the book. For instance, it introduces modernization theory and the notion of alternative modernities and provides the definition of modernization that I will use in this book. Remember I asked the question, What does "modern" mean? "Modern" in KSA does not look like modern in the United States. KSA (through state action) is "modern" in a uniquely Saudi and Islamic way, and so chapter 2 explains the concept of modern that I use in the remainder of the book. This chapter also includes a brief review of the anthropological literature on globalization, specifically including descriptions of theories of globalization and a discussion of questions about globalization that these theories generate, all of which I will put in the context of this Saudi example. I caution that this is only a brief introduction to the quickly growing and already voluminous anthropological literature on globalization and is provided for the purpose of placing this book in the context of that literature; it is not a thorough study of that literature. In addition, this chapter will introduce Edward Said's (1978) concept of Orientalism, as this concept was brought up to me repeatedly by Saudis and is important for any student of Middle East culture to understand. In my discussion, I will explain why my earlier description of the trip to the Kingdom Mall is an example of Orientalism.

Chapter 3 introduces the reader to the geography and history of the Arabian Peninsula, which is important to the understanding of the modern country of KSA. The Arabian Peninsula, home of important early civilizations and birthplace of an important early system of writing and significant scientific concepts as well as fine purebred horses and camels, was of vital significance to the world long before the discovery of oil. It includes a history of how the current state of KSA originated. Chapter 4 presents information on the early twentieth-century ways of life of Saudis, including descriptions of the culture of bedu pastoralists and the hadar oasis-dwelling agriculturalists.

Chapter 5 explains the steps in the modernization process the government has used to bring change to the Kingdom and provides examples of this process from the oil industry and the education system. It also looks at KSA's recent economic goals. This is followed in chapter 6 by a case study of the Tertiary Care Hospital of Saudi Arabia in Riyadh and an explanation of how this hospital exemplifies the change process. Chapter 7 examines research that describes how the culture has changed throughout the Kingdom, especially for bedu pastoralists and hadar oasis-dwelling agriculturalists whose culture was first introduced to you in chapter 4. It also touches on issues of identity for a new generation of Saudis.

Chapter 8 presents a picture of modern daily life in the Kingdom as I saw it during my stays there. What are the sounds and sights of life in the Kingdom? What is its pulse? How does an outsider experience it? I also emphasize the norms of Saudi culture that I consider as key to understanding Saudi today. Subsequently, chapter 9 turns to crucial issues for understanding the Kingdom today and covers two topics about which I find outsiders to be quite curious: women's roles, and political resistance and terrorism. Further, this chapter links Saudi Arabia to the global political and economic times with respect to oil, current events, and information access. Chapter 10 highlights the important points of the book. It summarizes the information presented in the previous chapters for easy recall and reflection.

As a Westerner who first entered the Kingdom of Saudi Arabia less than a decade ago, I bring my outsider and anthropological perspectives to understanding this most interesting of countries. The journey to comprehension has led me to appreciate the stark beauty of the landscape and the exuberant hospitality of its inhabitants. In this book, I hope to give the reader a look inside Saudi Arabia, at least as this anthropologist was able to discern it. Come with me on this journey into the Kingdom and learn for yourself.

Note

[1]Tertiary Care Hospital of Saudi Arabia is a pseudonym.

Chapter 2

The Anthropological Context

$\mathcal{W}$e are all part of a tangled web of action on the world stage that includes politics, economics, religion, and all manner of other cultural and societal forces. Anthropology plays an important role in the study of these transnational forces. Edelman and Haugerud suggest that "anthropologists would be well placed to explore how markets and the corporations and state and supra-national institutions that influence and administer them actually work" (2005b:18). My book contributes to this line of research. In this chapter I want to introduce the anthropological concepts and theories relevant to the tale I am about to tell. Below I discuss the concepts of modernization, globalization, complex adaptive systems, Orientalism, and rentier states.

Modernization

Explaining Modernization Theory

Modernization is a word of many meanings. More popularly, it means "current," and indeed, when we speak of the modern, we mean something "up-to-date." In social science, the word also refers to a theory of development that has been popular for over half a century. This traditional modernization theory is discredited in anthropology today, although it is still the mantra of many US politicians and makes up many of the assumptions of currently popular neoliberal political and economic philosophy. *Modernization theory* burst on the scene in the mid-twentieth century as a way to move all human societies to the economic levels of the Western societies. Accordingly, all societies were expected to go through the steps to modernization that the Western

9

countries experienced, resulting in a world of Western-style democracies with market economies, urbanization, widespread affluence, high mass consumption, and service-sector expansion (Lewellen 2002a:52; Rostow 1960). These characteristics are typical of Western societies and reflect Western values and this process reflects Western hegemony, which means an attempt to make the rest of the world to be like the West as well as the acquiescence by non-Western societies in accepting these values. In 1949, President Harry Truman used the term "underdeveloped" to describe some two billion people living in non-Western societies. The name stuck and was used in describing those to whom modernization theory was to be applied. By branding them "underdeveloped," as Esteva (1992) explains, they lost identity on their own terms, with all the diversity and richness of culture that two billion people reflect; in Western eyes, they became a homogeneous minority identified only by their lack of fit into the Western mold. It did not occur to the proponents of modernization theory that not all societies wanted to be like the West.

The Success and Failure of Modernization Practices

The statistics show us that modernization theory and the development process used to promote it were not the success many had hoped for in improving health, economic stability, and human welfare worldwide. There was definitely some success, however. Between 1960 and the late 1990s, the world GNP increased from $1.3 trillion to $30 trillion, and life expectancy in poor countries rose by 17 years. However, despite all the effort, in the late 1990s, 840 million people worldwide were undernourished and 1.3 billion lived on less than $1 a day. The wealthiest 200 individuals in the world had a combined income greater than the combined income of 41 percent of the world's population, and the nations with emerging economies were sending more money back to the West in debt repayment than they were receiving in loans and investments (Edelman and Haugerud 2005b:9).

Many anthropologists have documented the inadequacy of the modernist narratives (Escobar 1991). James Ferguson (1999, 2002), for example, describes the economic adversity of mineworkers in the Zambian Copperbelt. Instead of an improved life as a result of "modernization," the Zambians in Ferguson's study were worse off than their parents, with shorter life spans, smaller incomes, and less education. Other studies demonstrate how and why societies rejected the Western path to modernization. Manduhai Buyandelgeriyn (2008) shows us that cultural values and historical relationships often bring individuals to desire non-Western paths. In his review of ethnographic works on the former Soviet Union, he shows how former Soviets do not necessarily want a Western capitalist system. He singles out Humphrey's (2002) research, which explains that trading goods in the market was, under Soviet socialism, considered an immoral activity because one was making profit without labor. Consequently, for individuals in the former Soviet Union, making one's livelihood through trade could cause feelings of shame and guilt.

Trade, of course, is a valued part of the Western modern world; rejecting Western-style trade indicates a desire for a different kind of modernization.

Anthropological work, along with common sense, suggests that, when looking at the modern world, modernization should be defined more broadly than in terms of Western presumptions. People want to be modern, or current, in their own culturally appropriate way. Indeed, there are multiple paths to modernization, and societies see multiple modernities as their end goal. Ferguson describes this as:

> The realization that global modernity is characterized not by a simple, Eurocentric uniformity but by coexisting and complex sociocultural alternatives (Appadurai 1996), and that the successful negotiation of it may hinge less on mastering a unitary set of "modern" social and cultural forms than on managing to negotiate a dense bush of contemporary variants in the art and struggle of living. (2002:148)

Defining Modernization

Modernization is both a process and a goal. As I define it, *modernization as a process* is that process by which a nation, a people, an organization, or a village works to develop the technology and knowledge necessary to interact with any players on the world stage, while *modernization as a goal* is achieving a level of interaction on the world stage deemed sufficient by those pursuing it. In this book, I will explore one of those "contemporary variants" of modernity that Ferguson describes, because for Saudis, modernization does not include all facets of Western modernization. This case is especially useful for anthropology because most anthropological case studies of modernization are of emerging economies with few economic resources and little political power where the supranational organizations and Western superpowers seem to control the discourse. KSA, with its substantial economic resources based in oil and its resulting world political clout, is different. While no nation in today's interconnected world completely controls its own destiny, KSA is in a better position to shape its future than most emerging economies. Thus, this book provides a different tale of modernization than most told by anthropologists.

Globalization

At home in Texas, if I leave my office and walk to the edge of campus, I arrive at a shopping area catering to college students. I pass a store selling musical instruments from all over the world where I can buy a box guitar from India, a trumpet from Tibet, or castanets from Mexico. In the next block, I enter an Italian restaurant specializing in pasta but where I can also order an Arabic-style hookah to smoke. The restaurant is owned by neither Italians nor Arabs, but instead by Iranians. Recently, one of my favorite Mexican restaurants was sold by its Mexican owners to a family who is ethnically

Chinese, although it continues to serve Mexican food. Retailers in my town depend heavily on imported products to keep their costs down. Walmart, the largest retailer in the world, receives 10 percent of US imports from China (Sernau 2009:51). It is common to hear students speaking in four or five different languages, and many public signs in my town are written in both English and Spanish or in Spanish only. My town is no different from others in the United States. This is the globalized world with which we are all familiar. We are experiencing the worldwide movement of goods and people in our own lives, either as we encounter them in our hometowns or as we ourselves move abroad for work, study, or play. This movement is a characteristic of what we have termed *globalization*. Just where did the term come from and what does it mean?

Defining Globalization

In the 1970s American Express first used the term "globalization" in an effective advertising campaign about the worldwide acceptance of its credit cards (Harvey 2000:12–13). Since that beginning, "globalization" has become a household word, and in the twenty-first century it is a buzzword in academia as well as in the world at large. Knauft describes globalization as a "megatrope" and Tsing considers it "multireferential: part corporate hype and capitalist regulatory agenda, part cultural excitement, part social commentary and protest" (Knauft 2002:34; Tsing 2000:332; Edelman and Haugerud 2005b:21–22).

In anthropology alone, the definitions of globalization are legion. Abram states that it can and has been used to refer to:

- the spread of certain cultural forms,
- the concentration of capitalist power in the hands of a few, in particular transnational corporations whose activities escape the control of states,
- the increasing speed of transport between distant places . . . ,
- the growing accessibility of telecommunications across the globe, albeit unevenly,
- increasing colonial-style relations between certain capitalist forms and many countries, nations and states. (Abram 2003:138–139)

Given all these uses, Abram himself focuses on globalization as "social relations built up through translocal networks" (2003:138–39).

Inda and Rosaldo define globalization as:

> referring to those spatial-temporal processes, operating on a global scale that rapidly cut across national boundaries, drawing more and more of the world into webs of interconnection, integrating and stretching cultures and communities across space and time, and compressing our spatial and temporal horizons. It points to a world in motion, to an interconnected world, to a shrinking world. (2002a:9)

Lewellen prefers the following definition:

> Contemporary globalization is the increasing flow of trade, finance, culture, ideas and people brought about by the sophisticated technology of communications and travel and by the worldwide spread of neoliberal capitalism, and it is the local and regional adaptations to and resistances against these flows. (2002a:7)

In anthropology, globalization is used as both a descriptive term, describing how the world is connected, and a grand theory or theories explaining the processes that have led to this world connection and predicting where these connections will lead the citizens of this planet. Theories about world culture change and world culture connection have been a staple in anthropology since the beginnings of the discipline. Morgan and Tylor's theories of evolution, the earliest theories in the new discipline of anthropology in the late nineteenth century, were of this type. In anthropology the antecedents of globalization theory are found in modernization theory, world system theory, dependency theory, development theory, cultural evolution, and diffusion (Eriksen 2003; Lewellen 2002a; Edelman and Haugerud 2005a). Today, globalization is a catchall term that covers several important theories and/or discussions in anthropology about world culture change and connection. (See Appadurai 1996, 2001; Comaroff and Comaroff 2001; Hannerz 2002; Tsing 2000; and Friedman 2003 for further discussions of anthropology and globalization.)

Of all the works on globalization in anthropology, one individual's ideas seem to be the most discussed as an example of anthropological work on globalization. These are the ideas of Arjun Appadurai, and I will introduce them briefly here. Appadurai proposes that the modern global world is indeed different from what we have known in the past. It has long been an interactive system, but today, those interactions are as different from the past as to be of a whole new order and intensity (1996:27). The world cultural economy can no longer be explained by center-periphery models, which say that change begins in central places, like the United States, and then moves out from there to impact other geographic locations on the periphery, like Mexico or Ghana. Instead, Appadurai sees powerful economies like the United States as nodes of a "complex transactional construction of imaginary landscapes" (Appadurai 1996:31). We are confronting global cultural flows that Appadurai calls ethnoscapes, mediascapes, technoscapes, financescapes, and ideoscapes. These "scapes" are fluid and thus the reason they are frequently referred to as "flows"; they are streams of "cultural material," that is to say, people, information, technology, finance, and ideology, that move around the world. These flows are also disjunctive; they are disconnected from one another but relate to each other in multiple ways that are context specific and difficult to predict. The dynamics of global cultural systems are driven by the relationships among these flows.

Globalization can mean all of these things and more. I use it to refer to connections, to all those ways in which the world is so closely connected today, including the flows of trade, finance, culture, ideas, and people that Lewellen (2002a) and Appadurai (1996) mention. All of this is made possible by modern technology, also mentioned by Lewellen, which has caused the compression of time and space that Inda and Rosaldo discuss. The impact of this includes the Internet, satellite television, air travel, and other technologies that make possible everything from split-second, transnational, financial transactions among corporations to remote medical diagnosis for rural hospitals to the global spread of hip-hop music. Consequently, *globalization* is herein defined as the flows of trade, finance, culture, ideas, and people made possible by modern technology and the accompanying compression of time and space.

Explaining Neoliberal Capitalism and the Role of Supranational Organizations

Important to this discourse on globalization is another popular term: *neoliberal capitalism*. The worldwide spread of neoliberal capitalism is much discussed, debated, and either praised or lamented in academic circles. In anthropology, the most frequently used definition of neoliberalism comes from David Harvey (2005) who suggested neoliberalism is a "hegemonic project" with a stable package of characteristics (Hoffman, DeHart, and Collier 2006:9). Hoffman, DeHart and Collier (2006) suggest that understanding neoliberalism is complex in that particular elements of what is typically seen as neoliberalism diffuse and take shape differently in various societies around the world. Thus, neoliberalism does not always look like the stable package of characteristics Harvey suggested. In Guatemala, for example, indigenous activists invoked neoliberal values of efficiency, transparency, and accountability in order to criticize the state for its "neoliberal" policies.

Neoliberal capitalism herein refers to the presumption that allowing world trade to be regulated by a free market, free of government regulation, is the best strategy for global economic success and health. It supports the free circulation of goods, currencies, and labor across national and regional borders. Thus, the market, rather than the nation-state, should have dominance in resolving economic problems (Lewellen 2002a:17; Edelman and Haugerud 2005b:7; Tsing 2002). The role of neoliberal capitalism is important in studying globalization because many of the actions of those supranational organizations influencing the world markets are based on policies and laws grounded in neoliberal capitalist views. The worldwide recession of 2008 exemplifies the interconnectedness of our financial systems. There are international regulatory and finance organizations that monitor a variety of international activities from tariffs on goods and loans to nation-state governments to complex financial transactions by transnational banks.

Much of this international regulatory apparatus was developed in 1944 at a meeting of the Western allies at Bretton Woods resort in New Hampshire. In the aftermath of World War II, the allies were concerned about the global economy and also feared the future formation of military-economic blocs like the Nazi-controlled Europe they had just survived. Thus, they created supranational organizations to regulate world trade and the global economy. They created the International Monetary Fund (IMF) to establish exchange rates between world currencies and lend money to weak economies in danger of collapse, the World Bank to loan money for development projects intended to aid in the modernization of developing countries, and the General Agreement on Trade and Tariffs accords (GATT) to encourage the reduction of tariffs and promotion of free trade. GATT was replaced in 1994 by the World Trade Organization (WTO), which monitors world trade. Under the Bretton Woods Agreement, nation-states had powers to control movements of capital. Later, in the 1970s, the power of the nation-states was reduced as part of the developments that led to ascendancy of the current free market argument. The IMF, the World Bank, the WTO, and other supranational organizations, like the United Nations, play significant roles in world finance today, and they are one reason the modern world is so financially connected (Sernau 2009:63; Edelman and Haugerud 2005b:6). Saudi Arabia is part of this financially connected world; it recently joined the WTO and hopes to diversify its role in international trade. Just how the norms and policies of neoliberalism take shape in Saudi Arabia and whether they do so in a unique configuration as Hoffman and her colleagues have found in other locales is an interesting topic of study.

Questions in the Anthropological Debate on Globalization

Appadurai's work described earlier contributes to a series of ongoing debates in anthropology regarding globalization, some of which are relevant to this study of Saudi Arabia. I phrase these questions below and then provide for each the position that I take in this book.

1. Is globalization a new phenomenon? Appadurai seems to be suggesting to us that, while the world has long been connected through warfare and religions of conversion and there have been sustained cultural transactions primarily of commodities and travelers and explorers, the forces of connection for the last century have been of sufficiently greater order and intensity as to represent a new kind of interactive system. Thus, he considers globalization to be new in the twentieth century.

The position I take in this book is that while modern connectedness is, as Appadurai suggests, of a higher level of intensity, it does not seem to be so different from the processes that have been active in the world for centuries. If we characterize globalization as different, then we tend to ignore the lessons and the understanding a study of history can bring. David Graeber (2002:1226), for example, suggests that if we look at migration rates over the last 500 years, we see that migration rates today are down from 100, 200, and 300 years ago, rather than being higher. The history of global connectedness reaches back to the migrations of early humans. However, the process of modernization described in this book could not have occurred before the current phenomenon we call globalization. In order to succeed, the Saudi modernization process required that extreme connectedness that I defined as globalization.

2. Is the nation-state significant in today's world? Given the importance of supranational organizations like the United Nations and the WTO and the powerful global cultural systems created by the movements of people, technology, capital, ideology, and media across nation-states, Appadurai and others have suggested that the nation-state is under siege (see Huntington 1996; John Comaroff 1996, for example). Appadurai has stated that "the nation-state, as a complex modern political form, is on its last legs" (1996:19). Much of the world is deterritorialized as people migrate from their home states and establish communities in other parts of the world and as supranational organizations make rules that are supposed to supersede the authority of the nation-states. In this scenario, it does appear that the nation-state has lost its status as the major player in the world political economy.

Recent work, however, purports that the nation-state has maintained importance. David Graeber (2002:1225), for example, points out that the nation-state system with its regulated borders is a recent development in human history and that rather than replacing it, institutions like the WTO are premised on it. Terrance Halliday and Bruce Carruthers (2007) describe how supraorganizations like the World Bank, IMF, and United Nations are building an international banking structure through law. Using the example of China, they demonstrate the limited leverage these international institutions have in impacting the laws of those states with a "large transitional economy with geopolitical significance" (Halliday and Carruthers 2007:642).

Aihwa Ong (2006:75–96) cites Evans (1997) and Ruggie (1998) in support of the assertion that the question now is not whether states have retained power but rather what strategies are these, still powerful, states employing in the age of neoliberal economic and political globalization. She describes how some nation-states with emerging economies have developed strategies for interacting with global regulatory entities that both strengthen and weaken the state. For example, states in Southeast Asia like China, Malaysia, and Taiwan have used a strategy Ong calls "graduated sovereignty" in which they create special zones governed by rules amenable to international regulatory bodies (and thus to multinational corporations) in order to cash in on global enterprise. She further uses the concept of "graduated citizenship" to describe situations in states like Malaysia and Indonesia where citizens and foreigners alike experience differing levels of special treatment depending on their value in the global economy. For example, highly skilled and professional foreigners who are important to the success of the state's global economic aspirations may be especially nurtured by the government while other groups of foreign workers, female domestics for example, may find their rights curtailed.

Even though these supranational organizations have been given substantial power, if we ignore the role of the nation-state, we will misunderstand the globalization processes currently at play. After all, the Bretton Woods Agreement, which created several of these supranational organizations, was created by nation-states. Powerful nation-states like China and likewise Saudi Arabia continue to shape their own destinies while interacting with the supranational organizations in ways that impact all parties. The efforts of the Saudi Arabian government to modernize the country impact multinational organizations and global finance. Examples of this are: (1) along with the other nations of the Organization of Petroleum Exporting Countries (OPEC), Saudi Arabia's participation in and manipulation of the oil market impacts energy prices and consumption worldwide with repercussions throughout the world political economy; (2) KSA government immigration and modernization policies draw workers to the Kingdom, impacting global movements of people; and (3) as a result of its importance as the location of the two holiest mosques in Islam and its state-sanctioned support of Islam as taught by Muhammad ibn Abd al-Wahhab, it has played a significant role in the worldwide spread of religious ideology. Saudi Arabia is also an example of a nation using strategies like Ong's graduated sovereignty to improve its attractiveness to international business enterprise. It is creating a series of special zones in new economic cities, like the King Abdullah Economic City, which it is currently building. These and other examples of the continued importance of the nation-state, using KSA as the example, will be discussed in more detail later in the book.

   3. Is the core-periphery model of global development still relevant? Appadurai (1996:31) and others suggest that this model, which states that economic development moves out from core developed countries to the less-developed periphery of undeveloped and underdeveloped ones, no longer describes the world situation. Appadurai suggests that the United States is no longer a center from which development radiates; it is instead only a node of a complex transnational construction.

   Perhaps the core-periphery model has become more complex as world cities become nodes in the geographic dispersal of economic activities. Tokyo, Singapore, and New York City, for example, all play important roles in the global economic network (Sassen 2002). The core locations are no longer always in the West. Saudi Arabia, for example, may be considered periphery in terms of global political power but is core in terms of energy distribution and is important in many of the complex systems at play in the global world. The interplay of these systems is valuable to understand and studying those of which KSA is a part makes up one of the subjects of this book.

   4. Is the "construct culture" no longer viable? Appadurai and others have rejected the traditional anthropological notion of *culture* defined as the bounded, localized characteristics of a society, that "complex whole" of Edward B. Tylor's 1871 definition. Appadurai sees deterritorialism, the migration of people from their home states to establish communities in other parts of the world, as a significant force in the modern world, and thus culture, if the construct is to survive at all, must be decoupled from locality. People move; ideas move; pairs of blue jeans move from one locality to another while any single locality plays host to people of multiple ethnicities and various ideological beliefs who wear clothing made by or styles borrowed from yet other localities and ethnic trends. Anthropologists now study many subjects that are not geographically bounded—for example transnational corporations, virtual communities, and commodity chains.

Culture plays a role in this book, however. The state—the government of Saudi Arabia—has made a conscious effort to unite the disparate ethnic groups who have traditionally inhabited the Arabian Peninsula through a rhetoric of nation-building in which ethnic differences are celebrated in state-sanctioned festivals, dances, and theme parks at the same time that similarities are encouraged through standardized dress, religion, and values in order to impose a national cultural unity on the regional ethnic diversity. Appadurai (1996:39) calls this process "heritage politics," and similar efforts at national unification have occurred in nation-states around the world. While I think culture as a construct still plays a central role in the anthropological toolkit, I agree that it must be decoupled from locality and that the notion of a bounded culture with a list of culture traits does not and never did represent real human societies. Anthropologists have not supported this definition of culture in decades. I support Michael Fischer's (2007) plea for keeping culture as a tool of inquiry as it is a valuable way to discuss the multilayered discourse of modern difference that the flows Appadurai describes entail. In this work, I will invoke Saudi culture as a state-initiated unifying discourse and a social fabric that the Saudis themselves describe.

5. Are Appadurai's "flows" a useful construct for discussing globalization? Appadurai's work is used as a basis for studying globalization by some (Inda and Rosaldo 2002a) and is challenged by others (Heyman and Campbell 2009).

In this book, Appadurai's work is seen as useful; however, I see the process of globalization that I will describe as more carefully reflected by a model of complex adaptive systems in which organizations connect and intertwine in complicated patterns.

Complex Adaptive Systems

The modernization and change I describe in this book was possible only because of the ability of one complex organization, the Saudi government, to partner with multiple other complex organizations, including transnational businesses, other nation-state governments, and supranational regulatory agencies, to make this transformation occur. I use the construct of complex adaptive systems to explain these connections. Those partnerships are complex and numerous and form complex adaptive systems. The perspective presented in this book is that complex adaptive systems are a key ingredient of globalization.

A complex adaptive system is "a collection of agents that are involved in a process of coadaptation that can result in the formation of ordered networks of agents from disordered collections" (Falvo 2000:641—he references Holland, 1993; Kauffman 1993). Complex organizations, including nation-state governments, transnational businesses, and supranational regulatory bodies, are important, not just for their economic might and consequent political power, but also for the ways in which they couple, intertwine, divide, and recombine through partnerships, contracts, treaties, joint ventures, and other intraorganizational arrangements. These organizations form complex adaptive systems in which not only the individual organization adapts to its environment but the network formed by two or more of these organizations also adapts to the environment. In so doing, that network combines with more organizations and creates more networks so that what we experience is *a web of interconnected organizations all acting in their own interest but achieving their self-interest through partnerships with other organizations and other networks and through adaptations that appear beneficial to all network partners.* In this book I will attempt to show how this works by way of an empirical example: the process of modernization in the Kingdom of Saudi Arabia.

Orientalism

Said's Classic Work

Edward Said's *Orientalism* (1978) is a classic, much-cited work of the late twentieth century that brought home to anthropologists, other social scientists, and literary critics, among others, the ethnocentric and essentializing nature of much of what has passed as scholarship about the Arab and Muslim world. Drawing inspiration from the work of Michel Foucault (1972), Said demonstrates how the words *Orient* and *Oriental* were already fixed in the Western imagination. These terms, Said tells us, were coined by Westerners (for Said, this means primarily the English, French, and US Americans) as a way to describe a whole range of Arab and Muslim peoples, societies, and cultures with one oversimplified, stereotyping description. Further, that description depicted the way Westerners perceived this "other," the Orientals.

Said showed us how Orientalism is therefore more about the West than about the populations it described. It reflected Western perceptions and opinions that often had no basis in fact and little or no rigorous scholarly grounding. When seen through Western eyes, the world of the Arabs and Muslims looked exotic, different, not at all like the West. To Western eyes, their own Western world looked normal, the correct way to do things; thus, the Arab way must be the wrong way to do things. In this line of thought, Arabs needed to be more like the West; they needed to change. Furthermore, Arabs and Muslims were seen as inadequate and not able to speak for themselves, so others (Westerners) must do it for them. Said documents this thesis with numerous examples from political, literary, and scientific speeches and publications.

This misrepresentation of the Arab and Muslim world built up over centuries so that by the 1970s, when Said wrote his famous work, there was such a structure of Orientalism established in Western scholarship that any new works were built on earlier works, all of which created a closed system of scholarship built up around ethnocentric, Western ideas. Orientalism has *textuality*, meaning that texts use other texts as their authorization. The modern discourse of Orientalism, Said tells us, is a discourse of power rooted in colonialism. It was a discourse that allowed the West to legitimate its domination of not only parts of Arabia but also the larger Asian continent. The discourse was about wielding power over the "other"; it was about the West defining the terms by which the "Orient," a real place, was viewed. This, Said explains, tells us more about the West than it does about the Arab world. And it is a way that Westerners have defined themselves, in contrast to the "other." There was a power inequality between Western scholars and the non-Western populations they studied.

Said's argument has had a substantial impact in the scholarly world and has been extended to encompass Western scholarship about a host of less-powerful populations in the emerging economies around the world. Of course, the use of "the West" is another essentialism or stereotype. The West is as varied in geography, history, and society as the Orient. Anthropologists are aware that the tendency to stereotype others is present in all human societies. Said's research showed us that when there is a power difference, however, the tendency has long-ranging implications.

The Question of Area Studies

Said's (1978) work has prompted a rethinking of the academic division of scholarship into subject areas based on geography; these are known as "area studies." Universities and research institutions commonly had departments divided by geographical area of the world, so there was a Middle Eastern Studies Department, an African Studies Department, and so on. To follow Said's logic, this feeds the phenomenon of Orientalism, whether with regard to Arabs or Africans or Latinos. It singles out large, diverse peoples based on geography and lumps them together, encouraging the tendency to depict all the peoples within the geographic boundaries by the same, simplistic descriptors and to define them as so significantly different from the dominant West, as to need a special department for studying their ways.

In the aftermath of Said's (1978) devastating critique, Appadurai has suggested that area studies programs are a double-edged sword (1996:17). But area studies departments have allowed marginalized peoples and points of view to find voice in an academy that, for most of the twentieth century, focused almost exclusively on the male, Western canon. Thus said, area studies do anchor scholarly research to geographic places and makes difficult the study of the kinds of flows across geographies that Appadurai suggests in his work. By focusing on a particular locality, one misses the opportunity to focus on a flow across localities or to see that the geographic boundaries of these various area study arenas are false boundaries, created again by the West. Erasing the boundaries for study would provide a new and fruitful way of thinking. While the case study described in this book is of a Middle Eastern nation-state, the intention is to look at complex adaptive systems and show how that nation-state is linked to organizational systems throughout the world. There are two units of study in this book. One is the nation-state of Saudi Arabia; the other is the transnational complex adaptive systems of which the nation-state is a part.

Orientalism in Anthropology

Lila Abu-Lughod (1989) has provided a critique of anthropological work from the perspective of Said's (1978) thesis. According to Said, anthropologists working in the Arab world are Orientalists by definition because they teach, write, or conduct research on the Orient. I will review a few of Abu-Lughod's points here to show how she suggests anthropology reflects its Western context. Looking at anthropological work on the Middle East through Said's lens, Abu-Lughod suggested that it fell largely into three subject areas: segmentation, the harem, and Islam. Segmentation refers to *segmentary lineage,* a particular type of kinship and political system found among Middle Eastern pastoral nomads. For Saudi Arabia, the work of William Lancaster (1997) on the Rwala Bedouins is an example. The amount of the anthropological work on tribalism and the segmentary lineage theory in the Middle East is disproportionate to the 1 percent of the Middle Eastern population who actually live this transhumant, or pastoral, nomadic life.

Abu-Lughod notes that male anthropologists have conducted most of the research on segmentation and suggests that this overrepresentation of segmentation studies in anthropology is due to the association of men with politics in Western societies. Male anthropologists are pursuing a masculine discourse not only on politics but on violence as well. In Saudi Arabia, understanding segmentary lineage is important to understanding kinship and social relations. As I understand her, Abu-Lughod is not suggesting that lineage systems are unimportant in areas like KSA where they have significant impact, but instead she is suggesting that when considering the Middle East as a whole, the large number of segmentation studies is disproportionate to the importance of the topic.

The second subject area Abu-Lughod discusses is "the *harem,*" a provocative reference to studies of women. Here, the anthropologists doing the work are primarily women and the work fits into the larger category of feminist anthropology. She suggests that the number of works that satisfy the Western interest in seeing "behind the veil" give in to a colonial discourse. They feed the Western desire to view the exotic "other." The third subject area is *Islam*, and Abu-Lughod agrees with Asad (1986) about the charged

American students and Saudi children in Riyadh. (Anna Batta)

nature of this topic and that "how Western anthropologists begin to position themselves in relation to Muslim Arabs" will be important to the direction this research will turn in the future. Abu-Lughod is helping us understand how anthropological studies reflect the cultural context of the anthropologists who conduct them (1989:80–98). This is an insight developed from the work of Said (1978) and others.

Orientalism and the Trip to the Kingdom Mall

Let us return to the Kingdom Mall where I took you at the beginning of this book. I used that example in order to give you a description of Saudi life that is at once both familiar to a Western reader and unfamiliar. The descriptions of abayas and thobes and of the women-only floor in the mall were all attempts to draw you into an exotic landscape; this would be Orientalism in Said's (1978) view. On the other hand, the descriptions of the stores found all over the West and the standard mall behavior of buying a coffee and browsing the shops was intended to demythologize the subject matter and to place Saudis in a context familiar to big-city mall-goers worldwide. In this book, I hope to show Saudi Arabia in its complexity and its humanity.

Rentier State Theory

One more idea needs to be explained in this chapter. A theoretical approach that appears frequently in writings about KSA and other oil rich Gulf countries is *rentier state theory*. The term "rentier" derives from the term "rent," defined as the monies paid to a landowner for use of his land. The meaning of rent has been extended to mean the return on the use of a resource that one possesses. In this sense, the Saudi government possesses the oil and gas resources beneath its lands and by selling these resources is generating rent (income). Central to this theory is the fact that the state economy is supported largely by "rent." Giacomo Luciani explains the crux of the theory:

> A state that economically supports society and is the main source of private revenues through government expenditure, while in turn supported by revenue accruing from abroad, does not need to respond to society. On the contrary, a state that is supported by society, through taxes levied in one form or another, will in the final analysis be obliged to respond to societal pressure. (Luciani 1995:211)

The theory hypothesizes that states like Saudi Arabia, which have so much wealth from oil revenue that not only can they pay for the costs of government but they can also subsidize citizens' expenses, do not have to be concerned with citizen opinion. States like the US, which must use citizen tax dollars to pay for government operations, do have to be concerned about citizen opinion. When citizens are being taxed, they demand a voice in government; if they are not paying taxes, their allegiance can be "bought" with subsidies and services. Some theorists extend this argument to suggest that rentier behavior discourages democratization of the state because citizens have no reason to protest their lack of voice; in effect, they have been "bought off" by subsidies (Luciani 1995). Further, the state is legitimized through its redistributive role in which it provides services and stipends to citizens (Okruhlik 1999:296). Other critiques suggest that rentier states: (1) are subject to corruption as citizens try and succeed in garnering financial favors from acquiescent royal family members and high-ranking officials, (2) operate in secrecy since the financial transparency demanded by citizens who pay taxes does not apply to these states, and (3) exhibit bloated and inefficient public bureaucracy with acquisition of positions and contracts based on favoritism and demonstrate little incentive to improve efficiency as long as the oil revenue continues to flow (Moore 2004:207; Champion 2003). In addition to the oil-rich Gulf states, this theory is applied to other resource-rich nations like Venezuela, Bolivia, and Libya.

In Saudi Arabia, the state has periodically subsidized public utilities, gasoline, and staple foods like bread, rice, and sugar, and provided free education and health care (Champion 2003:81). Additionally it has sometimes assisted in citizen acquisition of land and the costs of house construction, subsidized costs of animal feed, and provided jobs in the government bureaucracy (Hertog 2009:16). Rentier theory, however, has been shown to be inadequate in the Saudi case. Steffen Hertog (2007, 2008, 2010) suggests that there never has been a fully developed and generally accepted rentier state theory but rather there are a number of recurring hypotheses regarding oil-rich states. He finds, for example, that having external income does not necessarily lead to an inefficient state bureaucracy.

With regard to the Saudi case, rentier theory oversimplifies the Saudi government's complex history and development and its dynamic relationship with its citizens. It incorrectly treats the Saudi government as a single monolithic entity with one voice rather than recognizing the multiple voices of powerful royal family members and some high-status commoners. These same individuals created a government of multiple ministries and bureaucratic institutions that, over time, have become relatively independent. This has created fragmentation in the state bureaucracy so that various pockets of government developed differently. For example, the national petroleum company, Petromin, was inefficient and riddled with rivalries as predicted in rentier state theory; however it was eventually dissolved and replaced as the state-owned oil company by the efficient, internationally competitive, Aramco.

Other scholars have also addressed specific concerns regarding rentier state theory. Gwenn Okruhlik (1999) observes that if providing for the population successfully bought citizen complacence, there would be no citizen resistance to the government in Saudi Arabia and thus rentier theory cannot explain the substantial resistance to the Saudi ruling family among KSA citizens. This resistance is a topic that will be discussed in chapter 9 of this book. David Long (2010) suggests that rather than being a new development that occurred with the flowing of oil revenue, the redistribution process described as a result of oil wealth in rentier theory is not a new phenomenon attributed to oil but is actually a continuation of centuries-old cultural behavior common in Arabia. This cultural behavior will be described in more detail in chapters 3 and 4 in this book. I agree with these scholars that rentier theory is overly simplistic in explaining the dynamics of Saudi government and politics and that a detailed review of KSA history and culture will provide a more complex understanding of the modern state.

As I write this, citizens are demonstrating for governmental change in Tunisia, Egypt, Yemen, Libya, and Bahrain. In this current spread of demonstrations for democracy, Bahrain is the only rentier state thus far demanding political change. As mentioned earlier, Luciani suggests that citizens in rentier states are unlikely to demand democracy because they have been "bought off" by subsidies. Will this fever for democracy spread to the rest of the rentier states in the Gulf? I cannot answer that question, but if it does not, this may be a validation of some aspects of rentier theory or instead may represent those more complex nuances of political economy found in the Gulf. It is not too surprising that the quest for democracy would spread to Bahrain, even though it is a rentier state. This is because the ruling elite there are Sunni

Muslims and the majority of the population is Shi'a. This was the case in Iraq under Saddam Hussein. The Shi'i citizens of Bahrain charge that they are underrepresented and their dissatisfaction is one of the factors fueling these demonstrations for change.

The Politics of Research

Said and Foucault have helped us understand that all writing is political. This is particularly obvious to me when reading work on Saudi Arabia. The state sanctioned-newspapers, like *al-Sharq al-Awsat,* are careful not to be too critical of the government or the religious establishment. Voices of dissent like Muhammad Al-Masari and Saad al-Faqih who are based in London use their outside location to speak their resistance to the Saudi government (Al-Rasheed 2007:70, 238). Saudi researchers are sometimes writing from a state-sanctioned point of view (Twal 2009) and sometimes from a dissatisfaction with the state government (Al-Rasheed 2007). Westerners can be either highly critical of the Saudi state (Baer 2003) or overly optimistic about it (Long 1997). As a result of this highly charged atmosphere, I present my own reasons for writing so that you can decide for yourself what my agenda might be.

Inspired by Abu-Lughod's work, I choose to place this book in cultural context. To do so, I will describe the time period during which this book was researched and written and my motivations for writing it. This will serve, I hope, to explicate some of the hidden agendas behind the work, many of which developed because of the political context in which the field-work was undertaken.

As mentioned in the Introduction, I first arrived in Saudi Arabia in July 2002, which was a politically charged time both in my native United States and in Saudi Arabia. This was less than a year after the terrorist attacks in the United States on September 11, 2001. Fifteen of the nineteen hijackers on that day were Saudis and, of course, the individual behind the attacks, Osama bin Laden, was a Saudi as well. Among people in the United States, emotions ran high. The Saudis were being vilified in individual living rooms, on television, and in the halls of the United States Congress. Saudis were painted as terrorists; Saudi men were viewed as sinister figures in sunglasses and strange cloth-ing who were deliberately anti-Western as an affront to the West; Saudi women in their black coverings were considered downtrodden creatures always under the control of men. People in the States shook their heads and saw the state of Saudi women as evidence of Western superiority because, in Western societies, women were free and there must be something wrong in KSA if women had to be veiled, equating veiling with lack of freedom. In the summer of 2002, I saw no efforts in the United States to present Saudis positively.

In Saudi, I found the atmosphere equally charged. Saudis had been dev-astated by the attacks of 9/11 and expressed strong support for the United States in that tragedy. However, they were now fearful of anti-Saudi rhetoric and behavior in the United States. In living rooms and shopping centers, they told me stories they had heard about Saudis being harassed in the United States, and almost everyone I talked to was afraid to go to the States. They were angry also for a different reason. They were furious over the recent violent attacks of Israelis on Palestinians and they blamed the United States. Their reasoning was that the United States provided Israel with the financial support to sustain its military and with political support at the United Nations and other international forums, and this support gave Israel the clout to avoid international condemnation. In this line of thinking, the United States was as guilty as Israel for the death and suffering of Palestinians.

During the eleven months of that first visit to KSA, the political electricity never diminished. I was there during the buildup to and the initiation of the current (as of this writing in 2011) war in Iraq. Saudis I talked to all opposed this war. The Kingdom has a long border with Iraq and, in the first Gulf War, the Iraqis had launched Scud missiles into KSA that reached as far as Riyadh, where I now lived. During that time, many Saudis had fled the city. So they were concerned that their city and their country would again become a war zone. They were frustrated that their government had so little say in the US decision to go to war when Saudis were likely to pay a heavy price for that war. When the 2003 war started, Saudis were spared danger as no Scuds were sent into KSA, but they watched in horror as Iraqis were killed and priceless relics of Middle Eastern history were looted from unprotected museums. Here again, the media played a significant role. Al Jazeera, the popular Arabic television network headquartered in Qatar, was closely watched by Saudis I knew, and they were well acquainted with the Al Jazeera version of war events.

I, too, was captivated by the television coverage. I alternated my viewing among Arab, especially Al Jazeera, and US and British channels. What I found was remarkable; it was as if the Western and the Arab worlds were broadcasting different wars. I wondered, how can we ever live in peace and understanding when we do not see the same "facts"? The US television showed American troops moving in convoys through the desert and Army generals giving briefings about the success of the troop movements. Arab television showed Iraqis wailing in the streets as they cradled dead relatives in their arms and morticians working over the bodies of children displayed in the cold, metal drawers of morgues. I left Saudi Arabia in May of 2003 shortly after terrorists blew up parts of three housing compounds in Riyadh where some of my friends were lucky to escape with their lives. I have returned to Saudi Arabia twice, both in calmer circumstances, but the goals for my research were formed in that first visit in tempestuous times.

Thus, my anthropological work in Saudi Arabia is charged with political and personal tensions. This book is a product of its time. Written at any other period in history it would have been a different work not only because the data would have changed but also because the particular confluence of world events would have been different. The introduction states the points I wish to make in this book. Behind these formal, academic goals, however, is a personal agenda. Anti-Saudi, anti-Arab, and anti-Muslim rhetoric continues to be prevalent in the West. I wish to contribute to the effort to humanize the Saudi people in the eyes of Westerners. I hope to contribute to creating an understanding of Saudi Arabia that allows Westerners to see its people as just another society of people who get up every day, go to work, visit with their neighbors, and worry about their children. I hope to help provide the cultural context that will make Saudi society understandable to those unfamiliar with it. At the same time, I have anthropologically significant research to describe in my explanations of the roles of nation-states and complex adaptive systems in the modern globalization process. The professional and the personal are one, no matter our effort to compartmentalize them. These are my reasons for writing.

Chapter 3

The Geography and History of Saudi Arabia

$\mathcal{S}$ince the late nineteenth century, anthropologists have appreciated the importance of studying the land in order to understand a people. The adaptation to survival includes not only the subsistence techniques humans use to feed themselves but the value system they develop to legitimate their relationship to the land. The Kingdom of Saudi Arabia occupies some of the harshest and most beautiful land on earth. Just ask any Saudi. To understand the story of the Kingdom, one must understand the land, the history of its human occupation, and the creation and development of the modern Saudi state. These topics are the subject of this chapter. To begin the tale of the Kingdom of Saudi Arabia is to begin at the beginning: the formation of the Arabian Peninsula.

The Creation of the Land

Amazingly for a land that is mostly desert, in its 600-million-year existence, Arabia has been under water more than it has been above it. Arabia was born in the clash and swirl of tectonic plates. One billion years ago, it existed only as a line of volcanic islands off the coast of Africa. Over the subsequent 400 million years, this tiny row of islands moved, collided with, and wedged up against other wandering segments of the earth's crust. It merged with these other maverick plates, eventually forming what is now called the Arabian Shield. For 100 million years more, volcanic activity caused by the pressure of these collided tectonic plates continued to shape the topography of the Shield. At the time, the Shield was attached to northeastern Africa as part of Gondwanaland, a large, wandering southern land mass made up of present-day Africa, South America, Australia, India, and Madagascar.

29

This was only the beginning of the violent movements that created Arabia. Five hundred and fifty million years ago, still attached to Africa, the Arabian Shield was submerged in an early sea. Only the area that is now the country of Yemen and the Tabouk area of western Saudi Arabia were above the water line. By 470 million years ago, the volatile movements of Gondwanaland carried Arabia as far south as the current tip of South America; the seas of the Shield receded and glaciers covered its western half. In subsequent ages, the Arabian Shield would repeatedly be inundated by water and once more be glaciated. Throughout these millions of years, the whole of the Arabian Shield slowly tilted downward in the east. Because of this tilt and because the western side of the Shield was still attached to Africa, flooding came in from the eastern, or coastal, side. With each successive flood, the waters crept less far inland and as the waters of these seas withdrew, they left behind rich layers of sediment laid down like layers of a cake.

It was to be another million years, however, before the final shape of the Arabian Peninsula emerged. About 50 million years ago, Asia and Arabia smashed together. The violent power of this clash pushed up landmass creating the Zagros Mountains of Iran and the Taurus Mountains of Turkey. Arabia and Asia were now forever linked. Meanwhile, on the western side of the Arabian Shield, a series of three faults developed along the eastern coast of Africa. One fault filled with water from the Mediterranean creating the Red Sea. The other two caused the formation of the Great Rift Valley of eastern Africa and of the Gulf of Aden. At its southern end, the Red Sea was still attached to Africa and did not break loose for another 25 million years when another fault developed that actually cracked Africa and Arabia apart (Thompson 2000:43). Meanwhile, fiery volcanic activity continued to occur in parts of the Arabian Shield. The results of this activity can be seen today in the *harrats* (lava flows) still covering parts of western Arabia and in the Wahba crater east of Jiddah.

Five million years ago, only yesterday in geological time, the Arabian Peninsula finally took its current shape. More fault activity caused the Gulf of Aden to sink and the Isthmus of Suez to rise. The Suez formed a plug, preventing the Mediterranean from flowing into the Red Sea while water flowed through the Gulf of Aden. And so, out of this continuous movement of the earth's crust, volcanic activity, clashes of fire, water, and ice was created the land that is Arabia today.

Even today, Arabia is still being created as it continues to swing toward Asia, and the Red Sea slowly widens while the Arabian Gulf narrows.[1] From sea inundations to glaciations, Arabia's climate changed violently from coldly inhospitable and covered in ice to pleasantly warm with gentle sea breezes. About seven million years ago, it contained well-watered plains teeming with giraffe, elephant, cattle, and antelope; subtropical forests of palm trees and mangroves; and vast flowing rivers full of hippopotamus. Four million years later, the Peninsula was hot, humid, and rainy with tropical forests and raging rivers. One million years ago, Arabia's climate became drier, with woodlands and grassy plains. Those riverbeds that had been carved deep into the sediment by rushing water were left empty and filled up with sediment. The climate continued to fluctuate. Then, about 17,000 years ago, with the end of the last Ice Age, the climate dried out for the last time and became the desert-like Arabian climate known today.

Rock formations in Al Hasa area.

The story of the forming of Arabia can be read on its face. The topographical features of today are the pages of its book of geology. Starting on the beaches of the Arabian Gulf, a walk across Arabia from east to west is a walk back through time, starting with the youngest land formations and moving through to the oldest. Moving west from the shore of the Arabian Gulf, the traveler passes through a maze of fantastical rock shapes that form the cliffs and caves of Al-Hasa. This is an old Pliocene coastline whose caves and cliffs were formed by the pounding of ancient surf. Walking again toward the west, the traveler crosses the Summam plateau, a layer of sediment laid down by the receding of an even earlier inundation of the Peninsula in the Miocene period. Embedded in this sediment are wonderful examples of fossilized marine animals, evidence that this was previously a sea floor. Approaching Riyadh, in the center of the Peninsula, the traveler moves onto an older layer of sediment from Cretaceous time and moves further back in time from the days of mammals into the days of dinosaurs. This is Mesozoic sedimentary rock. South of Riyadh is the Wadi Dawasir; a valley with no river at its center, which is one of these ancient riverbeds; now filled with nature's debris, the original river bed is 60 meters (65.6 yards) below the current surface. West of Riyadh, one reaches the spectacular Tuwaiq Escarpment, a feature so starkly huge it can be seen from space. The Tuwaiq Escarpment's sharp cliff face marks the edge of another of those inundations of the seas; the escarpment was caused by erosion. It appears that the land west of the escarpment is much lower in altitude than the land to its east, but this is simply an illusion caused by the limitations of the human perspective, that is, the inability of small human beings to see land formations on their own grand scale. Moving west, the traveler is moving slowly uphill, so that each successive escarpment is higher than the one to its east. One hundred kilometers west of the Tuwaiq Escarpment, the traveler finally steps onto the bedrock of Arabia, the actual Arabian Shield (Thompson 2000:61).

From here to the shoreline of the Red Sea, the 600-million-year-old Shield is visible, presenting the oldest exposed surface in Arabia. The Shield, of course, is covered in some areas by newer features that are recent changes in a living earth. Wandering across the Shield, the traveler encounters the harrats, those volcanic deposits scattered over western Arabia from geologically recent volcanoes. These are fields littered with great chunks of black rock and huge black swirls of molten lava now frozen as stone. A more burned-out-looking landscape would be difficult to find. A prominent feature of this area is the Wahba Crater, a giant hole surrounded by cliffs, where it takes a hearty hike to descend to the salt-covered floor. This walk across Arabia ends at the Red Sea shore, another recent feature, having developed with the formation of the Red Sea some 50 million years ago.

Throughout Arabia the traveler finds startlingly beautiful rock shapes, which are the dramatic effects of erosion by wind and water on a land with little vegetation to hold the soil. That these surprisingly bizarre, giant stone shapes have long impressed humans is evidenced by the many locations where

Rock formations in central Saudi Arabia.

ancient humans etched pictures of their lives into the stone faces and by the magnificent monuments they carved out of single giant monoliths. It is the deserts, however, with their variety of colors of sand, from white to peach to red to black, that are Arabia's best-known feature. The deserts of the Great Nefud in the north and the magnificent Rub al-Khali (the Empty Quarter) in the southeast are the deltas of formerly raging rivers and result from thousands of years of erosion during which the rock surface of the Arabian Shield was pulverized into particles of sand. It is the diverse types of rock weathered into sands of differing colors and weights that cause the great dunes to be multicolored. Outside of Riyadh, they are red and outside of Hofuf, white. Single dunes look like painted watercolors where shades of color fade into each other. A walk across Arabia could never leave one complacent. One is left to wonder about the people who have inhabited this harsh and beautiful land. As inhospitable as much of it seems today, it has been home to humans since ancient times.

Modern Climate

Saudi Arabia has a desert climate except in the southwestern province of Asir. In Nejd, the center of the country, which includes the capital, Riyadh, and in the great deserts, the temperature averages 45° Celsius (113° Fahrenheit) in the summer with high daily temperatures frequently at 54° Celsius (129° Fahrenheit). Winter temperatures rarely reach freezing although the dry cold can feel like it is at the freezing mark. Areas near the Red Sea and the Arabian Gulf are humid, usually above 85 percent and frequently at 100 percent humidity, while temperatures are usually below 38° Celsius (100° Fahrenheit). Average rainfall is 100 millimeters (3.9 inches) per year, but large regions may not receive any rainfall for several consecutive years. The mountainous Asir region of the southwest experiences a different climate altogether. Between October and March, it receives an average of 300 millimeters (11.8 inches) of rainfall because it is impacted by the Indian Ocean monsoons (Library of Congress 1992).

The Early Arabians (Paleolithic–CE 600)

Stone tools give testament to the presence of early humans in Arabia. The earliest forms of stone tools, those identified with early humans in Olduvai Gorge in East Africa, have been found in Arabia as well. At Sakaka in northern Arabia, for example, are stone choppers and cleavers dating from almost one million years ago. These tools, associated with Homo erectus, document early human travel out of Africa and through Arabia (Al-Hariri-Rifai and Al-Hariri-Rifai 1990:17; Thompson 2000:62). Other evidence includes tools of the lower Paleolithic, especially pre-Acheulian, Acheulian, and Levallois Mousterian tool industries. Most of this time, the climate was more amenable to human habitation than currently. When Arabia was wide grassy plains and woodlands, humans hunted and gathered from rich food sources. By 9000 BCE the evidence suggests subsistence was based on small to medium-sized mammal herds of probably cattle and sheep for humans living in partially settled communities with a seasonal pattern of long-range movements. Numerous petroglyph sites in the north-central area and the southwestern highlands date from 9,000–5,000 BCE. These include figures of humans and animals (Masry 62).

About 7,500 years ago, arid conditions in the southern Levant, the lands bordering the eastern side of the Mediterranean including Lebanon, Israel, Palestine, Syria, and Jordan, caused a migration of peoples into Arabia and northeastern Africa. They were pastoralists and agriculturists. As the environment became even drier, these agropastoralists spread through Arabia. From sites in the Rub al-Khali and Hail, there is evidence of agriculture, equipment for grinding grain into flour, fishing nets, and fired clay pots. They traded widely for prized items like central and southwestern Arabian obsidian, soapstone, and Red Sea shells (Hassan 2000:18–21).

Some 5,000 years ago, the people of Arabia began to use metals—first copper and then bronze. Trade networks were extensive; for example, archaeologists have established a link between the Bronze Age Indus Civilization of India and a port village at Ras al-Junayz in Oman. Indus artifacts found in the Arabian site include a copper stamp, or seal, and decorated pottery.

By 4,500 years ago, the climate in Arabia stabilized at the level of aridity known today. In oasis areas, the people were agriculturalists, while in the drier parts, they were pastoralists. Agriculturists were even using irrigation. It was about this time that agricultural city-states began to develop in Egypt and Mesopotamia. Through trade, these city-states were in contact with the oasis and desert dwellers of the area now known as Saudi Arabia. In the mix of activity of that time, Arabia was involved in extensive overland and maritime trade. Eventually, the camel was domesticated, date palms cultivated, and state systems and tribal organization both emerged in Arabia (Gogte 2000:7).

The camel, an animal that would play such a central role in life in Arabia, was probably found in the Peninsula as early as 4,500 years ago but was not domesticated for another 1,000 years. The camel became essential to the thriving cultures of Arabia because it made long-distance travel across the desert terrain possible. No other animal can last as long without water and carry such heavy loads. The camel was the key to travel and trade and to the development of long trade routes like those necessitated by the spice and incense business, ancient demonstrations of globalization.

The early history of the peoples of Arabia is written in stone. Carved into rock faces all over the Peninsula are images that tell the story of these early peoples. Possibly the earliest of these has been found at Kilwa and dates from about 10,000 years ago. Rock art images carved over thousands of years depict humans with swords, bow and arrows, spears, and shields. Some clearly have styled hair and elaborate headdresses. There are many carvings of animals, like cattle, camels, goats, sheep, lion, antelope, gazelle, and ibex, and some of plants, like palm trees. Some petroglyphs of camels show them being hunted; others indicate domestication, as the camels' feet are hobbled. There are depictions of humans on horseback and camelback. Some pictures even show motion. In one case, this is a group of running ostriches and in another, dancing human-like figures. Other carvings are the imprints of human hands and feet. A fascinating feature of this early rock art is the early presence of *wasm* marks dating from 8,000 years ago. A wasm is a brand typically found cut into the carved figure of an animal. They tended to be irregular geometric shapes and in some cases were similar to letters in early Arabian script. Early wasm symbols are found on pictures of cattle. As the climate became dryer and camels replaced cattle, wasm marks were carved into the etched figures of camels as well. While rock art ended with the coming of Islam, wasm branding is used in the present day to identify the livestock and belongings of a family or tribe (Alsharekh 2002:56–57).

Towns and trade routes were developing in Arabia, and by 5,000 years ago, the age of more complex kingdoms had begun. One of the earliest of these kingdoms was Dilmun (5,000–2,000 BCE), located on Bahrain and the eastern coast of Saudi Arabia. Bahrain was a green, fertile island and the city that developed there was an important stop on the trade routes to India. Other early kingdoms, like Thamuc, Midian, Dedan, and Kinda, were located in northern, eastern, and central Arabia. Of all these early kingdoms from the sixth century BCE through the fifth century CE, none left as spectacular remains as that of the Nabataeans.

Strategically located at the crossroads of both east-west and north-south trade routes, the Kingdom of the Nabataeans covered Jordan, southern Syria, and northwestern Saudi Arabia. Perfume and incense were transported overland from Saba, a kingdom in what is today Yemen, north to the Nabataean city of Medain Saleh in modern Saudi Arabia and then to Petra, a Nabataean site in present-day Jordan. In Nabataean times, Medain Saleh, an archaeological site in northwestern Saudi Arabia, was probably a prospering market. Today, the most stunning remains of Nabataean life found there are the tombs. The landscape at Medain Saleh is itself a marvel of mammoth, red sandstone monoliths that appear to be planted on a sandy plain. It is into these huge sandstone formations that the Nabataeans carved some 131 tombs in an area of 13.4 kilometers (8.3 miles). The origin of the Nabataeans is still mysterious. They seem to have moved into an area vacated by the Edomites when the Edomites moved north around 580 BCE. Mention of them appears in several early written sources. For example, the Zenon papyri dated at 259 BCE refers to the Nabataeans who traded frankincense from Minaean sources up into Syria. Archaeologists have identified hundreds of Nabataean sites and have found substantial evidence of Nabataean use of agriculture. Aerial photographs reveal the locations of ancient agricultural fields (Kennedy and Qatamin 2001:21).

Nabataean tombs at Medain Saleh.

In the second century CE, the Romans conquered the land and from then until the beginning of Islam in the seventh century CE, the peoples of the Peninsula were the victims of outside aggression, much of it from Byzantium and Persia. With the emergence of the Islamic state, large parts of the Peninsula were united.

The Origin of Islam

Muhammad, the prophet of Islam, (CE 570–632) was born in Makkah and raised by an uncle who was a trader by profession. Muhammad became a trader, too, and at age twenty-five married a widow, Khadija. At the age of 40, he had a religious experience and received divine revelations from Jibril, the Biblical angel Gabriel. These divine revelations were the first of many Muhammad had over a twenty-two-year period, and he began to acquire followers. By 622, he and his followers, called Muslims, meaning "those who submitted," were forced to leave Makkah for Madinah, where his religious movement grew into a political entity. Muhammad's movement gained strength, and through armed conflict he took Makkah in 630, uniting the two cities of Makkah and Madinah for Islam. He died in 632, the ruler of most of the Arabian Peninsula; his follower, Abu Bakr, became his successor. Abu Bakr moved into what are now Palestine, Syria, and Iraq, and 100 years after Muhammad's death, the Muslim Empire stretched from France to India. The story of Muhammad's successors is the story of the growth and divisions in the Islamic Empire, which was taken over by the Ottomans in 1517 and its last caliph deposed in 1924 (Bates and Rassam 2001:33; Akers 2001:104).

Battling for Control of Arabia (1500–1900)

Attempts at political control of the Arabian Peninsula by external powers are scattered through its history. However, to understand modern Saudi Arabia it is important to realize that most of the Arabian Peninsula was never under direct foreign control. The Ottoman Empire, based in Constantinople and influential from the fourteenth through the twenty-first centuries, made several attempts to add Arabia to its land holdings. Beginning in the 1500s and for the subsequent 400 years, the Ottoman Sultans held nominal control of the Hijaz region along the Red Sea in cooperation with the Sharifian family who ruled that area. The 1818 Ottoman–Egyptian invasion of central Arabia and the 1871 Ottoman occupation of Al-Hasa in the east and Asir in the southwest are further examples of Ottoman attempts to control the Peninsula. While Ottoman influence persisted until the defeat of its Empire in the First World War, it was never far-reaching. Much of Arabia was never under direct Ottoman authority; instead, local emirs, tribal leaders, ruled on behalf of the Empire and received subsidies in return. Thus, the Ottomans never disturbed Arabia's traditional forms of government and culture. When Ottoman territories were divided by the Western victors after the First World War, Great Britain gained the right to control of Arabia.

Britain, in fact, already had a presence in the Arabian Peninsula. To protect its trade relationships and other financial interests and to secure a position in the Peninsula against rival political powers, Great Britain employed wealthy Arab merchants as its agents throughout the nineteenth century. These individuals had extensive business and social contacts as well as political influence with local rulers. The British, therefore, operated within the local Arab political and financial system to maintain a presence; they never spread the mechanisms of colonialism over the Peninsula (Onley 2004:135). When Britain gained the right to control Arabia after the First World War, it was busily engaged elsewhere. In addition, the difficulty of bringing Arabia's various leaders under British rule and the inhospitable nature of the land, only parts of which had strategic value, gave the British little interest in turning it into a colony. Instead, Britain developed allies of its two most significant rulers: Sharif Husayn in Hijaz along the Red Sea and Ibn Saud in Nejd in central Arabia. Thus, although empires like those of the Ottomans and the British attempted to exert their influence over the lands that would become Saudi Arabia, none succeeded. Never was there a colonial government nor a colonial elite ruling the area; the Saudi state is an indigenous government developed from indigenous religious and political systems (Al-Rasheed 2002:1–2).

Tribal affiliation has been important in the Arabian Peninsula for centuries and, indeed, figures prominently in anthropological accounts of its peoples. Madawi Al-Rasheed (2002:7) explains that historically, the primary form of government in Arabia was the emirate (imara). Anthropologically, these governments would be termed "chiefdoms" so as to distinguish them from "states." An emirate was kin based, ruled by a patrilineage that lay claim to a territory with a mixed economy of trade, agriculture, and pastoralism. The lineage expected loyalty and tax or tribute from the peoples in its area in exchange for law and order and the redistribution of the wealth from the emirate back to the people. Boundaries were unstable, and warfare and raids were common as emirates attempted to increase their holdings.

The First Saudi State (1744–1818)

The story of the modern nation-state of Saudi Arabia begins in the eighteenth century. The Al Saud family hails from Ad-Dir'iyah, a settlement of some seventy households of farmers and merchants in Nejd, the heartland of central Arabia. Ad-Dir'iyah, a dusty community of mud-brick houses on narrow, winding streets, is still visible today on the outskirts of Riyadh. Traditionally, its government was of the emirate pattern; it was ruled in 1727 by Muhammad ibn Saud, a landholding merchant, to whom households paid tribute in return for protection. This relationship remained unchanged for fifteen years, until Muhammad ibn Abd al-Wahhab, a religious scholar, arrived from the neighboring town of Uyaynah. Al-Wahhab preached a singular view of Islam that stressed the importance of monotheism, which he defined as (1) no worship of saints or objects, (2) the requirement of *zakat*, an Islamic tax, and (3) the importance of war against those who did not follow Islamic doctrine as he saw it. He was outspoken about what he considered to be the right behaviors in daily life; for example, he required communal prayer for men and boys and discouraged tobacco use. In his line of thinking, Muslims had strayed off the path and needed to return to the true, pure Islam (Al-Rasheed 2002:16).

In 1744, Muhammad ibn Saud and Muhammad ibn Abd al-Wahhab formed a pact in which the former would be political leader and the latter would be religious leader. This pact was the beginning of the spread of Muhammad ibn Saud's rule beyond Ad-Dir'iyah; political expansion now had a religious legitimation. Those who joined al-Wahhab's religious movement could expect salvation and, in return, were requested to join in Muhammad ibn Saud's battle to regain his ancestral lands. This fit the traditional pattern of raiding to expand territory common in Arabia, but in this case it carried the extra legitimation of spreading the word of true Islam and giving salvation to those who joined. Al-Rasheed suggests that Muhammad ibn Saud was not of tribal background, although the modern Al Saud family disputes this. Al-Rasheed's argument is that without a tribal following to support them, the Al Sauds needed another form of support, which they found in al-Wahhab's religious movement. Later, in the spread of the modern Saudi state, Al-Rasheed contends, the lack of a tribal identity aided them. Their spread was not perceived by others in Arabia as the spread of a single tribal confederation trying to dominate other tribes, but instead they were perceived as mediators among various tribal interests and providers of religious salvation for all (Al-Rasheed 2002:27, 37).

Now armed with religious legitimation as well as swords and sturdy camels, Muhammad ibn Saud's troops moved through central Arabia, into Al-Hasa in the east and on toward what are now the countries of Bahrain and Qatar. In the west, they took control of much of the Hijaz region, including Makkah and Madinah. Saudi forces raided cities in Mesopotamia, Syria, and Iraq, although they were not able to establish control there. In 1814, the first Saudi state ended at the hands of the Ottomans who arrived in Ad-Dir'iyah with "2,000 cavalrymen, 4,300 Albanian and Turkish soldiers, 1,300 Maghribian cavalrymen, 150 gunners with around 15 guns, [and] 20 weapons technicians" (Vassiliev 1998:154). The Saudis surrendered. Ad-Dir'iyah was plundered, Wahhabi *'ulama'*, religious leaders, were killed, and the then Saudi ruler, Abdullah, was exiled first into Egypt and then Turkey where he was sentenced to death (Twal 2009:24; Al-Rasheed 2002:23).

The Second Saudi State (1824–1891)

With Ad-Dir'iyah sacked and Abdullah killed, the first Saudi state ended, but in 1824, Turki, the son of Abdullah, returned to Riyadh, a neighboring town to Ad-Dir'iyah over which the Al Saud family held great influence. He managed to retake much of Nejd and also the region of Al-Hasa, creating the second Saudi state. This state suffered from internal fighting among the members of the Al Saud family made worse by the political power of the Egyptians in Hijaz in the west and the Rashidi family in Hail to the north. Eventually, Muhammad ibn Rashid took Riyadh and Qasim, and his Saudi rival, Abdul Rahman, fled first to live in the great desert of the Rub al-Khali (Empty Quarter) with the Al Murrah tribe and then to Kuwait.

During the nineteenth and early twentieth centuries, the Al Sauds were not the only powerful family attempting to spread its control throughout Arabia. Other large and powerful entities like the Rashidi emirate in Hail (1836–1921), the Sharifian emirate in Hijaz, and the confederation of the Bani Khalid in Hasa had similar interests (Al-Rasheed 2002:26–37). The Al Saud family, however, would be the one to eventually triumph.

Abdul Aziz al Saud (Ibn Saud) and the Rise of the Third Saudi State

In 1902, after eleven years of exile, twenty-one year old Abdul Aziz al Saud, son of the exiled Abdul Rahman, returned from Kuwait to avenge his family's loss. Abdul Aziz was born in Riyadh in 1877 while his father was ruler of the second Saudi state. As a boy, he was privately tutored in reading, writing, memorization of the Qur'an, and Islamic theology. He learned the life of the bedu (bedouin) while living with the Bani-Murrah people before his family fled to Kuwait (Twal 2009:28). He returned to Riyadh in 1902 with forty to sixty men and, under cover of darkness, quietly stole into the city, attacked the Rashidi garrison in Riyadh, killed the Rashidi representative, and captured the city of Riyadh. This event is much mythologized and publicized in today's Kingdom and the garrison where it occurred has become a tourist attraction where tourists can rub their hands over a spear point still stuck in the garrison door from this surprise attack over 100 years ago. With the capture of Riyadh, Ibn Saud began three decades of military, diplomatic, and religious conquests that resulted in his uniting the lands of the current Kingdom.

A tall, imposing man sitting atop a finely bred camel, heading a squadron of supporters armed with rifles and swords and carrying flags representing his emirate, Ibn Saud moved across the deserts of Arabia. From Riyadh, he recaptured Qasim, also held by the Rashidis and then the Hofuf where the Ottomans had stationed 1,200 Turkish troops. He signed a treaty with the Ottomans that gave him authority in parts of Nejd, while the Ottomans supported the Rashidis in the remainder of Nejd. The First World War brought British interest in Ibn Saud. He signed a treaty with Britain in 1915 acknowledging his rule over parts of Arabia and giving him rifles and cash in return for his promise not to move against Kuwait, Bahrain, Qatar, and the Oman coast. The Rashidi family continued to ally itself with the Ottomans, and when the Ottoman Empire fell and World War I ended, Ibn Rashid was left without an ally. In 1921, Ibn Saud, with 10,000 troops, imposed a siege at Hail, the oasis that was the Rashidi home base. The Rashidis surrendered and Hail fell to the Saudis (Al-Rasheed 2002:42–44). In 1921, Ibn Saud put pressure on Kuwait. When Kuwait's rulers refused his request to collect fees on trade to Hail, Ibn Saud initiated a blockade, preventing trade between Nejd and Kuwait. This blockade endured into the 1930s and caused serious problems for bedu tribes whose normal mobility patterns involved crossing between Nejd and Kuwait. The blockade was eventually removed through an agreement between Ibn Saud and the Kuwaiti rulers (Toth 2005).

Ibn Saud turned his attention to the Hijaz, the greatest prize of them all, as this region contained Makkah and Madinah, the two holiest sites of Islam. Here, the Hashemite rulers enjoyed British support. Ibn Saud began by taking the Asir region in southern Hijaz in 1922 and then moving on Taif, in the mountains near Makkah. After three days, the town of Taif was taken and Husayn, the Hashemite ruler, was forced to abdicate rule of Hijaz to one of his sons. Encouraged, Ibn Saud moved his forces to Makkah and then to Jiddah and Madinah and forced Husayn's successor to leave. In 1924, he made the pilgrimage from Riyadh to Makkah, and in December 1925, he announced that he was now King of Hijaz and Sultan of Nejd. To assure Hijazi elites of their continued importance, he reintroduced the *majlis al-ahli* (council of the people) in 1925 and placed his son Faisal at its head in 1927. This entity would later be renamed the *Majlis al-Shūrā* (consultative council) (Twal 2009:26, 28; Lauziere 2000:70). Ibn Saud was not to annex Asir until 1930, and it was not until 1932 that he named his lands the Kingdom of Saudi Arabia and declared himself monarch. By that time, he was the ruler of Nejd, Al-Hasa, Hijaz, and Abha in Asir, the first time these four regions had been united since the first Saudi state. The borders of the Kingdom remain basically the same today, although the border with Yemen was not finalized until 2000 (Al-Enazy 2002) and at this writing is still experiencing unrest. Ibn Saud never succeeded in controlling Yemen, Oman, or the British-protected regions of Jordan, Syria, Iraq, Bahrain, and Kuwait.

Ibn Saud's success at uniting the disparate pastoral, agricultural, and merchant peoples of Arabia was due to more than military prowess; in fact, his military forces were at times well outnumbered. An important factor in his achievement was the religious legitimation stemming from the pact of his distant relative, Muhammad ibn Saud, with Muhammad ibn Abd al-Wahhab. Ibn Saud legitimated his rule by declaring that his purpose was the spread of the purest form of Islam, that of al-Wahhab. He professed that this was the only form of Islam appropriate for the land that was home to Makkah and Madinah, the two holiest cities in Islam; he would be the guardian of Islam in Arabia and of the two holy mosques in Makkah and Madinah. To enforce this branch of Islam, religious specialists from Nejd oasis communities, who were called *mutawaʻa* (plural form), were active through-out the Kingdom, assuring that its inhabitants followed the teachings of al-Wahhab. Al-Rasheed states that this enforcement of ritualistic Islam was sig-nificant in convincing a disparate people to accept Saudi political rule "under the guise of religious education, enforcing the *shariʻa* (Islamic law) and guard-ing public morality" (Al-Rasheed 2002:58). The *mutawaʻ* (singular form) role in enforcing the behavioral rules of Islam taught by al-Wahhab aided in con-vincing the population to accept the political authority of the Saudis. The mutawaʻa remain active in KSA today as the Committee for the Order of the Good and the Forbidding of Evil whose members patrol public spaces to oversee correct behavior in the name of religion. I see them walking the aisles of shopping malls and observing at public gatherings.

Another important force in state formation was the *ikhwān* (brother-hood). In the first ten years of his quest to conquer Arabia, Ibn Saud's forces were made up of Nejd townspeople, but later the ikhwān became significant to his success. The ikhwān was a fighting force recruited from the bedu tribal confederations and trained in religion by the mutawaʻa. Its members were tribesmen who agreed to settle in special camps, take religious training, and take up the holy cause of war. By 1926, there were 150,000 tribesmen living in the ikhwān settlements where they were given agricultural work and regu-larly received gifts from Ibn Saud. They formed a fighting force essential to taking the Hijaz. After taking the Hijaz, however, there was nowhere for Ibn Saud to expand his rule. He was stopped in the north and east by British pro-tection of Trans-Jordan, Iraq, Kuwait, and the other Gulf entities from Kuwait to Muscat. He no longer needed the strength in fighting forces that the ikhwān provided; his work had turned to state building. In 1929, the ikhwān rebelled against Ibn Saud and challenged his authority. He stopped their rebellion with military force. The ikhwān were part of the tribal system with its membership from the old tribal confederacies.

Al-Rasheed suggests that it was the move from tribal ascendency to a state system that caused the ikhwān to rebel (2002:69–71). By moving to a state system where it was in his best interests to reduce tribal independence and unify the country, Ibn Saud was negating the traditional power of the tribes, and, as part of the tribal system, the ikhwān did not accept the loss of tribal power. However, Ibn Saud's quelling of the ikhwān rebellion was due as much to his leadership skills as to his military ones. Some leaders of the rebel-lion were given lifelong prison sentences; others were pardoned and given positions of responsibility in Ibn Saud's developing government. For exam-ple, one leader, Majid bin Khuthayla, became responsible for Ibn Saud's cam-els and for gathering together loyal units of the ikhwān to serve Ibn Saud. These loyal fighters eventually became the Saudi Arabian National Guard (Habib 1978 as referenced in Teitelbaum 2005:3).

By 1932, Ibn Saud had become the first king of the Kingdom of Saudi Arabia, a modern state system. In the 1930s, however, KSA was a poor coun-try with few resources other than camels and dates and a master diplomat as a king. Education centered on learning the Qur'an. Transportation was by camel. The people were of diverse backgrounds with regional loyalties. Ibn Saud had much work to do to make his state a unified nation.

Strategies for Unification

> The network of power is a web of family and tribal relations that ensure both the rights and the safety of most Saudi citizens within an ideology of familialism and a network of patrimonial politics. (Fandy 1999:36)

Military conquest was only half the battle even with the help of the mutawa'a and the ikhwān. While Ibn Saud now controlled the lands that still make up the Kingdom today, the peoples of these lands were far from unified in his service. Consequently, he used traditional cultural behaviors—polygyny, the *majlis*, redistribution of wealth, and certain forms of dress—to bring the disparate tribes, towns and merchants together.

Polygyny: Marriage was an effective tool for creating alliances, subduing possible rivals, and creating his own royal lineage. Ibn Saud is reported to have forty-three sons and over fifty daughters (Al-Rasheed 2002:73). While the exact number of his marriages is difficult to document, he had a larger number than was characteristic in Arabia at the time. He married women of powerful Arabian tribes like the Shammar tribe, of important religious specialists like the Al-Shaykh family, and of well-known Nejd families like the Al-Sudayri family, as well as the women of other branches of Al Saud. Scholars agree that the King's polygynous practices were part of a political strategy. Some suggest that these marriages were actually a way of subduing rivals by turning them into affines. These families were wife-givers to the King, who in return gave them gifts and privileged status as an elite class (van der Meulen 1957:255; Al-Rasheed 2002:79–80). Others suggest that this was political alliance building, where marriages were used to cement relationships with powerful rivals-turned-allies. The marriages were like treaties cementing a relationship between powerful entities (al-Zirkili 1972; Philby 1952). Whatever his exact reasoning, it is clear Ibn Saud used marriage as a strategy for unification of the country. Equally as important, producing a large number of male offspring ensured that he had a large royal lineage of direct descendants. Thus, there was no need for the position of king to pass to any of his own siblings or other paternal kin. He marginalized his paternal kin and solidified the line of descent through his own sons.

The Majlis: Traditional Arabian hospitality centered on the majlis: individual tribal leaders, wealthy merchants, and the village influential would host regular gatherings where visitors, supporters, and the curious were welcome to come, visit, discuss, and eat. The host displayed his wealth through the sumptuousness of his dwelling and the lavishness of the feast; he displayed his virtue through his hospitality. It was said that the tent flaps of a great man were always greasy, referring to his ability to host many great feasts. As men walked out of the tent, their hands were so greasy from all the meat they had just eaten that they would leave grease on the tent flaps. Today in Saudi Arabia, the majlis continues. In a traditional display of hospitality, Saudi homes frequently contain a room for such entertaining and, in many cases, this room is left unlocked at all times and the materials for preparing coffee, along with platters of dates, are displayed so that anyone may stop and refresh themselves. Weary travelers can accept this hospitality.

Ibn Saud made use of this Arabian custom by holding several daily meetings. The *majlis 'amm*, held in the morning, was frequented by individuals with business to discuss. The *majlis 'asr*, after afternoon prayers, was attended by political leaders, especially those he had defeated in battle. His hospitality demonstrated his generosity and forgiveness; their acceptance of the same showed that they had surrendered their power to his leadership. The *majlis al-dars*, a study group, was held after evening prayers and centered on religious study. Throughout the day, the King held even more majlis sessions, where he was the primary speaker and delivered the judgments. He used these gatherings to demonstrate his power, leadership, and largesse. Like marriage, the majlis was a tool to aid in unifying his Kingdom and to demonstrate and reinforce his sole leadership. As in traditional Arab society, public access to personal contact with the King, his older sons, or other designated assistants was essential to the success of a ruler. The majlis was well attended as it provided the opportunity for countrymen across the Kingdom to develop and nurture these contacts with their new leader.

Redistribution of Wealth: Redistribution was a traditional economic mechanism in Arabia through which powerful leaders collected tribute, gifts, and other forms of revenue from wealthy subjects eager to show their allegiance, and then redistributed it to others in order to demonstrate their generosity and gain prestige and power. Ibn Saud used his subsidies from foreign powers, like the Ottomans and later the British, and the taxes he imposed on religious pilgrims to Makkah to reward local tribal and urban leaders (Al-Rasheed 2002:125). This cemented his relationship with those leaders. His place at the top of the redistribution system and the magnitude of the gifts of cloth, dates, and weapons he was able to provide underscored his authority as he displayed these old, traditional Arabian values of generosity and hospitality.

Dress: Prior to unification, proper dress throughout Arabia was regional. For example, men in the Asir region wore sarongs, long brightly colored sections of cloth wrapped at the waist and falling to mid-calf, while the bedu of Nejd wore the thobe, a long shirt, usually white, that fell to the calf or almost the ankle. After unification in 1932, Ibn Saud declared that men in government positions must wear the Nejdi traditional dress. Mai Yamani describes the changes this meant for men of the Hijaz in a study of the social, economic, political and religious connotations of Saudi clothing. Hijazi men previously wore turbans as a head covering but had to change to the Nejdi head covering of a *ghutra* with an optional *agal*. The ghutra is a long cloth, usually patterned red and white or solid white in color, and the agal is the black cord worn on top of the ghutra. This cord is in the form of a figure eight, and its original use was for hobbling a camel. Traditionally, Hijazi men wore a long, belted garment with trousers, which differed from the thobe worn by Nejdi men. Ibn Saud's declaration that all government employees must wear the Nejdi dress led to the decline of the wearing of traditional regional dress like that of the Asir or Hijaz regions. In women's dress, the veil was traditional in Hijazi dress, although prior to unification, it was often of a light color; after unification, Nejdi-style black veils were encouraged and came to replace the light colors of the past. Today, the black veil is encouraged by the members of the Committee for the Order of the Good and the Forbidding of Evil who chastise women whom they see as improperly veiled (Yamani 1997:56). Likewise, Nejdi dress is common among all Saudis and serves to reduce the individuality of the regions and promote the cultural hegemony of the Nejd region as the national culture of KSA.

The Birth of Bureaucracy

By definition, the daily work of a state is conducted by a bureaucracy. In the Kingdom, this bureaucracy developed slowly as needed. One of the first organized units developed by the King was a division to handle hospitality. Hospitality, as already noted, was an important symbol of power in the traditional Arab world, and Ibn Saud made use of this traditional method of signaling his power. The King set up a budget for providing feasts for his many guests. He provided lavish meals where whole cooked lambs or baby camels were brought on trays of rice accompanied by vegetables, fruit, more meat, and other foods. The hospitality enterprise was divided into three sections for the feeding of three types of guests: foreign delegations, bedu, and townspeople respectively. Throughout the 1930s and 1940s, bedu expected the King, if he were truly a leader with prestige and power, to feed them regularly, and the Batha section of Riyadh was designated as the place for bedu of no particular social standing to go and receive the King's largesse in the form of meals. Arab *shaykhs* (tribal elders or revered men) and foreign dignitaries went to the royal grounds to attend feasts (Al-Rasheed 2002:86). The need to provide banquets on a regular basis was thus the impetus for the development of a hospitality organization with a royal budget, one of the first examples of incipient bureaucracy in the Kingdom.

Throughout the 1920s and 1930s, Ibn Saud's employees did not receive salaries but instead received gifts, a place at the table, and sometimes living quarters at the palace (Al-Rasheed 2002:87). Throughout the 1930s, Ibn Saud's financial sources were traditionally Arab. Merchants were expected to contribute goods to his coffers when he had special needs and to regularly provide supplies. Most money came from one of two sources: (1) the zakat, an Islamic tax paid either in cash or in-kind in livestock, or (2) a customs duty imposed in Hasa and Hijaz. After taking control of the Hijaz, however, most of the royal income came from taxes and duties associated with the pilgrimage to Makkah. A Ministry of Finance was developed to handle these transactions, which added another layer of bureaucracy to the new state. In 1926, a foreign affairs directorate was initiated, which in 1930 became the Ministry of Foreign Affairs and was headed by Ibn Saud's son Faisal. One of its primary functions was issuing visas to foreign visitors.

In 1944, a Ministry of Defense was established that would come to include: (1) an army, initially made of the Hijazi army and police force, (2) the National Guard, initially made up of the former ikhwān and later a place of employment for members of nomadic tribal groups like the Shammar, and (3) the Royal Guard, fighters from urban parts of Nejd who had fought with Ibn Saud. In the 1950s, more ministries were established: Interior, Health, Communication, Agriculture and Water, and Education, and in 1953 the King established a Council of Ministers that advised the King but had no power to make decisions without his approval. In 1950, the ministries had a combined staff of 4,653 individuals, although few received regular salaries and most did not keep systematic records of their activities. The state bureaucracy was still in its infancy (Al-Rasheed 2002:95).

Ibn Saud died in 1953. The early years of his rule had been marked by conquest and the spread of Islam as taught by al-Wahhab; the later years, by diplomacy and state building. KSA had evolved from a chieftaincy into a monarchical state. While the various tribal leaders who were a threat to Ibn Saud had been subdued, tribal practices still held sway, and Ibn Saud succeeded in incorporating these practices into his new state. He encouraged the sedentism of pastoral tribes, which reduced their mobility as well as their independence. He also began to create central administrative bodies as described above. The British were anxious for all the states in the Middle East to solidify their borders, and Ibn Saud was obliging as this would benefit him in bringing profit from trade and pilgrims (Kostiner 1993:185–189).

Transfer of Power

Ibn Saud's son, Saud, succeeded him as King, and immediately there began a power struggle between King Saud and his brother, Crown Prince Faisal. During his rule, 1953–1964, Saud established additional ministries, founded the first university (1957), and abolished slavery (1962) (Al-Rasheed 2002; Twal 2009:37). In 1964, Saud abdicated the throne and Faisal became King. Faisal had represented his father on diplomatic missions since he was fourteen years old when Ibn Saud sent him to Paris and London. During Faisal's reign, Saudi oil revenues increased exponentially, giving Faisal the financial resources to set his country on a path of modernization. For example, in 1965, the Saudi GDP was 10.4 billion rials and by 1975 it was 164.53 billion rials, sixteen times what it had been ten years prior. Much of this increase was a result of the international oil embargo of 1973. Faisal established a Ministry of Planning, and in 1970 set in motion the Kingdom's first five-year development plan. Oil revenue and Faisal's personal determination to modernize the Kingdom resulted in the solidifying of state bureaucracy and the expansion of education, health care, and industry. Faisal placed his brothers as heads of the state ministries, a pattern that exists today, and made his brother Khalid the new Crown Prince. By so doing, he signaled that future Kings would come from his brothers, the sons of Ibn Saud, rather than from Ibn Saud's own brothers or from the sons of subsequent Kings like Faisal himself (Al-Rasheed 2002:123).

Faisal was committed to the idea that KSA could become a modern country with a modern economy and technology while maintaining its strong commitment to al-Wahhab's Islamic teaching; this is the vision still operating in KSA today. Faisal established the Ministry of Justice in 1970, and the senior 'ulama' (religious leaders) became state supported. He started Saudi television service and initiated girls' education on a voluntary basis (Twal 2009:39). With the immense oil wealth of the 1970s, Faisal was able to expand on his father's use of the traditional Arab norm of generosity. More than food and supplies, Faisal was able to use state revenue in the form of jobs, monthly stipends, and pay for medical care, homes, university scholarships abroad, land, legal documents, and much more. Additionally, the King and princes responded to requests for more gifts and money in their regular majlis meetings with the public. The state provided for its citizens and its citizens embraced consumerism.

The years of Faisal's reign were not without controversy. Some did not agree with his modernization plans and others felt he dealt too harshly with detractors. In 1969, members of the Saudi military plotted to overthrow him, a plot he stopped, but he was finally assassinated in 1975 by a nephew whose own brother had been killed by police after leading a demonstration against the opening of the television station ten years before. Al-Rasheed identifies Faisal's reign as the beginning of two types of tension in the Kingdom: one between Islam and the new materialism and technological transformation oil wealth allowed, the other between Islam and a reliance on United States technology and military expertise. These two lines of tension continue to exist in the Kingdom today and exemplify why understanding the history of the Kingdom is important to understanding the Kingdom today.

Faisal was succeeded by his brother Khalid, whose seven years as King saw several important acts of resistance. In 1979, the holy mosque at Makkah was seized by a group who denounced the Saudi royal family as corrupt and demanded they give up rule of the country. The siege was stopped and rebels were killed. Inspired by the 1979 Iranian revolution, in 1979 and 1980, Shi'a in the Eastern Province rioted against discriminatory treatment. These rebellions too were stopped with violence and their leaders were expelled from the country. After his death in 1982, Khalid was replaced by his brother Fahd as King. Fahd, one of seven sons born to the same mother, a member of the Al Sudayri family, was in a powerful position because of the support of his six full brothers, and they were all collectively known as the Sudayri Seven. Fahd named his half-brother, Abdullah, Crown Prince, gave his six full brothers important jobs in the ministries in order to consolidate his power, and adopted a new title, "Custodian of the Two Holy Mosques," at Makkah and Madinah. This title is in use by the current King, Abdullah.

Fahd, like his predecessors, faced internal discontent in the form of critical sermons from the 'ulama' and petitions signed by hundreds of Saudi citizens. In order to appease these negative forces, he passed legal reforms in 1992. These included laws regarding the Majlis al-Shūrā (the Consultative Council of Saudi citizens appointed by the King, who advised the King, although they held no power). This council was originally set at a size of sixty. It later increased to ninety members who were recognized scholars and men of expertise. Of the first sixty chosen by the King, over 50 percent held doctorate degrees and over 60 percent were educated in Western universities, indicating a preference for Western-educated professional elites. Almost 40 percent of them were from Nejd, indicating a preference for the Saud family's home region, even though the Asir, Hasa, and Hijaz regions were also represented. While this body has never had legal power and serves at the pleasure of the King, today it remains an influential body much involved in determining the future direction of the country and has continued to increase in size.

Additionally, Fahd's reforms created clear rules for administering the provinces. Previously, the emir of a province had no clear guidelines for rule, and the strength of his relationship with the King determined his powers. This new Law of the Provinces created clear rules of administration under the supervision of the Minister of the Interior, thus increasing the state bureaucratic apparatus. Fahd's rule saw continued discontent, as it encompassed the first Gulf War, the initial stages of the second one, and the terrorist attacks on the United States in 2001.

In 2003 Crown Prince Abdullah, representing his now physically incapacitated half-brother, King Fahd, oversaw efforts to placate dissent. He organized the first international human rights conference in the Kingdom and followed this with the establishment of the National Human Rights Commission in 2004. Additionally he set in motion the National Dialogue sessions, a series of prominent gatherings of intellectuals, religious leaders and business people of varying political and religious views to discuss topics of contemporary importance. For example, the topic of the second one in December, 2003 was "Extremism and Moderation, a Comprehensive View" and of the third one in June, 2004 was "Rights and Duties of Women." Further in 2003, the government began allowing half the seats in municipal councils to be elected, although only males could vote. This was the first experiment with democratic elections in the Kingdom. The role of the Majlis al-Shūrā was strengthened in a series of changes begun in 2003. While liberalizing the rules for women is a politically fraught subject and hard fought by religious conservatives, in 2003 the laws were changed so that women could obtain commercial licenses in their own names, a reform for which professional women had advocated (Kapiszewski 2006:464–471). Dissent in the Kingdom will be discussed further in chapter 9.

In 2005, Fahd was succeeded by Abdullah, who is the current King, and Sultan became Crown Prince. Under Abdullah's reign, KSA has joined the World Trade Organization (WTO), founded ten new universities, including the first coed university in KSA, and announced the development of new economic cities. These economic cities are planned urban spaces that will include all the necessities of a modern urban space including housing, entertainment and shopping and will focus on the development of new industries in the Kingdom. In 2006, Abdullah issued a ruling that will govern royal succession in the future. An Allegiance Commission, composed of all living sons of Ibn Saud and one grandson representing each of his deceased or incapacitated sons, will have the power to elect the Crown Prince (Twal 2009:44, 51).

The focus of this brief history of KSA has been internal matters; however, since the early movements of Ibn Saud, actions in Arabia have drawn considerable attention abroad. This will be discussed more fully in later chapters, but here a simple example will be used to underscore the point. Official records of presidential administrations of the United States include notes on state visits by Saudi kings during 1950–1970. These notes indicate oil was not the only US concern in KSA. The United States was also focused on how Cold War allegiances played out in the Middle East. The United States needed KSA as an ally to balance the support from the Union of Soviet Socialist Republics for other countries in the region (Mejcher 2004).

Conclusion

Arabia has both a long history of occupation, dating back to the Paleolithic Era, and a long history of climate change. The modern society developed out of adaptation to the current, mostly desert, climate that appeared some 17,000 years ago. Arabia became a land of merchants, camel pastoralists, and oasis agriculturalists, and, since 5,000 years ago, it has been home to a series of ancient kingdoms and many tribal confederacies and emirates.

The current Saudi state rose out of the defeats of two previous Saudi states; the first of these is the source of the Wahhabi version of Islam that is the official religion in KSA today. So the history of the modern Saudi sanction of Islam as taught by al-Wahhab began in the 1700s. Ibn Saud, the founder of the modern state, began his rule as a typical emir who conquered lands held by a rival. He then, through military action and diplomacy and with the religious legitimation of Islam, managed to take control of the lands that now make up the nation-state of KSA.

To unify these diverse regions and multiple emirates into a nation, he used traditional tribal tactics: marriage as a form of diplomacy, leadership behavior as demonstrated in the holding of the majlis and exhibiting the values of generosity and hospitality, and redistribution of wealth; in addition, he forged cultural unity by encouraging the dominance of Nejd (the Al Saud homeland) dress and other cultural symbols and of Wahhabi-sanctioned behavior throughout the Kingdom. At the same time, he and his successor sons slowly built a state bureaucracy out of a system that started as a traditional emirate form of governance. They added ministries as needed and moved from gifts as payment to employees to regularized salaries and formalized job duties.

Through all of this, the Kingdom has remained a distinctly Arab and Muslim state. For example, redistribution to citizens in the form of free health care, college tuition, and other financial aids, as well as the practice of the majlis, still exist today. The citizens of KSA continue to expect the King to fulfill the responsibilities of a traditional emir. Since the Peninsula was never colonized, there were no foreign structures to undo and no foreign presence to expel. KSA is one of a few such clearly indigenous state systems playing an important role on the world stage today, and its leaders insist that its uniquely Arab and Muslim version of modernity and statehood be recognized as equal in value to its Western counterparts.

Note

[1]Geographic place names reflect the views of those who create them. The body of water between Saudi Arabia and Iran is called the Persian Gulf in the US, "Persian" referring to the ethnicity of the population on the Iranian coast. In Saudi Arabia, it is called the Arabian Gulf, referring to the ethnicity of the population on the Saudi coast.

Chapter 4

Traditional Culture of Saudi Arabia

Personal Experiences

Within a few months of my first arrival in the Kingdom, I was invited to dinner at the date farm of a Saudi colleague. Like me, she was a professor at a university, in her case a Saudi university. To reach the farm, I was driven through the streets of Riyadh, down the Tuwaiq Escarpment, the sheer cliff face that can be seen from space that I mentioned in discussing the geology of the Arabian Peninsula, and then to the date farm on the outskirts of a small village. My hostess, dressed in Western casual skirt and blouse, greeted me and introduced me to the other guests, who included some of her family members, Saudi colleagues, and other Western guests. Guests were dressed in Western attire or in more traditional Saudi women's dresses, which were loose fitting, long sleeved, and floor length. None wore abayas as this was an all-female gathering. Single-sex gatherings are the norm in Saudi where women away from the eyes of men remove their abayas and enjoy each other's company.

We were served coffee, dates, fruit juices, chocolates, and tea (all part of a traditional Saudi greeting hospitality ritual) in the house and then my colleague took us for a walk around the farm, proudly showing us the date palms and pens of goats and other animals. The landscape was flat and the soil sandy, while the palm trees were tall and loaded with bunches of fruit. While we could have eaten dinner in the house, she preferred to serve us in the tent set to the side of the house. The tent was a permanent structure complete with a desert cooler, a device used to cool it during the hot day through water evaporation. Inside, the tent was decorated in Nejd style, with print fabric walls, seating on floor cushions, and rolled pillow armrests. We ate

51

from a low table piled high with more food than we could possibly eat. We had rice, several varieties of grilled meats, hummus, tabbouleh, and other Middle Eastern specialties.

After dinner, our hostess led us to an area where chairs were arranged on an Arabian carpet under the stars. She served us tea and told us her story. She is part of a strong, conservative, and close-knit Saudi patrilineal family from a rural area of Nejd. Some twenty-five years before, her father decided to send her to the States with her brothers for schooling. Her conservative uncles were outraged, thinking that sending a daughter to the United States for schooling, even though she would be in the care of her brothers, was a disgrace to the family. The idea was so distasteful that they even came to the airport and tried to convince her father to prevent her from getting on the plane. Her father triumphed, however, and she received schooling in the United States. Adjustment to the United States was difficult for her and she cried to come back home, but eventually she acclimated, and after many years of schooling in the United States, she received a PhD and returned to KSA to teach in the Saudi university system. Her uncles now express their pride in her accomplishments. Sitting in this peaceful setting with my feet rubbing the pile of a beautiful carpet, with the stars lighting the faces of my companions, I thought about how quickly times have changed in Saudi. While not all Saudi families would allow daughters to travel to the West for schooling today, many have, and during my friend's lifetime, the education system in Saudi was started and has grown to include not just primary and secondary schools but a university system as well. All this was unavailable to her mother, for example, since there was no formal schooling for girls until the 1960s. In fact, many of my Saudi friends with graduate school educations explained that their mothers were illiterate, since they did not have the opportunity to learn to read because they grew up before the establishment of a school system.

In a different instance, I was having coffee with a Saudi female friend who is a professional with advanced degrees. I was listening to her sadness as she expressed her grief over the recent death of her brother. In the process of telling me about the events of the days that had merged together in the aftermath of this tragedy, she frequently referred to the continual presence, help, and support she had received from her large family with uncles, aunts, and cousins all visiting her regularly and helping her cope. Then she looked me in the face and explained that family was such a comfort to her. She explained that while there were things she wanted to see changed in her country, there were very good things about it, too, and the importance placed on strong and cohesive families is one of those. As her country changes in the future, she hopes Saudis will be able to keep the importance of family. "It is such a comfort in hard times and it is my family that has gotten me through this crisis," she explained. I expressed my deep sorrow at her loss as well as my understanding of the value she placed on her family. Later in the day, I reflected on this interaction. I could feel her concern that her country is rapidly changing and care needs to be taken to keep the important cultural values.

What do these two visits with friends have in common? Both are concerned with traditional Saudi culture and the rapid recent changes in KSA. The first describes changes in fewer than fifty years in the education system and the changes in values and norms that accompanied the education changes. Fifty years ago, many families would not have allowed their daughters to go to school; now it is routine for girls to go to school locally; many even go abroad for schooling. In addition, the gathering at which my friend told her story combined elements of the new with elements of the old. We ate dinner in a modern version of a traditional-style tent decorated in traditional fashion but with a modern metal frame and cooling mechanisms. While this dwelling took advantage of modern technology, its style reflected a traditional Arabian dwelling. Thus, it exemplifies accepting what is useful in the modern but keeping what is valued in the traditional. The second example is concerned with future changes in the Kingdom as my grieving friend was acutely aware of the changes that her country is undergoing and expressed concern for keeping the treasured norms and behaviors that have been present for centuries. The strength of family is valuable to her.

I have had numerous experiences in KSA that exhibit the same themes evident in my two encounters described above: the importance of understanding traditional culture, the rapid rate of change and the significance of both of these in modern Saudi culture. Consequently, I consider a central theme of this book to be the changes in life in the Arabian Peninsula over the last 100 years, first, as a result of Ibn Saud's unification practices, and second, as a result of modernization processes employed by him and more intensely by his sons after the increase in the oil revenues in the 1970s. Change in the Kingdom was rapid from 1970 to 2000. Saudi Arabia today resembles other wealthy nations of the world in its material culture and modern technology and in the issues of day-to-day living that concern its inhabitants; however, its inhabitants share with other cultures in the Middle East a unique, complex, and ancient way of life. Here I describe the cultures of Saudi Arabia as they were recorded in the twentieth century in order to demonstrate the values and behaviors that continue to underlie life in the Kingdom today.

Regional Diversity

Saudi Arabia is often perceived as a single cultural entity symbolized by the thobe of the men and abaya of the women. In actuality, however, KSA includes a number of different economic, cultural, and geographic regions. Residents frequently speak of its division into three or four regions, but I prefer to describe it based on six internally diverse geographic regions (Akers 2001:59–76). Regions differed in cultural ways marked by outward symbols of these differences, like specific house types, craft specialties, and styles of dress. In all regions, pastoralism and agriculture were the main sources of income, and I will describe examples of these two economic strategies in more detail later in this chapter, but I first describe the six regions.

Nejd, the central plateau, which is home to the Al Saud family, the seat of Saudi political power, and the birthplace of the Wahhabi teachings on Islam, was long closed off from much of the cosmopolitan trade of other regions by its inaccessibility in the deserts of the center of the country. It includes the capital, Riyadh, and the second largest desert, the Nefud. The Riyadh climate is dry with annual rainfall of 100 millimeters (3.9 inches) and temperatures that range from 45° Celsius (113° Fahrenheit) in the summer day to 1degree Celsius (33° Fahrenheit) in a winter's night. While residents talk of fleeing the area in summer for the cooler climate along the coasts and while its temperatures are hotter than its important sister cities on the Arabian Gulf and the Red Sea, Riyadh's drier climate makes the intense summer heat less difficult than the humidity of the coasts. Traditionally, Nejd was home to both mobile pastoralists and settled agriculturalists.

The *Hijaz* is the area along the Red Sea from the Gulf of Aqaba to the Asir region and includes the two holy cities of Makkah and Madinah and the significant Red Sea port of Jiddah. Trade caravans have traveled through this region for centuries. Due to the influx of foreigners traveling to Makkah for Hajj or through the area in trade caravans, the Hijaz was the most commercial and cosmopolitan of the regions of KSA at the time of its unification. Many foreigners traveling in the region became residents, creating an ethnically diverse population. Ruled by the Hashemites who had British support and given its symbolic value as the destination of the Muslim pilgrimage and its economic value brought about by that same pilgrimage as well as extensive trade, the Hijaz was possibly the greatest prize of Ibn Saud's conquests.

Traditional male dress in the Asir region.

The *Asir* is considered the southern part of Hijaz and stretches along the Red Sea to Yemen. It is composed of coastal lowlands and interior mountains and receives the most rain of any region in the Kingdom. The region is recognized for its distinctive culture where many continue to live in traditional mud-brick houses, and one still sees the traditional male dress of a brightly colored kilt and a garland on the head.

Al-Hasa lies along the Arabian Gulf from Kuwait to Oman and the United Arab Emirates and also saw much caravan traffic in earlier times. It includes large oases important for agriculture and is known for its high-quality dates. Pearl diving was traditionally an important addition to the economy here, augmenting the pastoralist and agricultural livelihoods found throughout the Kingdom; in modern times the region is home to the oil business. Aramco, the state-owned oil company, is responsible for the current bustling urban settlements of Dhahran, Dammam, al-Khobar, and Ras Tanura, which have replaced Hofuf, an oasis settlement important in agriculture and trade, as the most significant urban drivers of this regional economy. This area is also home to KSA's large Shi'a population, which feels marginalized in a country that accepts the Wahhabi version of Islam, a branch of Sunni Islam, as its official religion.

The *Rub al-Khali*, or "Empty Quarter," is one of the largest deserts in the world and is larger than the country of France. Most of the area lacks water, and its sand mountains can reach as high as 305 meters (1,000 feet). This is the area of rolling sand dunes that so captures the imagination of the West. While more sparsely populated than other parts of the country, it is not "empty" of life. The Al-Murrah tribe, discussed later in this chapter, made use of it traditionally. Today it is also the source of much of the nation's oil wealth.

The *Northern Region* extends from Nejd to KSA's borders with Jordan and Iraq. It is made up of plateaus and a harrat (a stony area or lava field) where an ancient lava flow has left fields of jagged volcanic rock. It also saw caravan traffic in earlier times and was known for its good grasses used to pasture sheep and goats as well as camels.

All six regions contain peoples who lived by the two most important subsistence strategies of the Peninsula: pastoralism and agriculture. I turn now to a description of these two ways of life in the twentieth century.

The Bedu

With the domestication of the camel 3,500 years ago, a way of life evolved in Arabia, which continues to the present day, the lifeway of the bedu. While we do not have specific data on the size of this group, an aerial survey of the Kingdom in 1966 identified 227,000 nomad tents and based on that count Harold Heady estimated a population of a little more than one million. Herds of camels for each camp likely numbered less than 100 head (Heady 1972). Simply put, the bedu are the nomadic herders of the Middle East. They are contrasted with the *hadar*, or the sedentary peoples. Identifying who is bedu in Arabia is not simple. Most who would identify themselves as bedu no longer live as herders and, in fact, some of their ancestors may have lived sedentary lives for generations. The bedu are those whose values reflect bedu culture and who recently had family members who lived a herding existence. According to Al-Rasheed, the bedu value independence; animal herding; hospitality; defense of the weak; eloquence, especially in composing and reciting poetry; and the honor of raiding and war. Lancaster (1981:43) stated, the "bedu virtues [were] honour, bravery, generosity, political acumen and mediatory abilities. In the past when all men were economically equal . . . the only way of distinguishing one man from another in terms of worth was by his reputation." And while bedu family members might have taken up other occupations like wage labor or farming, they were still part of a larger bedu kinship unit. Today, only a small percent of the bedu still work in animal herding.

The Animals

The bedu developed a complex culture in one of the earth's harshest environments. Their economic activities centered on (1) trade in animals and animal products, (2) raiding or protection from raiding by other bedu, settled villagers, and passing caravans, and (3) providing animals for use by caravans. The most prestigious herding animal has always been the camel, although the herding of sheep and goats is common today. While sheep and goats provide meat, wool, and other products, the importance of the camel cannot be overstated. In the desert, it was the camel that provided transport. What other animal could carry such a heavy load, travel for so many days without water, and throughout it all provide its caretaker with food in the form of its milk? When the only water available was too brackish for human consumption, the camel acted as a water purification system: the camel drank the water and the bedu drank the camel's milk for liquid. Without the camel, the famously long and difficult travel routes across Arabia would never have developed. These routes developed as caravans carried goods from India and Persia (modern-day Iran) to the Red Sea and, after the emergence of Islam, were used also by pilgrims going to Makkah. Caravan routes tied the Arabian interior to the commercial and political world of the Middle East, the Far East, Africa, and the Mediterranean.

Donald Cole (1975) describes the life of the Al Murrah tribe with whom he lived for eighteen months from 1968 to 1970. The Al Murrah tribe in eastern Saudi Arabia inhabited a territory of 250,000 square miles with a population of about 15,000 in 1970. These tribal lands lay primarily within the Rub al-Khali (the Empty Quarter), although Al Murrah tribal members sometimes ranged as far as Kuwait and Iraq, and annually a household was likely to travel a minimum of 1,200 miles. Cole explains that, for the Al Murrah, the desert was inhospitable and dangerous only when they were without a camel herd; with one, it was a land rich in food. Camel's milk and dates were the staple foods; dates could be carried long distances through the desert and held for long periods of time without spoiling. Thus, when the bedu were away from fresh food sources other than their camels, they relied on dates, which are high in sugar and provide quick energy. They frequently carried wheat flour and made a kind of camp bread using the sands beside the fire as an oven and coals to provide the heat. They also regularly consumed rice. Most protein came from the wild animals they hunted; camels were too valuable to kill for their meat and were only killed if the animal was sick and dying.

The Al Murrah explained to Cole that the desert satisfied all their needs; it had "clean sand, fresh air, the best plants for camels, good hunting and only one's brothers." Only members of their own tribe, their "brothers," frequented the Empty Quarter so there was no danger of raiders, and only there, they said, could they find the plants that would allow them to raise such prize thoroughbred camels with such good milk production. The Al Murrah named their camels and created poems, stories, and songs about them. Arabic contains an extraordinary number of words for "camel," and the Al Murrah used different words depending on the sex, age, color, use, and breed. A tribesman, in fact, might know the genealogy of a particular camel as far back as ten generations (Cole 1975:23–31, 57).

In a time of raiding, the camels had to be swift, quiet, and possessing of great endurance. The camel that brayed could give the raiders away as they attempted a surprise attack on a camp or herd. A swift camel was not only fast of foot but also did not need to be watered often and could graze on the run, thus requiring fewer stops. To appreciate the hardship of desert travel, realize that at the end of a long journey through the barren desert, the fat camel had become lean and its hump nearly gone. Riders were completely dependent on their camels on these long trips. It is therefore no surprise that camels were well tended. Riding camels were usually females without calves as they were easiest to manage. The stronger male camels were used as the pack animals. Males were also used to carry the litters in which women and children rode. Many tribes had herds of special camels, matched in color, and a special herd would be much admired and of interest to potential raiders. The strongest warriors were asked to guard this special herd. A tribe's reputation was known by the quality and health of its camels because healthy camels had grazed in rich pastures to which only the most honored of tribes would be able to gain access. Camel herds were often named and their names were used as battle cries. Lancaster (1997:99) who studied the Rwala on the northern edge of the Great Nefud desert between 1972 and 1980 estimates that a family of six needed a herd of fifteen or twenty camels to survive; most Rwala had herds that were much larger.

With the coming of the automobile, the camel's economic value declined as it was no longer the only way to travel long distances through the desert. Since the automobile, sheep herding has become economically more profitable because sheep reproduce faster than camels; with the availability of water trucks, sheep can now graze where lack of water made it impossible before. Also, the government drilled wells in the desert allowing for herds to

Camel herd outside Riyadh.

graze in places only camels could go before (Cole 1975:160). Camel herds have retained their cultural value, however, and while the herding of sheep and goats has increased as the herding of camels has decreased, camel herds are still kept as insurance against hard times. Should vehicles not be available, families could return to the old ways. Thus, camels hold a special place in the hearts of the bedu. The camel remains a symbol of bedu culture itself, and a bedu with fat, beautiful camels is still to be admired.

The other animal of importance to the bedu is the horse. The famed Arabian horses admired the world over are prized by the bedu as well. The horse was used in raids because it is nimble and quick. Camels were ridden on long journeys, but the warriors led their horses, and if attacked, they jumped on these swifter animals to hunt down the attackers. So the tribe's success at defending its assets depended on the quality of its horses as well as its camels. Like the human, however, the horse's survival in the desert depended on the camel. It was camel milk that kept it alive in the waterless desert. A common theme of bedu poetry is the praise of beautiful camels and horses. This emotional importance attached to the animals is a common characteristic among pastoralists in societies all around the world. For example, the Navajo in the American Southwest held sheep in similar high regard.

Raiding

Another characteristic behavior of pastoralists in many parts of the world is dependence on raiding, and in this the bedu are typical. This made economic sense as a means of renewing spent resources. Water is of course the most precious of resources in the desert; when rain does not come, the pastures dry up. Rain in the desert is variable; one might say it is fickle. In any given year, some areas will be well watered and others will receive no rain followed in subsequent years by a reverse pattern. If the rains do not come to the pastures owned by one's tribe, the tribe's camels die and so do the humans. How does one even out the rain when it falls so indiscriminately? By raiding. If the tribe's herds were decimated because of drought, its members could raid the herds of a tribe more fortunate with the rain. Raiding was not always conducted because of need, however.

Cole distinguishes between raiding and war for the Al Murrah. Raids were conducted against tribes of equal status with the purpose of capturing camels. The object of war, on the other hand, was to gain territory, to pillage, or to take control of another group (Cole 1975:95). Bedu raiding followed elaborate codes of behavior, and those who did not follow the codes lost something precious: their honor. According to Saad Abdullah Sowayan (1985), the rules included the following: (1) a formal declaration of war had to be made against a tribe before raiding it; (2) a surprise attack at night was considered cowardly and one during the day was brave and brought honor; (3) only healthy men could be attacked; and (4) women, children, the infirm, and even the sleeping were not to be harmed. If a group undertook a raid on a distant camp, the warriors rode to the site with camel riders who carried them and their equipment and provisions. The warriors led their horses, which were not ridden until the actual raid.

The best times to raid were (1) when a camp had just packed up to move, (2) in the morning as the herd was being driven out to pasture, or (3) in the evening when the herd was returning. At these times, the herd would be together and the warriors would be able to acquire more animals. Once the herd was off grazing, the animals would be scattered and difficult to round up in a raid. Since all bedu knew the best times for raids, a camp was always cautious at those times and posted lookouts who scanned the horizon, watching for raiders. If a raiding party was spotted, the warriors in the camp decided whether they had sufficient numbers to ward off the intruders; if not, they retreated and let the invaders take the spoils. Then they likely chased the raiders back in the direction from whence they came. The route of the invaders was easily determined because, of necessity, they headed for the nearest water source. Another battle was likely at this location, and the wronged parties might win back their camels.

When a tribe's pastures were bare, their leaders might decide to try to take the pastures of another tribe. This was cause for a large battle. The invading tribe moved into the desired pastures signaling its intent to take them. Both tribes pitched war tents and a serious battle ensued with the pastures going to the victors.

Raiding was an honorable activity and success in raiding, when this meant acting with courage and honor, was revered. It was a way for a young man to improve his social status. The prestige of being an honorable and brave warrior was more important than the material reward of acquiring stolen wealth. In fact, Alois Musil (1928) comments that a warrior was likely to give the stolen goods away and might even give them to the very family from whom they had been taken. Giving away the camels just stolen increased one's status, as the giver proved himself a successful raider and a generous man as well. Before guns, raiding caused comparatively little loss of life but allowed a man to demonstrate great bravery. It was considered a badge of courage to fight in hand-to-hand combat with one's enemy in an attempt to protect one's property and the women and children of the tribe. Battle should always reflect one's bravery and skill. It was wrong to kill a wounded or ill man who could not put up a good fight. Actually, in combat, if a warrior saw that he was losing, he could ask pardon from the victor and his life would be spared. Here, the winner got what he was fighting for—an increase in his own prestige—and the loser lost what he was fighting for—his own prestige and honor. Many bedu poems reflect these values. Below are a few lines from a poem by Nasir ibn Emir ibn Hadi of Ghatan as an example.

> Fortunate are those who were absent the day we were attacked at
> Amelah, those who did not witness the uproar of our frightened
> camel herds.
> The panicked beasts threw off their loads. My heart was inflamed
> by the urging shouts of our ladies.
> When I charged the enemy lines, they met me with lances and spears;
> but when I fled, the lady with the beautiful eyes cried out after me.
> After the spear broke I unsheathed Abu Lah, my sword, the only
> weapon left in my hand.
> I fought in their midst until I repelled the attacking multitudes. I
> chased them away like the rutting male camel after she-camels in
> heat.
> Slow down, mounted lady with thick eyelashes! I shall defend you
> as long as my swift mare can run.
> For the sake of your eyes, I shall run down the foe, and his soul
> shall leave his body before reaching the ground. I shall leave him
> for the lame hyenas and spotted vultures to sup on.
> It is my custom to risk my life on the battlefield while the cowardly
> run away.
> These are the words of a fearless man. I am a noble hunting bird.
> (Sowayan 1985:38)

Raiding ended throughout the Kingdom in the 1930s due to two factors: (1) Ibn Saud unified the country and forbade raiding, and (2) camels lost their economic value due to the arrival of the automobile.

Agriculture and Trade

While animal herding is the primary economic activity of bedu, it is not the only one. For generations, some bedu have been agriculturalists. For thousands of years, this most likely took the form of date plantations in oases within the tribal area. These were worked by peasants who received a portion of the proceeds for their labor or by slaves. Other crops of fruit, vegetables, wheat, and barley could be grown, too, but dates were the most important as they, along with camel's milk, formed the basis of the bedu diet. Bedu who did not own date palms had to trade their animals and animal products (wool, meat, and butter) for dates. Both mobile bedu and sedentary people in the oasis areas needed access to products neither could produce. These included coffee, salt, rice, sugar, clothes, weapons, rope, and perfume. To acquire these, they were dependent on caravan trade. Depending on the location of the bedu tribe, this trade could be from India, Iraq, the Mediterranean, and the Arabian Gulf or beyond. As caravans came through their areas, the bedu derived further income by selling them the following: (1) camels for transporting goods, (2) protection for the caravan from possible raids by other bedu, and (3) guide service to show them the way to the next water location.

Small oasis villages on major caravan routes became large, thriving towns fed by the economics of the caravan trade. If the location also happened to be on a pilgrimage route to Makkah, there was additional wealth to be gained from guiding, outfitting, and protecting pilgrims. The small oasis of Hail is a good example of the economic success the right location can bring. Located on a route used for trade from Iraq and Persia (modern-day Iran) to the Hijaz and also used by pilgrims to Makkah, the Shammar tribe's ownership of this small oasis led to economic and political prosperity, and Hail grew into a prosperous trading town. It was the regional location for trade between sedentary agriculturalists and pastoral nomads and an important stop on the caravan route. Members of the Shammar tribe served as guides and protectors of caravans through their territory. The town also supported artisans who made copperware, camel saddles, embroidered material, and other items that could be traded. The success of this town was important in the rise to power of the Rasheed family of the Shammar tribe.

The Annual Cycle of Movement

While the bedu are referred to as "nomads," they were not free wanderers: they traveled primarily in their own tribal territory or risked confrontation with another tribe, and their movements were not random; they followed the good pastures and, of course, the available water. When Pleiades left the night sky, it was summer, the driest time of the year, and they congregated in large tribal groups at reliable water wells owned by the tribe. At this time of year bedu visited widely with local settled agriculturalists and other pastoralists. It was a time for making and renewing relationships, alliances, and reputations for hospitality. It was a time for trading the tribe's surplus for items needed in the coming year and trading information and gossip with tribal relations. The camels were sent out to pasture away from camp, as the pasture close at hand was quickly grazed. Herders and guards were sent with the herds, returning every third day to fetch water from the wells for the camels. The time when the herds were out was fraught with anxiety as this was the best time for enemies to raid and steal the herd. Herds were large and their guardians few as most men were back in the camp so the guards had to be extra vigilant. If an enemy did come, the guards tried to fend them off and to stampede the herd. In camp, the tents were usually placed in rows beside the wells; often, wells had to be deeply dug in order to reach water. To bring the water up from such a depth, they used a pulley system with a bucket, a rope, a water wheel over the well, and a camel to do the pulling. Today, in the spirit of ingenuity and conservation, the water wheel apparatus at many wells is made of an old car frame and a hubcap.

When Canopus was in the east at dawn, it was September and the time of the coming of the rain. Water was again available in seasonal locations so that the large camps broke up and small groups traveled in various directions. Scouts would have already reported on the best locations for pasture and water, and a traveling group was likely to move every week or ten days. Even though the camps were small and scattered, they continued to have contact with each other. Often a camp was within shouting distance of the next one. Winter was not free from the threat of raid from one's enemies, however, because although the herds were smaller, a few wandering raiders could sneak into camp and lead away a prize camel or two. These small camps defended against raids by placing their tents in a circle with ropes stretched between them. The livestock was in the center. Should anyone try to lead a camel out under cover of darkness, the movement of ropes was intended to wake the unsuspecting owners.

To see the bedu move camp must have been an impressive sight. The decision to move was made by the leader in consultation with the other men of the group. When and where to move was determined by water and pasture availability as well as by the movements of hostile bedu as reported by the scouts. The women took down the tents and loaded tents and belongings on the pack camels. As the caravan got under way, first in line, riding their camels and leading their horses, were the well-armed warriors on the lookout for enemy raiders. Following them were the pack camels loaded with the belongings of the group, and then other members of the group followed on riding camels. Women were hidden away in litters, which were frames covered with fabric and placed on the camels' backs. At the rear of the caravan, moving here and there to graze, was the camel herd. The move was a momentous event with groups traveling in sight of each other and covering 30–50 kilometers (18–31 miles) a day moving from water source to water source, allowing the herds to graze as they went. Such a move might take two months (Finan and Al-Haratani 1998:352–354). This annual cycle was captured in a poem by Ibn Sbayyil.

When the hot wind begins to blow and the green stalks wither,
when milk no longer allays the thirst of the herders.
Then the nomads come back to their summer camps, their camel
herds covering the hills. The loaded camels are couched, and the pitched tents
Are lined up like a chain of black hills. The sheep herders yield up
the water wells.
The nomads fill the vast plain around the wells of fresh cool water. . . .
They remain by the wells for ninety days and there is no mention
of moving camp.
But the cool winds of the rainy season begin to blow and Canopus
appears in the east shortly before the morning twilight. . . .
The next morning the ladies roll up the tents, and the camel herds
are watered before they are driven off.
The herds spread out in the countryside on their way to a pasture
which the scouts have recommended.
The camp is left desolate; it has reverted to wilderness, with wolves
howling about. . . .
After they have bought all they need, without regret they quit the
settled country. They go wherever the rain falls. (Sowayan 1985:25–26)

When the caravan finally reached a destination intended for a long stay, tents were pitched by the women. The number of poles supporting the tent indicated its size, and inside every tent a divider separated the men's and women's sides. The horse of the male owner of the tent was tied outside and his camels brought in front at night. The leader of the group usually had the biggest tent since this was where men gathered to talk. It was located at the most dangerous spot in the camp in order to serve as a sign to passing enemies and to be an easy location for visiting friends to reach.

Since tribal boundaries restricted bedu movement and wandering without permission into others' lands would bring warfare, one of the reasons for political alliances was to negotiate in which lands one could safely pasture one's animals. The alliances also served the function of information sharing, as such information could be life saving. One of the values of traditional hospitality was that it gave the camp an opportunity to learn all the information about routes and grass levels and rain possibilities of areas through which their guests had recently traveled. The bedu exhibited a sophisticated knowledge of plant, animal, weather, and topography patterns across the desert as well as specific and current knowledge of alliances, enemies, and movement patterns of other bedu groups.

For several reasons, this traditional pattern of movement protected the fragile desert pastures. Since animals had to be close to water, grazing lands too far from a water source were not used; this allowed those undergrazed areas to provide seed for range restoration. The fact that one had to have permission of the owners in order to graze in an area meant choice pasture might not be used by all, and this limiting of the number of groups grazing in an area prevented overgrazing. Furthermore, the bedu population and their animal population were not sufficiently large as to stress the environment (Finan and Al-Haratani 1998:342–355).

Women and Work

Work in a bedu camp was not all camel herding and raiding. Women's jobs included making and repairing the tents. While a woman did not shear the sheep, she carded and spun the wool, wove the tent fabric, and stitched the pieces together. She made the clothes and necessary cloth objects, like quilts and pillows. She collected firewood and water and prepared and preserved the food. Among the Al Murrah, the senior woman in the family owned the tent (Cole 1975:64). Tents were typically made of goat hair or sheep wool, although today it is common to see white cloth tents. Tents had from one to five rooms, but most needed at least two in order for the women to have a room separate from that of the men. A one-room tent was likely to be used only for a temporary shelter.

The fabric that formed the divider between rooms was beautifully decorated in designs specific to the owner's tribe; the tent's outer walls were plain by comparison. A tent divider may have been 7.6 meters (25 feet) long and 2 meters (7 feet high) and was made of woven strips sewn together with iron needles and heavy yarn. When visiting in the women's side of one of these tents in 2002, I remarked on the slits in the fabric of the divider wall. My female companions explained that this allowed them to look through and see which men were visiting in the men's side. I exclaimed, "Well doesn't that also allow them to look in at you, unveiled in the privacy of your home?" They quickly responded, "Oh no, the men would never do that." It would bring extremely serious consequences. The slits were for one-way viewing only. While women were separated from unrelated males, their work of collecting water and moving tents made them part of the activity of the camp.

Hospitality

While raiding and the accompanying hand-to-hand combat are no longer in evidence in Arabia, other important desert virtues are very much alive. These are the virtues of hospitality and generosity. It is part of bedu culture that no stranger should be turned away from camp. Rather, any visitor will be well fed and protected, not only for the length of the stay but for three days afterward, which is considered to be the time it takes to digest the last meal provided by the host. As mentioned in chapter 3 when discussing the majlis, in Arabia today one finds houses unlocked, coffee pots available, and plates of dates on display so that at any time of day or night, a visitor may partake of food and drink. A foreigner driving through the desert who meets a bedu out tending his animals is likely to have the bedu chase after him, insisting that the foreigner return to his home for dinner. I have had this experience more than once myself when bedu women were present to offer the hospitality. The coffee-making ceremony is an important symbol of this hospitality. This uniquely Arabian coffee made with cardamom is still the first offering a guest receives in a modern Arabian home, at a formal reception, or even in an airport lobby. It is likely to be followed by dates and tea. Arabic coffee and dates, along with camel milk, are the symbolically significant foods of bedu culture and the signs of bedu hospitality.

Still today at Saudi homes, large quantities of meat and rice are served on huge platters providing more food than the guests can possibly eat. A host never refuses food or drink to a visitor, unless with the intent of gravely insulting him, and never refuses a cry for help. Generosity in helping others is a reflection of honor and builds reputation; the gracious hospitality of the people of Arabia is internationally known.

Poetry

The bedu are also famous for poetry. In my travels in Arabia, Saad Abdullah Sowayan's book was several times referenced to me as a good place to start my reading about traditional Arabian culture and values. Sowayan, a Saudi anthropologist, has written a book explaining the significance of Nabati poetry, the popular vernacular poetry of Arabia (Sowayan 1985:1). The composing and reciting of poems was a time-honored tradition, and any large gathering was likely to include the reciting of poems that were memorized and passed on orally. Their subject matter reflected bedu values and the bedu way of life. General themes were warfare, camels, and honor, and poems were often composed about a particular individual well-known for his valor in battle, his generosity to his guests, and his honor in all things important. Bedu poetry is part of the ancient tradition of Arabic poetry and literature. Poetry composition continues to be valued in Arabia today as a performance art, although much of it has now been captured permanently on the printed page. However, old bedu poems and the stories that accompanied their creation are still part of the lore of Arabia known to many modern citizens.

Organization through Kinship

The bedu were organized by kinship into a complex structure usually referred to as the tribe. While the definition of this term varies, Al-Rasheed's explanation for the Shammar in central northern Saudi Arabia in the early twentieth century is a good example of a typical Arabian tribal structure. In the nineteenth century, the Shammar were estimated by one source to have numbered 4,000 tents and by another to have been composed of 150,000–200,000 people. With peoples who were so mobile, exact numbers were difficult to acquire. The Shammar were a *gabila*, translated as tribe—a loose association of people who recognize that they are related to each other by kinship. Given their frequent movements over a large geographical area, there was little unity and in fact no recognized head leadership until the 1830s when the Rasheed family began to dominate from the oasis area of Hail. The Shammar were further divided into four *ashair*, each with a recognized leader, the tribal shaykh. The members of an *ashira* understood themselves to be united politically and militarily. Within each *ashira* was any number of smaller units, *fukhud* (plural), which were lineages whose members inhabited from 100 to 150 tents. The members of a *fakhd* (singular) camped together and herded animals together. These units owned pasture land and water wells. A fakhd had a recognized wasm, or brand, which marked its wells and announced the well ownership to all. A fakhd was further divided into smaller lineages, *hamula*. Each of these had the right to use the wells of its fakhd. The members of a hamula placed their tents close together and grazed their animals as one herd. This unit was closely related patrilineally. Its likely composition would be a man and his wife or wives, his sons and their wives, their sons, and their wives and children. Thus, it might entail four generations related through the male line to the oldest couple; this unit of patrilateral parallel cousins is called *ibn amm*. The smallest recognizable kin unit is the *beit*, the residential tent. Upon marriage, a man establishes his own tent and becomes owner of part of the herd. He and his family are then self-sufficient in providing for their own milk and meat (Al-Rasheed 1991:20).

To summarize, the functions of these various levels of kinship structure are as follows: the gabila and ashira have political functions and the fukhud, hamula, and beit have economic functions and camp or live together. At its most inclusive level, the gabila, the Shammar recognized their common kin-

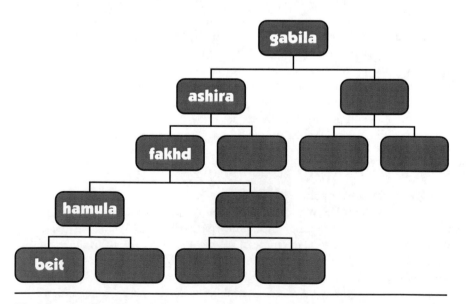

Kinship units, Shammar tribe.

ship identity and trusted that they would come to the defense of other members against outside threats. While Al-Rasheed explains that it is hard to imagine all 150,000 Shammar uniting in a military activity, and there is evidence of splits within the tribe when faced with outside pressure, Shammar unity did represent a culturally held prescription, and all Shummar recognized their allegiance to help, protect, and share resources with other Shummar. Cole's experience with the Al Murrah was similar; he found that to know someone as a fellow Al Murrah tribesman was to know that he was a brother, to know his lineage was to know where his family camped, who his ancestors were, and what they had accomplished (Cole 1975:84; Al-Rasheed 1991:21). Tribal identity remains strong in Arabia today. It is a basis for marriage arrangements and holds importance across the Kingdom as a key to one's identity and one's standing in society.

In Partnership with the Land

Few modern lifeways are as successful and sustainable as traditional bedu culture. In a desert land, the bedu developed an existence that allowed them to thrive. Their feelings for the land were strong. The following lines from a poem by Al Oni in which he praises his homeland give a sense of the emotional pull of the land. Al Oni is lamenting the loss of his group's land to a rival.

> Were I to find solace in crying, O camel, I would cry every white
> day and every night. . . .
> I would cry over the homeland where we grew up, bordered on the
> north by lofty escarpments,
> And bordered on the east by the sand dunes of al-Arazim; it is
> situated between al-Lwa and as-Sirr. I remember those sand dunes—
> oh, how beautiful they are.
> A homeland in Najd that was once a haven, a refuge sought by
> those burdened by hard times.
> She resembles a fair chaste maiden; in her beauty my homeland
> outshines all fair maidens. . . .
> She is our mother—oh how sweet was her flowing milk; she
> nourished us, she raised us, we are her children. (Sowayan 1985:82)

While bedu possessions seem meager by today's standards, they were sensible. Mobile societies rarely acquire great numbers of possessions for it is impractical to transport them. The bedu, however, had wealth in their animals, possessions that could move on their own. Furthermore, their way of life left them plenty of time to appreciate beauty and art. There was beauty in the sleek, fat, thoroughbred camel, the intricately woven pattern of a tent divider, and the elaborate patterns stitched into clothing and painted on bodies with henna. That they valued art is well established in their love of poetry. Few mobile societies have developed the art of poetry to such a degree as the bedu.

Bedu possessed many skills that seem incredible to others. For example, the members of the Al Murrah tribe are still renowned for their tracking ability. They can tell by the tracks what color a camel is or whose car has passed and when. They can identify the footprints of individual camels, including all those in their own herds. In earlier times, this was a useful skill, as a traveling family member might return to the desert to find that his family had moved camp. Imagine returning home to find that not only had the locks been changed but your house had been moved! Donald Cole explains how for the traveling Al Murrah tribesman, this was no cause for alarm because in order to find the new camp, he would track the camel herd. In the twentieth century, Al Murrah tribesmen were employed by the police due to this tracking ability. They were able to recognize human footprints as well as camel ones and could tell if the maker of the print was young, old, male, or female, and even if a female was pregnant. Prior to the popularity of wearing shoes, a tribesman might help the police find a criminal suspect by sitting in the market observing the activities until the person belonging to a footprint sought by the police happened by. The Al Murrah knowledge of the geography of their lands and their sense of direction were equally unparalleled (Cole 1975:54–55). The bedu were well adapted to their environment, and they took nothing from it that would not be replenished by the next rains.

As mentioned in the previous chapter, Ibn Saud was able to bring the independent bedu into his incipient state system by enlisting their help as warriors fighting for the cause of Islam through their participation in the ikhwān. The intention was to stop their volatile raiding and shift their allegiance from the tribe to the state and to settle them permanently in agricultural villages. He replaced the old system of tribal laws with shari'a, Islamic law. As the Arabian Peninsula was turned into nation-states, bedu found it more difficult, although still possible, to move across national boundaries. Today, many formerly pastoralist families are settled in urban areas and those still living the pastoralist life have family members who have moved to urban areas. They take part in the formal education system and work in jobs of all types. They are taxi drivers, oil field workers, doctors, accountants, teachers, and business persons. Many bedu participate in the Reserve National Guard of Saudi Arabia for which they draw salaries. In order to maintain the family herds, they frequently employ foreign laborers to work as herders. In driving across the desert, however, one still sees the scattering of white tents with a white pickup truck and a huge water truck nearby. Somewhere in the vicinity is a herd of camels or goats and sheep.

Distinguishing the Bedu and the Hadar

Donald Cole (1975:23) described the ways in which the economies of the bedu pastoralists and the hadar agriculturalists were intertwined in Arabia. Urban dwellers often owned animals that they sent to the desert with pastoralists to graze, while pastoralists might own date palms in the oases that they depended on their sedentary neighbors to harvest in exchange for a portion of the profit. Pastoralists turned their animals into the fields of their agricultural neighbors so the animals could graze on the stubble left after a harvest. In turn, the resulting manure fertilized the fields. Nomads also provided protection to their neighbors in settled villages from other raiding pastoralists. Al-Rasheed (1991:16–17) commented that desert life was based on a single economy with three parts: trade, animal herding, and agriculture. Settled peoples relied on the pastoralists for animal products, like meat, butter, and wool; pastoralists depended on the agriculturalists' products of dates and other foods; traders imported grain, rice, coffee, sugar, cloth, and weapons on which agriculturalists and pastoralists alike depended.

Al-Rasheed, in her description of the political life of the Rashidis of Hail, further explains the meaning of bedu and hadar in her own Hail homelands. Bedu referred to more than an occupation of pastoral nomadism. Members of pastoralist families who moved into oasis towns were still considered to have bedu identity. Bedu referred to a cultural category that indicated a person (1) had tribal origins traceable back for generations that had been kept pure by patrilineal endogamy, (2) exhibited a value system of hospitality, defense of the weak, and eloquence, and (3) prized a lifestyle of raiding and camel herding. There was always smoke coming out of the tent of a generous bedu leader, as food was continuously in preparation for his many guests (1991:120). Al-Rasheed lists the social classes of Hail, from the perspective of an aristocratic bedu: (1) aristocratic bedu who were camel herders, (2) herders of sheep and goats, and (3) Sulab, who were hunters with no tribal origin and did not participate in tribal raids. These classes were reinforced in marriage arrangements. An aristocratic family would never marry into a family of herders or marry with the Sulab, for example. Marriage patterns, in turn, reinforced the class system.

The bedu/hadar distinction is salient in other countries in the Arabian Peninsula as well. In Qatar, the bedu, who trace descent from nomadic Arabian Peninsula tribes, settled in towns after the discovery of oil while the hadar are the village dwellers who settled long before the bedu and some of whom are migrants from Persia (modern-day Iran) (Nagy 2006:129). In Kuwait, which could be described as a city state so urban is the country, the hadar are again distinguished from the bedu by their longer residence in the urban spaces. The bedu arrived in the country after the oil discoveries and primarily between 1960 and 1980. They are viewed as having moved from Saudi Arabia, although they are members of tribes whose traditional lands straddled the Saudi–Kuwaiti border. In Kuwait, the hadar see the bedu as newcomers reaping the benefits of Kuwaiti citizenship (Longva 2006:171).

The Hadar

In KSA, hadar refers to settled populations in towns and oases. Along the coasts, these populations were frequently engaged in maritime activity while inland they were typically agriculturalists. From the perspective of aristocratic bedu of Hail, the hadar were of lower status, partially because they had either no tribal origins or they had failed to keep their tribal descent lines pure due to tribal exogamous marriages. Al-Rasheed (1991:118–132) explains that the hadar were outside the bedu value system because they did not participate in raiding and warfare. The hadar did not have the power to defend themselves and depended on their bedu allies for that service, which placed them lower in status than their camel pastoralist defenders. The hadar were divided into the following occupational groups in Hail: (1) farmers; (2) artisans who made weapons, saddles, cooking utensils and other items necessary to the life of all desert dwellers; (3) merchants who were frequently foreigners and, while wealthy, were not of sufficient social status to marry aristocratic bedu; and (4) slaves of African or Caucasian origin. Marriages served as boundary markers for these social groups. One was not likely to marry into a group of higher or lower status than one's own.

Al-Rasheed (1991:50) gives us a description of the early twentieth-century oasis town of Hail, which was located on important trade routes and was ruled by her ancestors. The heart of the town was a walled palace built by the emir. Across from that were the mosque and the market. The palace opened onto a central square where the emir held his daily majlis. Bordering the square were the emir's storehouses. Hail was on a trade route that started in Karbala, Iraq, and ended in the Hijaz, a trip that took approximately ten days. The route was used by traders as part of a larger trade network extending from India to Europe and involving the movement of carpets, jewelry, spices, coffee, perfumes, weapons, and rice and by pilgrims making their sacred journey to Makkah.

Soraya Altorki and Donald Cole provide a description of a medium-sized provincial city prior to the influence of the Al Saud. This village, 'Unayzah, was the home of Altorki's father and will be used here as another example of early twentieth-century village life in Nejd. The villages in the area where Altorki and Cole worked date to shortly after the birth of Islam in the seventh century. In the thirteenth century, a number of small walled villages were joined in one larger walled city to make the city of 'Unayzah. Each of the original villages retained its own space and became a neighborhood within the new walls of the city, and each is recognized as a distinguishable neighborhood today. Members of two tribes, the Bani Khalid and the Subay', made up many of these neighborhoods. The public space held a market and a mosque. The economic basis for the city was agriculture; however, many families practiced pastoralism as well.

Homes were of mud brick, the favored building material of the desert and the same material used in the American Southwest, where it is known

Ruins of traditional homes.

as adobe. Homes had three entrances: a men's entrance, which led to the majlis room that was left unlocked so that visitors could refresh themselves when needed; the women's entrance, which led to the kitchen and the bedrooms upstairs; and the animals' entrance, as animals were kept on the ground floor. The houses had storerooms filled with dates, firewood, and wheat that were under the control of the senior woman in the family. Houses were close together and people of mixed origin and economic status occupied the same neighborhood. This old, dense city began to be replaced in the 1950s, and at the time of Altorki and Cole's fieldwork, most of it lay in ruin (1989:22–23).

Residents were distinguished by occupation, usually inherited, and tribal affiliation. Occupational groupings were (1) the learned (religious), (2) the rulers, (3) farmers, (4) merchants, (5) cameleers or caravanners, and (6) artisans. Affiliations were either *qabili* (tribal), *khadiri* (nontribal), or *'abd* (slave). The emir was always a tribal person, and the artisans in leather, silver, gold, blacksmithing, and butchering were always nontribal. Women were active in farming and commerce. The economic livelihood of the area involved city dwellers, pastoralists, and traders alike, as the pastoralists sold camels, horses, sheep, goats, ghee, and other milk products in the market, in return purchasing dates, wheat, coffee cardamom, tea, sugar, rice, cloth, leather buckets, rope, and household utensils. The animals provided by the pastoralists allowed for long-distance trade to Syria, Egypt, Iraq, and even India.

Agriculture was irrigation dependent. Water was drawn from wells using a pulley system and leather buckets, and it was the job of women to lead the camels who pulled the buckets of water up from the depth of the wells. During this process, the women sang to the camels and fed them alfalfa and other plants. They worked with up to twenty camels in four shifts of five, working through the night to bring up enough water to irrigate the fields. In stories told to Altorki and Cole during their fieldwork in 1987, community members remembered fondly the sound of the women singing and the noise of the water as it was emptied into the basins. These were pleasant sounds of a life now gone.

Date palms were important, not only because the fruit provided dietary nutrients and fiber but also because the wood from the trees was used to make a variety of household items. Date production was a time-consuming and dangerous enterprise done only by men in a cycle of care that followed the seasons. The trees were watered once or twice a day in the summer months. They were pruned and inseminated in order to grow fruit; then, a month later, the branches bearing fruit were disentangled and supported with sticks; ten days after that, these branches were tied together in clumps. A month later, the harvest was ready. Caring for date trees thus required men to climb the trees many times during the production season. This was a dangerous task and men had been known to fall and die. Thirty different varieties of dates were grown in 'Unayzah. They were distinguished by color, size, sugar content, moisture, flavor, and time of maturity (Altorki and Cole 1989:42–43).

The extended family, which was the typical work unit, owned or share-cropped the land on which they grew crops. Males worked with the date palms, prepared the fields, distributed the water in the irrigation system, and threshed the wheat while women did the weeding and harvesting. Sometimes farm work required a larger number of participants than the extended family, and then neighbors worked together in each other's fields. While dates and wheat were the most important crops, farmers also grew pomegranates, figs, millet, barley, alfalfa, pumpkin, squash, peppers, eggplant, okra, black-eyed peas, watercress, onions, leeks, coriander, cumin, and melons and raised cattle, sheep, goats, camels, donkeys, and chickens.

The *suq* or market of 'Unayzah is hundreds of years old and lies in the open space between the original settlements. A Western observer in 1918 commented that there were some 1,000 shops in the suq of 'Unayzah. In this suq were all items needed by the camel-herding bedu while nearby another suq sold meat, fruit, vegetables, alfalfa, coal, and firewood. In a third suq, women sold items for women, like henna, cooking utensils, spices, and cakes, and, in yet another suq, men sold metal products of iron, copper, silver, and gold. In front of the mosque was the majlis area where the emir sat each morning and talked with the people and settled disputes (Altorki and Cole 1989:61–62). 'Unayzah was a thriving market town and well into the 1930s 'Unayzah residents were still active in the long-distance camel caravan trade that linked the city with the ports on the Arabian Gulf and with

Kuwait in the east and with the cities of the Hijaz in the west. The trip from 'Unayzah to Jubayl, an Arabian Gulf port, took about twenty days one way. Much of the life of 'Unayzah as described above has now changed. Altorki and Cole explain:

> In order to understand the contemporary development of 'Unayzah, one must comprehend the foundation on which that development rests. For a very long time and until not too long ago, 'Unayzah had a complex economic structure and its population had a high degree of occupational specialization. It was a center tied into various networks that operated locally, regionally, and at an international level. There was also a great deal of symbiosis between the various actors who operated within the structure of these networks. . . . The farmer, the craftsperson, the trader, and the caravanner were as indigenous and as essential to the economy as the Bedouin herder. Today, only the Bedouin herder is widely remembered. (1989:81–82)

Conclusion

In the popular imagination of KSA inhabitants today, their traditional way of life and especially bedu history is much lauded, discussed, and re-created. Dates remain an important symbolic food, and any Saudi can describe for you a number of different varieties of dates and their properties. At harvest times, dates continue to be an exciting topic of conversation in the Kingdom. Upon arrival as a dinner guest, one is always offered coffee presented in the traditional manner and at least one variety of dates. Camels continue to occupy an important place in the imagination, with camel races held in cities like Riyadh and urban dwellers owning herds of prized thoroughbreds that they graze in the desert. In Riyadh, it is not uncommon to be invited into a modern version of the traditional bedu tent for an evening of hospitality where the diner will be presented with large platters of food, typical of bedu feasts of old.

The importance of the past goes well beyond nostalgia and runs deeper than the simple behaviors described here. Many themes from these earlier lifeways run through the lives of modern Saudis. The importance of tribal identity and status differences still guide marriage arrangements, and values of hospitality, generosity, honor, and closeness of family still govern behavior. Much has changed in the Kingdom, however, as the move from camel caravans to crisscrossing highways demonstrates. The next section of this book focuses on those changes and the processes used to achieve them and brings this story into the age of globalization.

Chapter 5

The Process of Modernization and Continued Economic Development

The Rapid Rate of Change

*T*he rate of change that the Kingdom has undergone in the last seventy years, even the last thirty years, is so rapid that it is difficult to appreciate. In 1918, the population of Riyadh, the current capital, was 19,000, and by 1940, it still covered an area of 10 square kilometers (less than 4 square miles). Today, it is a city of 1,036 square kilometers (700 square miles) of gleaming modern buildings, streets jammed with traffic, suburbs of new homes, and a population of 4.5 million. As another example of the rapid rate of change, consider the changes in transportation since the camel-driving days of the 1930s. While cars were introduced in the 1920s, they were of limited importance throughout the Kingdom due to the rugged terrain and lack of roads. After World War II, KSA began to develop a road network, but by 1970 the Kingdom still had only 60,000 vehicles registered. Thirty years later, however, eight and one-half times that many vehicles were registered (507,700 vehicles).

The Kingdom's air transportation system began in 1945 when US President Franklin D. Roosevelt gave Ibn Saud a DC-3 airplane. It was the first plane in the state-owned airlines, Saudi Arabian Airlines, which some fifty years later, in 1999, was carrying 12.7 million passengers annually between

Date processing plant outside Riyadh.

twenty-four airports in the Kingdom and fifty-two airports around the world. KSA has three international airports; all are modern structures of marble and steel built since 1980. In Jiddah, the international airport has a special Hajj terminal used only during the month of the annual Muslim pilgrimage to Makkah. The increased use of electricity tells the story of the transition from bedu tents and traditional mud-brick houses to cement block and marble Egyptian-style houses. In 1970, there were only 216,000 subscribers for electrical service in the entire Kingdom, but by 1999, there were 3,372,000 (fifteen times the number in just thirty years) (Al-Farsy 1990:225–230). And, consider this dramatic change in cities. The urban population grew from 560,000 individuals to 18 million in 50 years. It was 30 percent of the population in 1960 and 88 percent by 2003 (Al-Sharideh 1999:12, Tabutin et al. 2005:571, 606).

Perhaps it is easier to understand this transformation through human stories. Living in the Kingdom today are people who have lived the transition, like Sara, a not-so-old grandmother, who crossed the country on camelback in her youth and as an adult crossed the Atlantic on the Concorde.

The Formula for Modernization

How has KSA managed this rapid transformation to a gleaming, modern Kingdom? How has a country that had no modern education system and no modern technology or infrastructure been able to develop all of these and to become a player on the world stage in economic and political issues in just a few short decades? Of course, part of the answer lies in the oil resources used to fund such a transition, but money alone could not bring about this transformation. The mechanism for change has been the use of networks of transnational partnerships forming complex adaptive systems to bring about knowledge and technology transfer; the Kingdom has repeatedly used this mechanism to effect change for eighty years. The suggested steps of this change process are as follows:

1. Enter into a foreign partnership with a complex organization like a transnational business to bring needed expertise into the Kingdom, including foreign management of the necessary companies.

2. Set up foreign-led training programs in KSA for Saudis and send Saudi students abroad for further education.

3. Train Saudis in all areas of expertise needed to execute the desired business.

4. *Saudization*: Slowly replace foreign experts with Saudi experts until all the enterprise has been Saudized.

5. Dissolve foreign partnership.

The Saudi government has used this process in many and varied types of industries. Some of the individual steps of the process have become formal policy. For instance, the government has had a formal policy of sending students abroad for study when no equivalent program was available in the Kingdom. Also, the policy of Saudization is an explicitly stated goal and one that has been codified in law for some occupations. Beginning in 1970, the government instituted a series of five-year plans aimed at development in the Kingdom. The three objectives of the first were: (1) increase the rate of growth of the gross domestic product, (2) develop human resources, and (3) diversify the Kingdom's economy to reduce dependence on oil revenue (Al-Farsy1982:141). These objectives remain primary in the Kingdom's modernization process today.

The five-step process of modernization has been used repeatedly to effectively jumpstart the economy and move the Kingdom into the modern age. The way in which the process has been applied is organic. It has simply been a workable solution applied over and over again to areas where knowledge and technology were needed to modernize the Kingdom. So, partnerships have been formed as the need arises and dissolved when the need is gone. Partnership networks can change, morph into different forms, dissolve, reconstitute. These are instigated by multiple players in the Kingdom. While here my focus is on government initiatives based on the perceived needs of the Kingdom, individual Saudis and groups of Saudis also participate in these partnerships based on their own strategies for economic gain. This is the way complex adaptive systems work. Given the global nature of today's business world, it is unlikely that the Kingdom will ever be without some number of transnational partnerships. While it will eventually acquire the levels of expert knowledge and technology use that it desires, no modern state can be without transnational partnerships, and KSA will not be an exception. These networks of transnational partnerships, functioning as complex adaptive systems are one of the mechanisms of globalization.

Strategic Use of a Foreign Workforce

Important to the desired rapid development was the necessity of foreign experts to assist in all aspects of development. The second five-year plan (1975–1980) specifically called for a doubling of the number of non-Saudis in the workforce from 314,000 to 812,000. Government analysts projected that it would take more time to educate and train the Saudi workforce, and therefore more foreigners would be needed in the short term. There was concern that this large foreign workforce would negatively impact the Saudi Islamic way of life, even though many of the foreign workers would be drawn from Islamic countries. Because of this concern, the government attempted to keep the foreign workforce at one-fifth the size of the Saudi citizen population. In the mid-1970s, it was estimated that the need for foreign workers would reach one million individuals in the subsequent ten years. The government weighed its options. To bring in the foreigners would allow the country to keep up its rapid pace of modernization. To curtail their numbers would mean slowing the rate of development projects as sufficient numbers of Saudis were not yet trained to fill these technical jobs (Al Farsy 1990:223).

The government planners feared that international efforts to conserve oil use and to develop alternative energy sources meant that the vast oil wealth the Kingdom enjoyed would last only until the end of the century (Al Farsy 1990:224). If so, then the task of modernizing the country needed to be completed by the turn of the century, which was less than thirty years away. Therefore, the decision was made to proceed with modernization projects at full speed and bring in the necessary number of foreign workers. Thus, from the beginning, the danger of foreign cultural behaviors and values was one reason for the plan that would become Saudization. It was intended that foreigners would leave the Kingdom as soon as the need for their services was gone and that the government would consciously work toward that end (Al-Farsy 1990).

Saudization

The reason for the importance of Saudization is the country's large number of unemployed youth and the prospect that this number will only grow. Thirty-eight percent of Saudis are under the age of eleven (Rugh 2002:53). Faced with a future of so many youth with no employment prospects, the government is Saudizing occupations as fast as practically possible in order to provide jobs for its youth. Andrew Inkpen and Steven Carroll (1998) and Randall Schuler (2001) describe how increased learning increases the bargaining power of the learner in a partnership by reducing the learner's dependence on the teacher partner. This is exactly what the Saudis have intended in many of their transnational partnerships.

In addition, the high percentage of expatriates working in the country means that substantial income is leaving the country as these expatriates send money home to their families or invest it in their home countries. The Saudi government would like to recapture and reinvest income flowing overseas by replacing expatriate workers with Saudis (Looney 2004), Taecher (2003) estimates that 9 percent of GDP or $14 billion was remitted to families outside the Kingdom in 1999 (as stated in Al-Dosary and Rahman 2005:497).

Examples of Saudization abound. In 1974, the Saline Water Conversion Corporation (SWCC) was established with the goal of producing desalinated water to supplement the meager water supply available from fresh water sources. The SWCC gave high priority to training Saudis to work in desalinization facilities leading to the subsequent Saudization of jobs. In 1999 the Council of Ministers established a Saudi Geology Survey Bureau that would conduct all geological surveys for KSA. One of its stated aims was to "develop a skilled workforce in this field as part of the Saudization program" (Al-Farsy 1990:133). During my fieldwork in 2003, the government Saudized the gold suq, meaning that henceforth all merchants in the jewelry shops must employ a Saudi salesman. Previously, this occupation was held primarily by foreigners. In other occupations, Saudization has occurred more slowly, through the process of attrition and filling vacancies with Saudis. The administration of the Tertiary Care Hospital, discussed in the next chapter, was Saudized in this way.

Despite efforts to Saudize since 1970, unemployment among Saudis remains high. The Ministry of Planning stated that only 29.9 percent of working age Saudis (54.4 percent of men) had jobs in 1990 (Kapiszewski 2001:233). The Saudi Ministry of Labor and Social Affairs estimated in 1997 that the workforce contained 2,500,000 Saudis and 4,500,000 expatriates (Kapiszewski 2001:69; *Arab News*, 4 May 1998). Adel Al-Dosary and Syed Rahman (2005) of King Fahd University of Petroleum and Minerals in Dhahran describe some of the problems Saudization is encountering. The pay is typically higher for government jobs than it is for comparable private sector jobs making Saudi citizens less interested in the latter and most available jobs are in the private sector. Also, in order to fill government quotas for Saudis in the private workforce, private companies are hiring Saudis for nonexistent jobs so as to reach their quota. Al-Dosary and Rahman suggest the government accompany Saudization with even more skill development opportunities for its citizens than it is currently providing and address the pay equity issue (2005:500-501).

Other frequently discussed problems for Saudization are Saudi nationals' lack of interest in menial jobs (Champion 1999; Gardner 2003, 2005) and lack of a work ethic (Kapiszewski 2001:234; *Arab News*, 27 December 1997). Interior Minister and Chairman of the Manpower Council Prince Naif told a meeting of the Majlis al-Shūrā in 1997 that "Saudization has become an urgent national issue that requires joint efforts by the government and the private sector" (Kapiszewski 2001:234; Business Monitor International 1997:63).

Prince Naif was later quoted in the *Arab News* (May 18, 1998) encouraging youth "to be ready to do any job, no matter how insignificant, and have the competence to take up the challenge of certain jobs" (Kapiszewski 2001:234). Thus, while Saudization has been a goal for decades, its success thus far is limited. The government is still anxiously working on ways to provide adequate jobs for all its citizens.

Saudization is not a drive to remove all foreigners from the country, as any country with state-of-the-art technology, cutting-edge knowledge workers, and multinational business interests must have an expatriate population. Such a population is a necessary part of maintaining multinational business ties and a global edge. Instead, the five-step process, including the step of Saudization, is intended to position KSA as a modern and global leader in control of its own destiny and with a vibrant economy capable of providing jobs for all its citizens. This will mean reducing the numbers of expatriates in the country as jobs are increasingly filled by Saudis, but it will not mean eliminating expatriates all together. A similar effort to "nationalize" the workforce is in process in all of the six Gulf states (KSA, Bahrain, Kuwait, Oman, Qatar, and the United Arab Emirates) under similar monikers like "Kuwaitization" and "Omanization" and for similar reasons (Bahgat 1999:132; Louër 2008:50; Kapiszewski 2001:210-243). Sharon Nagy provides the following quote from a senior official in nearby Qatar who describes this process in his country:

> In the beginning, we were completely and totally dependent on foreign consultants. We had no databases, no technicians; not even any Qataris sophisticated enough to discuss the issues with them [the foreigners]. So, we just turned everything over to them and completely relinquished control. They even had to bring their own pens!
>
> [Eventually] with more Qataris returning from being educated abroad, these educated Qataris began to take positions in the administrations involved. . . .
>
> You will see, now we have Luis Berger [a foreign planner] coming to do the new PDP, a twelve million-riyal contract. However, this time there is a steering committee working with them made up of all but one Qatari. The technical committee is also all Qatari, except one. (Nagy 2000:132)

So KSA's oil wealthy neighbors have also used the tactics described here to modernize their countries.

Factors in Saudi Success

KSA has been blessed with two factors that are a large part of the reason for the success of this five-step process; in fact, this five-step process would not have been possible without these two important factors that were not present for most countries developing during the twentieth century. Those factors are:

1. The Kingdom of Saudi Arabia was never colonized. There were no Western laws or ways of proceeding that had to be dismantled. Ibn Saud, the first King of modern KSA, began from an Arab and Muslim culture base and built an Arab and Muslim modern state.

2. Natural resources provided ample capital to fund this modernization task. While oil was discovered in the 1930s, the resultant abundant financial resources did not start to appear until the 1970s. It was in the 1970s and under the rule of Ibn Saud's son, King Faisal, that the Kingdom began applying the above-mentioned formula to areas of modernization other than the oil industry.

Many developing nations are using transnational partnerships to accelerate their modernizing process. Few, however, enter these partnerships from as strong a position as KSA. Most others do not have the economic resources; at best, they are able to provide human resources. Consequently, these partnerships have typically not been as successful for other developing countries (see Andreosso-O'Callaghan and Qian 1999; Machado 1989–1990; Dent 2003 for examples of transnational partnerships in other developing countries). The resources that oil provides are an essential component of this success. An example of the five-step process is the founding of the modern Saudi education system.

Transnational Partnerships in Education

Ibn Saud established a Directorate of Education in 1925. Formal education at that time included four private schools in the Hijaz region, some military

Signs of the times. Cars have replaced camels as the primary mode of transportation.

academies, and Islamic schools that existed at some mosques. The Kingdom did not begin to develop a national education system until 1949. In 1950, there were twenty-seven state schools and twenty-two private schools in the country (Al-Rasheed 2002:95). In 1962, UNESCO estimated that 98 percent of Saudis over the age of fourteen years were illiterate (Shaker 1972:256). Public education for girls did not begin until the 1960s. By 1970, there were only 3,200 schools in KSA and 550,000 students. Boys outnumbered girls two to one in elementary school and seven to one in secondary school. A majority of the students (387,000) were in elementary school. Only 16,000 of the total were in high school. Thirty years later in 1999, the sex ratio had evened out as half the students were female. There were almost five million students in school, with 734,000 of these being in secondary school. In higher education the story is similar. The oldest university in KSA is King Saud University founded in 1957 (Al-Farsy 1990:256–260). By 2002, KSA was spending 23 percent of its budget and 7.5 percent of its GNP on education, more than almost any other Arab country (Rugh 2002:42). Today the Kingdom has a university system that includes public universities as well as private colleges, and faculties are made up overwhelmingly of Saudi PhDs.

The Kingdom made this rapid change in education through transnational partnerships using the process described earlier. Given the lack of a national education system, few Saudis were trained to develop the national education system and few were trained as teachers. Consequently, non-Saudis were brought in. The ranks of teachers were filled primarily by Egyptians, who brought not only their specific knowledge but also Egyptian pedagogical ideas and techniques. In 1983, 66 percent of the 34,000 intermediate and secondary teachers were non-Saudi. At the same time, KSA was educating its young people abroad in large numbers, training them to be the next generation of teachers in the Kingdom. In 1976, there were over 3,000 Saudi students studying in the United States, and the numbers reached a high in 1981–1982 when over 10,000 Saudi students were studying there. By comparison, this figure is five times higher than the number of Egyptian students (Egypt has a significantly larger population) in the United States during the same year. By 2001, there were still over 5,000 Saudi students in the United States, roughly one-fourth of the Arab students studying there that year, even though the Saudi government had decreased the amount of scholarships it awarded to its students to study abroad. This effort to educate Saudis abroad paid off at home. By 1993, not only had the number of teachers in KSA grown, but increasingly Saudi nationals had become teachers, so that only 33 percent of the 85,000 intermediate and secondary teachers were non-Saudi (Rugh 2002:43, 49). An example of the success of this process can be seen in the University of Petroleum and Minerals in Dhahran. As a result of the Kingdom's education effort, by 1999, 76 percent of adult Saudis were literate, giving KSA a rank of seventh out of sixteen Arab countries in adult literacy (eighth in female adult literacy, with 65.9 percent) (Rugh 2002). Transnational partnerships were an important aspect of the education effort. The use of this process started with the oil industry, however, and it is the development of that industry that served as a model for subsequent uses of the five-step process. I now turn to a discussion of oil.

Complex Adaptive Systems and the Oil Industry

The story of the Kingdom's modernization begins in 1923 when Ibn Saud partnered with a British company for exploration for oil in the Eastern Province. This is the first important application of step one of the five-step modernization process outlined earlier.

Oil and Step One: Enter into Foreign Partnerships

In 1923, there were no Saudis with oil expertise and so Ibn Saud entered into a foreign partnership with the British to bring that knowledge to the Kingdom. Four years later, when they had not found oil, the British did not renew the partnership. In 1932, however, oil was discovered in neighboring Bahrain, and in 1933, Ibn Saud entered into an agreement with Standard Oil Company of California (SOCAL) for the exploration of oil and extraction of the same should it be found in Saudi Arabia. Persia (present-day Iran) and Iraq had previously entered into contractual relationships with the West for oil exploration, and their contract terms served as a basis for the Saudi negotiations.

While oil had been found in Bahrain and similar geological formations in Saudi Arabia caused the Americans to assume they would find oil in KSA, it was a risky time to take on such financial commitments. This was 1933 and the height of the Great Depression in the United States; President Roosevelt had just closed the banks and the country had just gone off the gold standard. Oil was selling for less than 50 cents a barrel. SOCAL committed itself to loans of $250,000 in gold, annual rental payments of $25,000 in gold for concession rights, royalty payments of about $1 in gold for every ton of oil produced, and an advance to the Saudi government of $250,000 in gold once oil was found in commercial quantities. Given the economic times, this was a gamble for SOCAL. While they knew there was oil in nearby Bahrain and they could see topographical features on the eastern coast of Saudi that indicated the possibility of oil in KSA, there was by no means a guarantee of finding oil, and the task of exploring, drilling, and bringing oil into production seemed daunting, given the desert environment, the remoteness of the area, and the lack of technology or even the barest essentials of communication and transportation in the Saudi Eastern Province. The economy of the Eastern Province was based on fishing, pearl diving, and small-scale agriculture in the oases. There were few schools, illiteracy was the norm, and there was an absence of people with the technical and clerical skills an oil company needs to operate (Clark and Tahlawi 2006:219).

However, SOCAL proceeded, and through this effort, the California Arabian Standard Oil Company (CASOC) was founded. The agreement stipulated that CASOC would hire Saudi nationals for all jobs for which Saudis were qualified and would start training programs for them. Since Saudis in the area were unfamiliar with Western technology and business practices and were mostly illiterate, they did not have the training necessary to work in a business office or an oil field. Early training was informal, as drillers, craftsmen, and office workers were taught on the job. By 1935, a few Americans and 115 Saudis worked for the company.

By 1937, the American nature of the company was beginning to show. The first two wives of American employees arrived, and Western-style houses were built near the drilling rigs. Other oil companies joined the partnership, and in 1938 after five years of exploration and test drilling, the Kingdom's first commercial oil field was discovered. In 1938, the first well, named Dammam number 7, came in and the oil business in Saudi Arabia was born. That well eventually produced 32 million barrels of oil in 45 years before it was taken out of service because of reduced demand. In the spring of 1939, Ibn Saud came to the oil fields to celebrate the send-off of the first oil tanker. He traveled from Riyadh in a caravan of 500 cars and 2,000 people and a tent city of white tents was set up near Dhahran to house this entourage. Two days of festivities followed and Ibn Saud opened the valve to let the first barrel of oil flow into a tanker at Ras Tanura (Nawwab et al. 1995).

In 1940, the first school for Saudi employees was established, but World War II soon brought activity in the oil fields almost to a halt. The war at sea made shipping too dangerous; in fact, one ship was torpedoed and sunk. American families were sent out of the country and food was in such short supply that oilmen grew their own. By 1943, however, the United States placed a high priority on Saudi oil to satisfy its growing need, and oil activity in Saudi opened back up. In 1944, the joint operating company was renamed the Arabian American Oil Company, or Aramco. By the end of the war, Aramco was busy again. It posted its first two-million-barrel month. Schools were reopened and ten US children enrolled in a one-room, American-curriculum school. One hundred and seventy-five men were in training classes at Aramco; many of these would become Aramco executives in the future. In 1946, TWA made the first commercial passenger flight out of Dhahran, and the following year, Ibn Saud came to visit Aramco again; this time his entourage arrived by airplane rather than car as the Kingdom now had its own fleet of aircraft.

In the 1950s, the Kingdom developed additional oil partnerships with Japanese and French companies, and four oil companies had shares in Aramco (Al-Farsy 1982:43–45), more examples of step one of the modernization process. By 1952, Aramco had 24,000 employees. Aramco, however, retained its distinctive American culture. US families had re-created an American suburb in the heart of Arabia complete with Boy Scout troops and turkey for Thanksgiving. US business structures and principles formed the backbone of Aramco, an American company set down in the middle of the Arabian desert.

In 1962, the Kingdom created the General Petroleum and Mineral Organization (Petromin). This was the nation's first national petroleum company whose mission was to develop KSA's oil, gas, and minerals, including the creation of partnerships with foreign entities (Al-Farsy 1982:40). As will be seen, however, Aramco eventually became the state owned oil company and Petromin was dissolved in 2005. By the 1970s, Aramco had grown into a thriving international enterprise. In 1970, there were 10,000 employees, and by the end of the decade, that number was six times as large, at 60,000 employees with an additional 20,000 contractor employees. In 1974 Aramco had the capacity to train 5,000 employees, continuing its commitment to train Saudi nationals.

Oil and Steps Two and Three: Train Saudis by Establishing Foreign-Led Training Programs at Home and by Sending Students Abroad for Education

The original 1933 agreement with SOCAL included a provision that the company would employ Saudi nationals to the extent possible and so training programs were begun immediately. These are steps two and three of the modernization process. At first, the training programs were for drillers and office workers. By 1950, 4,000 Saudis (40 percent of the Aramco workforce) were in Aramco training programs learning some 144 crafts, trades, and skills from a teaching staff of 250. This training ranged from academic subjects to blueprint reading, electrical wiring, and plumbing. At the same time, the government was interested in opening its own university to train Saudi students for the oil business. In 1963, the College of Petroleum and Minerals was established in Dhahran, and the first year (1964) it had sixty-seven students, primarily Saudis, and fourteen faculty in programs of applied engineering and engineering science. In 1971, the college had ninety-five faculty, mostly from the United States, Great Britain, and Western Europe, and in 1975 it became a university with five colleges: Engineering Science, Applied Engineering, Sciences, Business Administration, and Environmental Design (Rashid and Shaheen 1987:108–117).

By 1978, student enrollment was 2,350 taught by 388 faculty of whom only thirty-seven were Saudi, although over 100 future Saudi faculty members were in PhD programs at US universities receiving the training that would eventually lead them to return to the university to teach. In addition, the King Faisal University Faculty of Medicine and Medical Sciences in Dammam was established through a partnership with Harvard University initiated in 1975 (Al-Farsy 2001:266; 1982:59). For the first ten years the faculty members were mostly Western but by 1985 the renamed King Fahd University of Petroleum and Minerals had some 670 faculty, 50 percent of whom were Saudi. Tuition, books, and room and board were free to Saudi students who also received a monthly stipend. The university sent many of its promising students abroad for further education with the agreement that they return and teach at home. In fact, the Saudi government was sending vast numbers of promising students for university degrees abroad, primarily to the United States and Europe. By 1974, Aramco had the capacity to train 5,000 employees, and by 1994, the training program had 1,800 teachers and support personnel and some 10,000 students. In addition to government-sponsored education, Aramco itself sponsored students to go elsewhere for advanced university degrees.

Oil and Steps Four and Five: Saudization and Dissolving Foreign Partnerships

In 1973, the government began to purchase Aramco shares from its shareholders (Standard Oil, Texaco, Exxon, and Mobil) and by 1980 had completed the process, giving the Saudi government ownership. Aramco continued to operate and manage the oil fields. In 1988 the company's name was changed to Saudi Arabian Oil Company (Saudi Aramco) by royal decree, as the new company took over the operation and management of the oil fields. In 1989, John J. Kelberer, an American, relinquished his job as head of Aramco, the world's largest oil company, to Ali Naimi, a Saudi. Ali Naimi's career history highlights the government's strategy of Saudization at Aramco and exemplifies the five steps of the process outlined earlier. He began working for Aramco 40 years before as an office boy. He went to university and earned engineering and management degrees and slowly climbed the corporate ladder. In 1975 he became the second Saudi to be named a vice president and in 1979 he became chairman of the Saudi Arab Manpower Committee with the charge of further integrating Saudis in senior management positions (Hertog 2010:655). Ten years later he become the chief executive at Aramco. The turnover in power at Aramco from an American to a Saudi was noted in the United States in an article in the *New York Times*.

> At a quiet dinner a few days ago, the last American to preside over the world's largest oil company handed over power to its first Saudi boss. The Saudi, a man who started working there more than 40 years ago as an office boy, earned engineering and management degrees as he climbed up the ladder.
>
> The transfer of the Arabian American Oil company from the American John J. Kelberer, to the Saudi Ali Naimi, took place at Hamilton House, named after an American lawyer who negotiated the first agreement that opened this kingdom to American oil companies 45 years ago and led to the formation of Aramco, as the company is known to the world.
>
> While the formal transfer of power was low-key, in the Aramco tradition, the event was one of great moment both in Saudi and international terms. (*New York Times*, April 6, 1989)

Today, Saudi Aramco reports to the Supreme Council of Petroleum and Minerals Affairs. This council is chaired by the King, and its membership is drawn from both the government and the private sector. It sets the broad mission and objectives for Saudi Aramco. The board of directors of Saudi Aramco is chaired by the Minister of Petroleum and Mineral Resources. Saudization has been a success at Saudi Aramco. It employs 56,500 people from over fifty countries, yet 80 percent of its employees are Saudi and Saudis hold most of the management and the operating posts at the company (Al-Farsy 1990:113–114).

Oil's Extended Economic Impact

The thriving oil business fueled the economic growth of the Kingdom. Such a large operation needed housing for employees, schools for them and their children, recreation facilities, health care establishments, and shopping venues selling food, clothing, and all the necessities of a Western life.

In the 1930s and 1940s, employees at Aramco were primarily from the United States, the Arabian Peninsula, the Arabian Gulf countries, and India. With the need to expand in the late 1940s, workers were added from Eritrea and, after World War II, from Italy. By the early 1950s, Sudanese were joining the workforce, and as a result of the 1948 Arab-Israeli war, Palestinians came as well. Ibn Saud had requested that Aramco make a special effort to employ as many Palestinian refugees as possible. The 1970s brought British, Irish, and Asians, especially Filipinos and Sri Lankans.

With its large workforce, Aramco was also in the business of creating a home environment for its workers. In 1933, Dhahran was a small village. Housing, schools, shopping, and recreation venues for employees all had to be created. In 1951, KSA began a home-ownership program in which eligible Saudis could acquire free plots of land from the government. They then received long-term interest-free loans from Aramco to help pay for construction or purchase of a house. By 1994, $3.7 billion had been loaned to employees and more than 36,000 homes had been built or purchased.

School construction began in 1953. The Saudi government had regulations requiring certain industrial employers to build schools for workers' children. Aramco built elementary schools for males ages six to fourteen and in 1959 added grades seven through nine. In 1960, the Kingdom started an education program for girls, and the following year, Aramco built schools for girls. In 1984, it added high schools. By 1994, Aramco had built and continued to maintain 103 schools with a student capacity of 51,000. The government required that all schools be turned over to the government after they were built, although maintenance was to continue to be provided by Aramco. Health care followed a similar path. The government required the company to provide health care for its employees, and hence by the 1990s Aramco medical facilities provided care for more than 200,000 people and supported private medical care as well.

The government depended on Aramco to provide electricity to the Eastern Province. KSA created Saudi Consolidated Electric Company in the Eastern Province in 1976 and designated Aramco as the managing company for the first five years. Aramco's task was to develop a major regional power grid. Management passed from Aramco after five years, and by 1991, the electric company was serving 400,000 customers. Aramco was additionally required to use Saudi vendors when possible. In 1970, purchases from Saudi suppliers amounted to $36 million and by 1978 had reached $737 million. In 1994, the value of Aramco contracts with hundreds of Saudi-owned and joint venture businesses totaled $2.7 billion; in addition, Aramco purchased $1.1 billion in materials, with Saudis supplying nearly 90 percent of that amount. Thus, Aramco was "required" to bring jobs, housing, schools, electricity, and medical facilities into the community, effectively becoming the agent of change and modernization in the Eastern Province.

The strategy successful at Aramco has been used by the Saudi government in all sectors of the economy, generating hundreds of transnational partnerships combined into complex adaptive systems that bring foreign expertise and technology to the Kingdom and then eventually replace the foreign experts with Saudi-born ones. Next we'll look at the modernization process used to free Saudi Arabia from its dependence on oil and to generate income for its ongoing five-year plans.

The Continuing Focus on Economic Development

Finally, in this chapter, we take another look at how business has affected modernization and change in Saudi Arabia and made it a global player.

Offset Investment

Saudi Arabia was the first of the Gulf Cooperative Council (GCC) countries to begin an offset investment program, which it started in 1984. The concept of offset companies is used in various parts of the world and is a mechanism that assists in the economic growth of developing countries. When a foreign company sold products and services worth a substantial sum to Saudi Arabia, the company reaping the profit was required to reinvest a portion of its profits in Saudi Arabia. Thus, the amount of Saudi funds leaving the country due to the purchase is "offset" by the portion of those funds that the seller returns to the Saudi economy through reinvestment. That reinvestment may involve (1) producing some of the purchased goods in KSA, (2) increasing imports to the seller country from KSA, or (3) transferring technology from the buyer country to KSA. Globally, offset can be direct, meaning the buyer country is assisted by the seller country in providing some of the elements of the purchase, like supplying parts for the product, or indirect, meaning the seller is involved in investment in the buyer country unrelated to the purchase. Saudi Arabia was interested in technology transfer and indirect offset, as these would best serve the government's goals. The goals of the Saudi offset program are as follows:

1. provide advanced technical training and resulting high-value employment for Saudis;

2. increase foreign investment;

3. reduce imports, through in-country production, and increase exports;

4. develop professional and managerial expertise in high-technology fields;

5. foster technology knowledge transfer through research, development, and manufacturing processes;

6. make use of the Kingdom's raw materials.

The government was especially interested in offset programs in the fields of non-oil-related, high-technology industry, defense, services, and agriculture. The list of goals for the offset program underscores the needs KSA has defined as critical for its future economic, political, and social growth. It must find quality jobs for its citizens; in order to do this, it must provide the training from foreign experts, since in 1984 there was little expertise among Saudis in high-technology fields, as well as create the jobs by increasing foreign investment and increasing economic productivity. It must diversify its economy so that it is not so heavily dependent on oil and create more production at home so as to decrease dependence on imports at the same time that it builds its own export business.

By 2005, KSA had entered into twenty-two offset programs with contractors in three countries: the United States, the United Kingdom, and France (Ramady 2005:74). An example of one of these offset companies is Advanced Electronics Company (AEC) begun in 1988. It was a joint venture with Boeing, Arabic Computer Systems, National Commercial Bank (the first one established in KSA), National Industrialization Company, and Saudi Arabian Airlines (Saudia) (Ramady 2005:74). The offset obligation is that the investing foreign company must keep the investment for ten years; Boeing sold its share of AEC after fifteen years. AEC has been profitable almost from the start. In 2009 it had 2,061 employees of whom 29 percent were engineers. Of the entire staff, 77 percent were Saudi, including most of the engineers. AEC designs and manufactures electronics for military, telecommunications, and industrial customers. For example, it has built electronic components for Boeing for F-15 airplanes and for Lockheed Martin for F-16 airplanes. Other customers include the Saudi Armed Forces; the US Army, Navy, and Air Force; Saudi Aramco; Lucent Technologies; Siemens; Nokia; and Raytheon. AEC partners with international companies like Cisco that are seeking to increase their market share in the Kingdom. Prior to the offset program, which includes seven companies developed in the advanced electronics field, there was no advanced electronics expertise in the Kingdom. Thus, AEC's success demonstrates the type of technology transfer and new industry the Kingdom hopes to develop to employ its citizens (Ramady 2005:88).

In a 2005 study of the success of the Saudi offset program in reaching its goals, Mohamed Ramady determined that only six of the twenty-two offset programs had the goal of developing technical and managerial skills for the Saudi workforce, which was important not only to create high-value jobs for Saudis but also to ensure the long-term success of technology transfer in the Kingdom without relying on expatriate workers. Ramady (2005:83) refers to this as the all-important "human capital transfer," and he points to the lack of science and engineering training in Saudi universities where only 8 percent of graduates specialize in science and engineering. The International Monetary Fund cites four areas of needed improvement for the Kingdom to continue its aggressive growth: education, financial sector deepening, contract enforcement, and modernization of the legal system (SAGIA 2009:10). One of the strategies being used to tackle this program is the establishment of the King Abdullah University for Science and Technology, which opened in the fall of 2009 and is discussed later in this chapter.

Attracting Foreign Investment

The Saudi Arabia General Investment Authority (SAGIA) was established in 2000 to generate foreign investment in the Kingdom. Saudi Arabia is aiming for rapid and sustainable growth that capitalizes on the country's geographic location situated between the East and the West. It instituted the 10X10 program, where the goal was to position Saudi within the ten most competitive economies by 2010. To benchmark how KSA ranks among the world's competitive economies, SAGIA is using three internationally recognized competitiveness measures (the World Bank's Ease of Doing Business Index, the Institute for Management Development's rankings, and the World Economic Forum Global Competitiveness Index). At the time of this writing, the country was working toward its 2010 goal. In the World Bank/International Finance Corporation's report measuring ease of doing business, the Kingdom ranked 38th in 2007 and 23rd in 2008. Its 2008 ranking put it first in the Middle East North Africa region (MENA). It was ranked 35th in the World Economic Forum's Global Competitiveness Index (GCI), where it was listed for the first time in the 2007–2008 edition and was ranked third in the world for its macroeconomic stability (SAGIA presentation May 2009; www.sagia.gov.sa). The International Monetary Fund tracked the Saudi economy as growing an average of 4.5 percent between 2003 and 2007, largely due to expansion in the financial and construction industries (SAGIA 2009:4–5; Council on Foreign Relations 2008:2).

In order to reach its 10X10 goal, the government of KSA has been making numerous improvements reflecting further modernization for a country that began this process only forty years ago. These include judicial reforms intended to improve the court processes, which businesses use to resolve disputes, and infrastructure improvements, including additions to railways, roads, seaports, airports, and a monorail between Makkah and Madinah. Literacy rates in the Kingdom have grown from 33 percent in 1970 to 83 percent in 2009, and in 2009 more women than men were studying in universities. Yet, the government has seen the need for further improvement, and in 2007 KSA began a strategy to improve the public education environment, teacher training, curriculum development, and extracurricular activities with the addition of a 12 billion SAR ($3.2 billion) public education fund. In addition, while 400,000 students graduated from high school in 2008, there were only places for 90,000 of them in the universities. Thus, more postsecondary educational opportunities must be opened up (SAGIA 2009). A universal coverage program began in 2008 with the goal of providing voice and Internet coverage to the entire country by 2015 (www.sagia.gov.sa).

To make doing business in Saudi Arabia more attractive to foreign investors, the government has made numerous changes in laws and procedures. Commercial law in KSA is an example of Western laws adapted for use in an Islamic country ruled by shari'a (Islamic) law. Saudi companies are regulated by the Commercial Court Regulation of 1931, which identified several types of Islamic companies, including general partnerships, limited partnerships, limited liability, and corporations. However, while Saudi Arabia is governed by shari'a law, much of its commercial law is based on Western law, specifically French commercial law, which was adapted for Saudi use in the mid-1960s. In an analysis in 2000, Thabet Koraytem explains that the Great Ulamas Committee, which he describes as the highest Islamic institution in KSA, determined that contracts for French-style companies were acceptable due to a principle of the Hanbali Islamic school of thought of which the followers of al-Wahhab are a part. This principle states, "In profane activity, everything is allowed as long as no evidence (from the Koran and the Sunna) forbids it (explicitly)" (Koraytem 2000:65). A cultural factor frequently noticed by Western businesspersons is the Saudi interest in personalizing the relationship between business partners, as their personal relationship is considered more important than the written contract between them (Koraytem 2000:66; Yavas et al. 1994:73). Saudi commercial law from the 1960s strengthens the personal relationship between the partners compared to the French laws from which it borrows.

More recently, KSA has been attempting to change its commercial laws and laws of foreign investment to become more open to foreign investment. In 2000, it passed a new Foreign Capital Investment Law (*Arab Law Quarterly* 2001:49). Recently, Saudi Arabia joined the World Trade Organization, which required the government to make changes in commercial law in order to meet WTO requirements (Middle East Policy 2006:24). Between 2004 and 2009, for example, it has reduced commercial registration fees, cut the procedures required for starting a business, increased the protection of minority shareholders, developed an electronic system of registering property titles, reduced the minimum capital requirement for new companies to start up a business, and streamlined business start-up procedures. The new economic cities discussed below allow 100 percent foreign ownership in investments (SAGIA 2009:6, 11).

The business sectors in which the Kingdom can or does have the most competitive advantage and thus is hoping to develop are (1) energy, (2) transportation, and (3) knowledge-based industries. Low taxes, excellent incentives to invest, and a stable currency that is tied to the US dollar make investment attractive. KSA is ranked 20th in the world for least burdensome regulation for business and least wasteful public spending (Schwab, Porter, and Martin 2007).

Economic Goals

The government views four economic goals as imperative for the Kingdom to achieve. They are: (1) promote regionally balanced economic development such that the population profits economically with jobs in every region of the country, (2) diversify economically since the current 90 percent dependence on oil is too risky for a healthy economy in the future, (3) create jobs to give the 60 percent of youth under eighteen years of age employment as they become workforce age, and (4) upgrade economic competitiveness vis-à-vis the rest of the world. An important strategy for accomplishing these is the new development of economic cities. The Kingdom is spending $60 billion to construct four new economic cities, with the intention that the four

American students learning about the planned new economic cities. (Angela Sortor)

cities will contribute over $150 billion in annual gross domestic product, create over a million jobs, and have four to five million residents by 2020. Two additional economic cities are in the planning stages. These locations will be true cities with residential sections, hospitals, shopping areas, mosques, and all the necessities of a city in addition to the businesses and industries that will provide jobs. KSA partnered with a developer of the city of Singapore to create the master plans for these economic cities (SAGIA presentation May 2009; www.sagia.gov.sa). The first to be up and running is King Abdullah Economic City (KAEC), located on the Red Sea an hour from Jiddah. It opened Phase I in September of 2009. Ultimately, it will be the size of Washington, D.C. and will be fully developed in 2025 at a cost of $26 billion. It focuses on clean energy and was built on the best environmental standards in the world. The city will be wired for broadband at a speed ten times faster than the current fastest speed through a partnership with Cisco.

Part of the twenty-first-century Saudi strategy is aggressive investment in plastics. In 2008, KSA had only a 1 percent share of the world's plastics market, but SAGIA hopes to raise that to 15 percent by 2020, which would mean doubling domestic production and increasing numbers of foreign producers who relocate their businesses to the Kingdom (Mansi 2009). They hope to attract investors for plants that would convert plastic resins into finished products for export to Europe and other locals. In King Abdullah Economic City, the government is devoting 23 square miles to a "Plastics Valley" that will house all sorts of related industries. Low worker wages (no minimum wage in Saudi), easy access to cheap resins and energy, and state-of-the-art warehouses are part of the attraction (Grace 2007). These companies will be more joint ventures that lure more foreign workers, as well as Saudis, increasing the number of business ventures with work staffs of twenty-plus nationalities.

KAEC will have a seaport, industrial zone, central business district, resort district, educational zone, and residential areas. Almost 30 percent of global shipping passes through the Red Sea, and the seaport in KAEC is designed to accommodate that sea traffic and bring additional economic benefits (SAGIA presentation May 2009). Companies that have already reached agreements to build factories in KAEC are as diverse as Mars, which will build a chocolate factory, and Emirates Aluminum, which will establish a $5 billion aluminum smelter (SAGIA 2009:19). Adjacent to the city is King Abdullah University for Science and Technology, a new university offering only graduate degrees in math and science, which is the first coed university in the Kingdom. As is the case in some other universities in the Kingdom, the courses are taught in English, considered the international language of science (SAGIA presentation May 2009; www.kaust.edu.sa).

The three other cities under construction are in different geographic areas in order to foster regional economic development, and each of these focuses on a specialty. Jizan Economic City is south of Jiddah and will also have a seaport. Seventy percent of the investment attracted to Jizan is Chinese; Mandarin will be the second language spoken there. The Madinah Economic City will be a knowledge city for the furthering of religious knowledge but also for knowledge-based industries like health care, education, and research and development. For example, KSA is partnering with Microsoft to develop a Microsoft academy in the Madinah Economic City. Because currently non-Muslims are not allowed in the holy city of Madinah, in the new economic city, 30 percent of the city will be open to non-Muslims. The last of the planned cities will be in Hail. Here the Prince Abdul Aziz bin Mousaed Economic City is scheduled to be the largest logistics and transportation hub in the Middle East (SAGIA 2009:10–15; SAGIA presentation May 2009; www.sagia.gov.sa). All of this demonstrates how the Saudi government has increased its focus on private, rather than government, business development in the past two decades. Additionally, private Saudi business groups have emerged as leaders in investment across the Arab world (Hertog 2009:17).

Conclusion

Complex adaptive systems were important throughout the development of the oil industry. In the original 1937 partnerships with SOCAL, the mechanism was already in place. In this case, a nation-state government (KSA) and several transnational businesses (SOCAL and the other oil companies) have combined in a network, creating another complex organization (CASOC). The network is a system adapting to its natural, political, and economic environment in order to promote the mutual economic interests of the individual organizations (KSA government and the oil companies) and of the network they have formed. Later, in 1950, the Saudis partnered with Japanese and French companies, partnerships that provide more examples of the coupling, intertwining, and recombining of organizations into complex adaptive systems.

Saudization continues to be a stated goal. The strategy successful at Aramco has been used by the Saudi government in all sectors of the economy, generating hundreds of transnational partnerships that bring foreign expertise and technology to the Kingdom and then eventually replacing the foreign experts with Saudi-born ones. The complex organizations formed in the Kingdom, whether oil companies, school systems, or economic cities, are impacted by the forces of globalization and modernization. They are a result of the state modernization strategy, are defined by their international workforces, and are impossible without the intense interconnections of globalization. The necessary coupling, mixing, dividing, and recombining of government, transnational organizations, and local enterprise repeatedly form complex adaptive systems. Every year Saudi Arabia develops new businesses using this model.

The Seventh Development Plan (2000–2005) specifically lists "developing the potential of the Kingdom's human resources through training and coaching, to meet the needs of the national economy, and to enable the Saudi workforce to replace the non-Saudi workforce" (Al-Farsy 1990:182). The need for jobs for young Saudis continues to be crucial as does the need to diversify the economy so that the Kingdom is not dependent solely on oil revenue. These are important foci of the economic expansion and the partnerships of complex adaptive systems currently underway in the Kingdom. In the next chapter, I look inside one of these complex adaptive systems in medical care.

Chapter 6

The Tertiary Care Hospital of Saudi Arabia

A Case Study of the Modernization Process at Work

*O*n 2002, I conducted a study of a hospital in KSA because, as an organizational anthropologist, I was fascinated by the fact that this hospital employed people holding passports from over sixty countries and I was interested in how that worked in an organizational context. What I found was not only a story of cultures interacting but also an example of the modernization process. This chapter tells that story. Like other areas of development, in 1970 KSA had relatively few modern health facilities. There were only seventy-four hospitals, 591 health centers, and 1,172 physicians. As part of its first five-year development plan, the government set out to improve this situation and contracted with medical establishments in the West to help build a medical system.

The Creation of a Modern Medical System

In 1970, King Faisal laid the foundation stone for the new Tertiary Care Hospital of Saudi Arabia (TCHSA), which was to be a special facility to treat patients referred by their physicians due to the seriousness of their illnesses. The government had contracted with a British firm to build the facilities. On the edge of the desert, on the outskirts of Riyadh, a modern hospital was built, along with a housing compound to provide living quarters for the foreign physicians and other specialists. In 1975, TCHSA opened with 120 beds. Today, TCHSA still has its own housing department, utilities department, and transportation department, all of which were originally necessary because the hospital was so far outside the city of Riyadh that those services were not available to its employees. One of the employees remembers:

> People used to come and sit out in front of the hospital under the street-lights because there weren't any lights out this far and they would sit there and read their books at night. There was no airport out here. We couldn't get a taxi here. We had to walk down as far as where the Intercontinental Hotel is to get a taxi. They wouldn't come out here. Too far out of town. There was very little food in the grocery stores. This was in 1975. There was not much food here. You couldn't make a telephone call easily. You couldn't buy a flower. Now they import flowers from Amsterdam and you can get anything you want overnight.

To manage the hospital, the government partnered with a US firm, Hospital Corporation of America (HCA). So, while a British company created the buildings, a US company actually created the working hospital. HCA created all the procedures, hired the staff, and managed the development of a modern tertiary-care facility. Doctors and nurses were hired primarily from Europe and North America. Employees remember "[a] bias from the beginning to hire Americans." Furthermore, they report:

> Almost 100 percent of the staff was American at that time. . . . The Americans were here and they put in an American system, turnkey. . . . There was an infrastructure in place at one time. I tell them, the hospital has really good bones. It was constructed well originally. The policies and procedures were fabulous. The human resource policies [were] really good, financial, everything.

Meanwhile, the Kingdom sent its most promising students to Europe and the United States to attend college and medical school. The students' tuitions and living expenses were paid by the government with the understanding that the students would return to practice medicine in the Kingdom. Even though today KSA has its own medical schools, it is still a TCHSA emphasis that students leave the Kingdom for part of their training. "It is sort of a requirement for this hospital that you have to have, like, an international training. And I think it is very healthy. I really appreciate the few years that I spent outside. It definitely broadened my mind. . . . I think it is a written requirement." Two Saudi physicians, one male and one female, who are now employed by the hospital, describe their training:

> I was sponsored by this institution to do training in nuclear medicine and radiology. And I spent about five years in Canada and then after I completed my training in nuclear medicine, I decided to do training in PET [positron emission tomography], which is an equipment we have had here since 1995. But we never really had anybody who was trained in

PET. There were no training physicians available in Canada; in fact, they did not have this equipment in Canada. We had enjoyed very good collaboration with Duke University and my previous section head recommended several institutions; one of them is Duke. So I took the time to visit Duke University and I met my mentor, Dr. Coleman, And I got accepted into the program; I did two years of training and I came back. The hospital here has credentialing requirements. One of them is that you have to have the American board or the equivalent plus seven years of training in order to be eligible to be a consultant [job title for staff doctor]. So I had to fill those requirements and so I was credentialed as a consultant in nuclear medicine. That was back in November of 1999.

And:

I did my medical school here in Saudi Arabia at King Saud University and then I did my four years of residency here in this hospital and I had my boards here before; at that stage it was the Arab Board. So, I had my board, which was my specialization. And then I went to London for three years to do my subspecialty. So, and then I came back here to work as a subspecialized consultant now for the last six years or so.

By the late 1970s, 9–10 percent of HCA's revenue was from its partnership with TCHSA. Other Western medical organizations were also partnering with TCHSA, evidence of complex adaptive systems at work. For example, in 1978 the hospital partnered with Baylor College of Medicine, in Houston, Texas, to begin performing cardiac surgery. The partnership with Baylor would continue until 1985 when TCHSA cardiology services became offered entirely by in-house medical staff. The management of HCA ended in 1981, and Saudis took the lead in hospital administration. In 2003, the last non-Saudi administrator, a US citizen, left the hospital. In 2003, over 50 percent of the physicians were Saudi. The Kingdom also has its own medical schools. The teaching physicians in those schools were mostly trained in the West; the students, however, will be a new generation of Saudi doctors whose education was acquired entirely within the Kingdom. Most nurses are still foreign born, as KSA is just beginning to train its own nurses. Thirty years after its opening, TCHSA is a world-class tertiary-care hospital and a leader in health care in the Middle East. The process of development through transnational partnerships that was outlined earlier is the reason for the rapid, successful change and an example of complex adaptive systems.

Ongoing Transnational Partnerships: A Necessity in Modern Health Care

Not only were transnational partnerships and the complex adaptive systems they form essential in developing a modern medical system in KSA, they continue to be essential in operating a modern medical system anywhere in the world. World-class biomedicine is a global business. Saudis at TCHSA made it clear that they could not remain a world-class facility and a leader in the Middle East without the continual making, breaking, and recombining of transnational partnerships. As one of the staff at TCHSA described it:

> It is essential to keep up with the latest in medical knowledge and technology, which requires constant participation in the world market for medicine. In medicine, the exchange with different physicians, knowledge, learning about new applications, new medication: this is how you improve your standard of medicine. You cannot work without it, especially [with] the US because most of the inventions and the discoveries occur in the US. So, to have medical cooperation is of utmost importance for people, for all mankind, not just Saudis but everybody. We will be not improving or somewhat retarded, if you will, if we don't follow the new technology and all the development that happens.

TCHSA has collaborated with numerous institutions including Massachusetts General Hospital, the Mayo Clinic, Johns Hopkins Hospital, Memorial Sloan-Kettering Cancer Center, and the UCLA Health System. Also physicians from these institutions visit TCHSA to give lectures and see patients, and physicians from TCHSA visit these institutions to learn new procedures firsthand. TCHSA has partnered with WorldCare, a company that contracts with numerous hospitals for providing second opinions and consultations. When the physicians at TCHSA need a second opinion on a case, they contact WorldCare to make the connection with specific medical institutions for them. In 2003, TCHSA signed an agreement with the Cleveland Clinic for such services. TCHSA is developing electronic diagnostic systems with hospitals in the United States. In these systems, all the information that pertains to the patient can be sent electronically. A physician located anywhere in the world can actually diagnose disease without seeing the patient lying in a hospital bed in Saudi Arabia.

TCHSA is, in turn, a leader in the region and provides expertise within KSA's borders and in the larger Gulf area as well. The hospital has established an Internet medical information site, Healthgulf, which was developed through a partnership with Medunet, a Saudi enterprise. Medunet provides medical and educational resources to all corners of the Kingdom through modern telecommunications technology. The Healthgulf site has 12,000 subscribers from the Gulf area and beyond. It contains two actual sites: one in English for the medical professionals, offering current medical information and second opinions, and one in Arabic for the general public, offering medical educational information. The Healthgulf Internet site was created through partnerships with Malaysian software companies. The site includes notices of symposia held in the Kingdom. Examples are: The Second Women's Health Update Symposia, held in Jiddah in March 2004 and the Microvascular Surgery Intensive "Hands On" Course, held in Riyadh five times during 2003 and 2004. The site includes treatment guidelines (for example, RH-Isoimmunization Prevention, Identification, and Management), case studies (for example, Spontaneous Renal Artery Dissection in a Normotensive Young Male), and articles (for example: "Shaken Baby Syndrome" republished from the *American Family Physician*) (www.healthgulf.com). In this Internet site, TCHSA shares medical information gleaned from the world over with its subscribers who are primarily in the Kingdom and the Gulf area.

Not only were networks of transnational partnerships essential for developing and maintaining Saudi expertise and its leadership position in the region, they remain essential for conducting business efficiently. Outsourcing has become a way of life in Saudi just as it has in the United States. For example, TCHSA contracts with CBAY, a US company, for medical transcription. The Kingdom has few trained medical transcriptionists and has tried in the past to entice foreign transcriptionists to move to the Kingdom to work. TCHSA tried to recruit from the United States, South Africa, and the Far East but with little luck in recent years. Faced with a backlog of transcription needs, TCHSA contracted with CBAY to handle medical transcription. Each day they transmit their medical records electronically to CBAY in the United States, where records are in turn transmitted to India, where transcriptionists actually transcribe them. Then the records are transmitted back to the United States, checked for errors, and sent on to Saudi to the TCHSA, *all* within twenty-four hours. The administrator for clinical services learned of CBAY at the Health Care Information and Management Systems Society annual meeting in the United States.

TCHSA may be initiating robotic prescription filling, through another company, Pyxis, found through attending professional meetings in the States. Attendance at international professional meetings is essential to TCHSA's success. One administrator explained, "It is a challenge. Since you are considered to be a leader [in] tertiary care in the Middle East, you have got to be like those big hospitals and you cannot do it by isolating yourself." These are again examples of those networks of partnerships that are beneficial to each of the partner members respectively and together form an adaptive system.

Thus, the example of TCHSA sheds light on another aspect of the five-step process. While transnational partnerships were essential for modernization of the Kingdom, Saudis assume they will continue to be essential for the running of a modern Kingdom. In medicine, as this author was informed numerous times, traditional partnerships are essential to maintaining a cutting-edge medical institution, whether in Saudi Arabia or in the United States. The Saudi experts at TCHSA, like their counterparts all over the world, will go wherever necessary in the world to establish partnerships that allow them to maintain their leading edge in tertiary care.

Hybrid Culture at TCHSA

The transnational partnerships that brought the miracle of modern medicine to the Kingdom have been fraught with problems. An important set of these are cultural issues.

TCHSA is staffed by 7,488 employees of sixty-three different nationalities. They proudly refer to themselves as a "mini United Nations." While initially it was necessary to draw skilled workers from outside the Kingdom, slowly TCHSA is becoming Saudized with 38 percent of the total staff being Saudi in 2003. One important aspect of this multicultural mix is salary and salary differences cause problems. First, the hospital recognizes eight salary "zones," which are based on nationality. One's pay is determined by one's job type and one's zone. For example, a nurse from the United States (zone 1) or Canada (zone 2) makes almost three times as much as a nurse from the Philippines who is doing the same job. People of different nationalities are placed in zones based on the economy of their home country. How much money does it take to get a nurse from the United States to come to Saudi? Almost three times the amount of money it takes to get a nurse from the Philippines.

> [We] have an entire world here that [we] are drawing from. In the US, if you are doing the same work you are going to get roughly the same pay. And [in the US] if we take advantage of the fact that there is this global workforce, what we tend to do is build the factory in Mexico or Indonesia and pay the people there 25 cents an hour. But here we bring all those people together and do that. So we have set up different pay scales based solely on what your passport is.

Tension arises when workers doing the same job are paid differently. An additional problem is that the Saudi rial is tied to the US dollar. So as the dollar rises or falls on the international market, those not from the Kingdom or the United States see the value of their paycheck change. European doctors at TCHSA have effectively taken a pay cut in recent years because of the rise in the Euro, while US doctors have *not* seen their salaries erode even though doctors from the United States and Europe are paid with the same pay scale. The differences in culture and in pay, of course, cause tension.

But many see this cultural mix as a good environment. One physician describes her department:

> We have one American, one Canadian, three Danish, and one South African. That is for the physician staff. And the rest [of the physicians] are Saudis actually, six or seven. . . . Our nursing staff we have a whole mix of everywhere. . . . And we have 50, 55 nurses. They come from all over. South Africa, a lot of Canadians, a lot from the Philippines, a lot from other Arab countries as well. . . . The support staff, . . . I have one from South Africa and one is Filipino, and one is Arab—she is from Palestine. Case managers and coordinators, most of those are Saudis because they have to interact a lot with patients. They have to be native speakers. Secretaries are mostly from the Philippines. We have pharmacists, dieticians, physiotherapists. And they are a mixture from all over. If we all know the mission, if you know what you are doing, it doesn't matter what the nationality or background of the staff members are. Because your aim is really to serve the patient. So on a work basis, I don't think it makes much difference. Maybe on social background it might. People with the same background or the same country will socialize together more. But when it comes to work, it really makes no difference whatsoever. Under-

stand that I have been working in this hospital for 16 years, and we have not ever had any problems just because people come from different backgrounds, different nationalities. We have here like a team and you have to work as a team; otherwise, you can't really serve your patients.

Others describe the kinds of cultural clashes this involves. For example, the following perceptions are culled from interviews with nurses: (1) British doctors clash with American nurses because the United Kingdom has a more rigid system than the United States. British doctors do not expect nurses to question them. (2) English nurses are not taught to do a physical assessment (listen to breathing and heart, check pulse, and so on) when a patient first arrives at the hospital, while US nurses are. (3) Indian nurses do not have the clinical experience or nursing education for this kind of high-tech hospital. (4) Filipinos are excellent at cardiac and pediatric specialties.

Saudization is systematically sweeping the hospital. All hospital administrators are now Saudi as well as about one-half of the physicians. Other positions have been Saudized en masse. Patient-care assistants (individuals who push wheelchairs and do other patient-related tasks) were for twenty years primarily Sudanese. In an eighteen-month period, these positions were Saudized and the Sudanese were forced to move to other, lower-paying, jobs or leave. Given the unemployment in the Kingdom, Saudis jumped at the chance to become patient-care assistants. One administrator remembers that there were "ten applicants for every position" and that the applicants "filled up our entire lobby." Other jobs recently Saudized in the same way are case managers and ward clerks.

Part of the unique nature of the culture at TCHSA is this multicultural mix that creates the hybrid culture. Although the staff includes workers with some sixty-five different national passports, a few nationalities make up large percentages of the total staff population. In 2003, Saudi Arabia made up the largest percentage of the workforce at 38 percent, followed by the Philippines (17 percent), the Sudan (8 percent), Canada (6 percent), India (4 percent), and the United States and South Africa (3 percent each). While all these cultural groupings impact the dynamic of culture at TCHSA, two have extraordinary influence on hospital culture: Saudi Arabia and the United States. Since the hospital was originally created by an American corporation, HCA, staffed with Americans, and using an American hospital structure, policies, and procedures, it initially had a strong American hospital culture. This is voiced by American old-timers still employed at the hospital: "There were very few concessions to the Islamic way. We were an island and it was very American." As the hospital has increasingly been Saudized, that culture has been altered in Saudi ways so that by the time of this study, there was a hybrid culture of which Saudi and US elements were the most prominent. The following stories, culled from interviews with hospital staff, illustrate the transition from US domination to strong Saudi influence:

The Swimming Pool: Originally, the hospital amenities center had a swimming pool that was for Westerners only. The reason originally for the "Westerners only" rule was to avoid the Saudi rules of segregating men and women. It allowed the Western population to use the pool the way they would use a pool in their own countries. Muslims, of course, wanted use of the pool, especially for their children. In 1981, the Muslim staff, primarily Egyptians, "forcibly occupied" the pool and the rules were changed. New, Saudi-style rules were put into place, which are still in effect. Some days of the week are reserved for men only, others for women only, and others still for families. One's religion or nationality is no longer an issue.

The Cafeteria: Originally, the staff food area was an American-style cafeteria with one general seating area for all. At some point in the early 1990s, it was changed so that there were separate eating areas for men and women, and a third eating area for families. This third area, however, is used by unrelated men and women eating together and thus not used in a strict family sense. This would never be allowed in a public eating establishment outside the hospital, and so it remains a bone of contention among some Saudis who see this behavior as strictly forbidden by Islamic and Saudi law.

The Mosques: When the hospital was built, there was no mosque or chapel in the hospital. The absence of a mosque is real evidence of the initial strength of the American role as Saudi Arabia is a country of mosques. In the major cities it is not uncommon to find locations where one is in hearing distance of the call to prayer from twenty or thirty mosques. Even gas stations sometimes have a mosque attached to them. Thus, no mosque in a facility as large as TCHSA with its thousands of employees is astounding. For decades the hospital sported makeshift prayer areas for the employees. Eventually, two mosques were added, and recently, a nicer, official prayer area was built. While it would not be unusual to find a mosque at any hospital in the world, it is highly unusual for it to have taken so long to add mosques at a facility in the Kingdom.

Housing Compounds: Expatriate employees lived in the compounds mentioned earlier. At the hospital's inception, there were separate compounds for: (1) families, (2) single men, and (3) single women, respectively. Additionally there were no restrictions on the movements of single men and women. In 1979, however, the rules were changed so that single men could not visit the single women's compounds and vice versa. Security guards actually enforced this rule. Thus, rule changes put the compounds more in keeping with the religious rules of other public spaces in the Kingdom.

Dress Code: The hospital dress code also reflects the tension between US and Saudi culture. All male physicians at the hospital, including Saudis, wear Western suits and lab coats while at the Saudi university medical schools, male Saudi physicians wear ghutras (head coverings) and thobes, of traditional Saudi male dress. Women physicians at TCHSA wear the *hijab* if they are Muslim, meaning they cover their hair and may also cover their faces including their eyes. When examining a patient, they leave their eyes exposed. They do not, however, wear the abaya. The abaya would be the appropriate dress in such a public place as a hospital, and it is worn by women visitors to

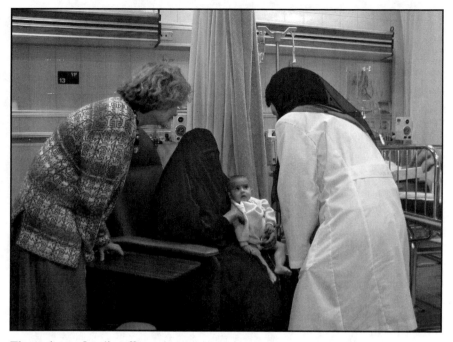

The author, a Saudi staff member, and a patient's mother exemplify female dress in the hospital.

the hospital. Women physicians and nurses, however, wear pants or long skirts and lab coats instead of the abaya. Lab coats have become an acceptable alternative to abayas for women physicians, nurses, and other medical specialists. The response to this dress policy indicates the tension between the two cultures in the hospital's hybrid culture. Some Muslim women enjoy the greater freedom by leaving their hair uncovered, placing a scarf in easy reach around their neck. Traditional Saudis at the hospital complained, however, about the indecent dress of women in the hospital. In a further conflict about dress, some Saudis believe that nurses in scrubs should wear scrub uniforms with long sleeves so that their arms will not be exposed and that they should veil. Westerners, however, rationalize issues of dress as issues of sanitation. A woman in a veil or a man in a ghutra, while putting in an IV or dressing a wound, could endanger the patient by allowing the veil or ghutra to touch the sterile field. The same argument is made about long-sleeved scrubs for women. The sleeves could touch sterile fields. Western dress is seen as more sanitary. (No mention is made of the danger of Western neckties touching a sterile field.) When examining a patient, however, it is perfectly acceptable for a female physician to wear hijab, including covering her face, with the exception of her eyes. Female patients are typically covered including their eyes. The most difficult area for a male physician to get permission to examine on a female patient is her face.

Male–Female Interaction: For Saudis unaccustomed to Western ways, the hospital is the locale of a bewildering array of inappropriate behaviors. Just stopping a colleague in the hall to discuss a patient can be misinterpreted. Under Saudi codes, it is inappropriate to speak to someone of the opposite sex. A Western nurse who smiles and says hello to a Saudi male is acting completely inappropriately. Another issue is that women and men are working too closely together: "Completely mixing, all together. This is against our way." In one case, a male patient-care assistant handed a tray to a female coworker and his hand touched hers. This is *haram* (forbidden) and there was an outcry. Other Saudi women, discussing the incident, stated that if this had happened to them, they would have told him, "Don't you ever touch me again or I am going to tell my father, or I will report it to my head nurse."

Female Leadership: Given these rules, an outsider might expect women to have little influence in the medical community. Yet, female physicians hold places of leadership in the hospital. Several Saudi women physicians are department heads. The chief resident at the time of this research was a Saudi female. All of these are positions one is elected to hold, and women were elected to these positions by their male and female colleagues alike. Some female physicians, in fact, insist that they have never been treated disrespectfully by their male Saudi colleagues, only by male colleagues from non-Arab countries.

Muslim Time / Western Time: The hospital time schedule is set to the Western clock as normal work hours for administrators are 8:00 AM to 6:00 PM and medical staff keeps shift hours similar to those in the United States. A Saudi workday is typically 8:00 AM to approximately 3:00 PM. This gives Saudis time to fulfill their other time-consuming obligations to their family and their religion. As one Saudi described it:

> The problem is that we inherited all the American [ways] from those who established this hospital and the changes, they are very difficult. Change is very, very slow. . . . The culture here [in KSA] is completely different. . . . The culture is completely different in the States. Here [at TCHSA] we work from 8 to 6, killing us. We don't see our children. We don't see our people. . . . So this is the American system. But all the country are working from 8 to 3 or 2:30. So that we can—we are not to work all the day. We have children, we have families, we have ourselves. We are not here only to get money and to just collect money. We have a social life.

These Saudi hours are also impacted by prayer times. The end of the Saudi workday is prior to the late afternoon prayer call.

Thus, the culture at TCHSA is a confusing mix of influences. Pieces of the hospital culture come from a multitude of cultures geographically dispersed around the world. All are joined together at TCHSA to create the organizational culture lived by those who enter the hospital's doors. Upon walking into the lobby, one immediately sees the ways in which behavior is different from behavior out on the street. One sees women in lab coats, not abayas, and groups of unrelated males and females walking down the hall talking. But this is only the surface, what one can see from a single vantage point. Below this surface, multiple layers of interconnected pieces make up the true hybrid culture of TCHSA.

Without question, this is a hybrid culture in tension. As is the case in any national culture, the Saudis on the hospital staff are not of one mind regarding the propriety of hospital rules and regulations. Some Saudi staff are strict Wahabbi traditionalists who see the hybrid hospital culture as containing many elements that are forbidden in Islam and who are disgusted by allowing what, to them, is immoral behavior. Other Saudis find the rules acceptable and enjoy the freedom the hospital environment gives them. As for the other nationalities working in the hospital, their opinions and comfort levels with the rules and behaviors in the hospital are as varied as their nationalities and the diversity in their own countries. Some Westerners, for example, think the Saudi rules inside the hospital, and certainly those outside it in Saudi public space, are silly and backward while other Westerners take a more culturally relative position. Some of the hospital staff cope with the tensions by sticking to procedure during the workday and isolating themselves "with their own kind" after hours. Others make an effort to socialize with staff from a variety of cultural backgrounds. None of the staff interviewed for this research disputed the value of the American "bones" of the hospital. They agreed that all procedures in the hospital must be up to the most exacting of international standards. The disputes, rather, were over issues of behavioral rules, like who sits where in the cafeteria. Of course, time and again, behavioral rules impact Western hospital standards, like the dispute over whether Saudi dress endangers the sterile field when cleaning a wound.

The hospital culture is slowly moving from an all-American culture toward a Saudi culture, but it is doubtful that it will ever lose all of its Western characteristics. Many of these are too integrated into the international procedures and standards of a modern health care facility, and the West is driving international standards in health care. Just as English is the official language of international medical journals, the lab coat and scrubs are the international dress alternatives for physicians. In a medical evaluation of a patient, doctors and nurses, whether males or females, must talk to each other, even though similar communication between unrelated males and females in other public spaces, such as shopping malls, is forbidden. Thus, while the culture of the hospital may continue to move closer to general Saudi culture, it will probably never lose its hybrid quality. There are just too many other cultures represented in the mix. While the Kingdom will continue to Saudize hospital jobs whenever practical, it will not do away with the transnational partnerships that create this hybrid culture. Saudi doctors and hospital administrators alike emphasized the essentialness of maintaining transnational partnerships in order to maintain a state-of-the-art facility.

The hybridity of the hospital culture is always in flux—the pieces of the culture are always in movement—as if no one is satisfied with how they mesh and everyone is always looking for a better fit. This is a characteristic of hybrid cultures. They inherently contain tension.

The External Environment and TCHSA

Like other global businesses with multiple networks of transnational partnerships, TCHSA is impacted by the geopolitical economy. Understanding this impact is essential to understanding transnational partnerships generally as well as those in KSA specifically. The September 11 terrorist attack in the United States is an example of an external event that had serious and long-reaching effects on TCHSA. An important reaction was the reluctance of Westerners to come to the Kingdom and of Saudis to go to the West. TCHSA had been dependent on the West for nurses, for example. Prior to 9/11, some 25 percent of the nurses were from the Philippines, 25 percent were from Canada and 12 percent were from the United States. Eighteen months after 9/11, the numbers from Europe, the United States, and Canada had dropped. For the United States, this was a drop to 5 percent. The US-led invasion of Iraq caused a new wave of resignations. The shortage of nurses was critical world-wide, and the Kingdom's rulers were especially concerned that the country's loss of nurses was due to perceived terror links in Saudi Arabia. TCHSA was scrambling to solve its critical nursing shortage.

Another post-9/11 problem was caused by the new US rules about mail. The hospital sent many tests to the Mayo Clinic and other US hospitals for analysis. Some of these tests could only be done in the United States or Canada; however, the United States was reluctant to accept specimens from the Middle East. Packages entering the United States were irradiated; because the specimens were live cells, the cells were killed. The hospital labels such packages clearly "Please do not irradiate. These are live cells." Of course "live cells' were exactly the kind of materials the US irradiation system was meant to kill in an attempt to reduce the chance of biological terrorism. Consequently, TCHSA had difficulty getting samples through to US laboratories.

Additionally, Saudi physicians and other Saudi medical specialists from the hospital frequently traveled to the United States for meetings, seminars, and visits to hospitals to learn new procedures and test new equipment. After 9/11, many of them were reluctant to go to the States. There was a perception in Saudi that Saudis were mistreated by US immigration officials and were in danger in general of being hassled in the United States. Several Saudis interviewed stated that they planned to skip the meetings they had expected to attend in 2003 and 2004.

TCHSA also had planned to establish two offices in the United States to facilitate arrangements for Saudi patients being transferred to the United States for care. These plans were temporarily scrapped. Fewer Saudis were going to the United States for care. Also, fewer physicians were choosing to complete their training in the United States. The difficulty of getting visas was one of the reasons for this problem. One interviewee described the case of man in need of emergency medical care who waited for a visa to the United States for one year. He finally went to Western Europe for the care. (The author checked with the US Embassy and found that this story was indeed true.) Thus, world events are significant to the success of the hospital. Networks of transnational partnerships are part of an open system that includes political and economic forces on the world stage. Environment is a critical factor in their success. There is great concern in the KSA government over the impact of world politics on its networks of transnational partnerships. Government leaders see these networks as essential to the Kingdom's continued success and anything that threatens them potentially limits that success.

TCHSA Today

In 1970 the government's goal for health care was to bring modern biomedical care to the Kingdom, and the establishment of TCHSA was part of the plan for achieving that goal. The hospital was targeted to become a modern, tertiary care facility for the Kingdom and a leading medical facility in the Middle East. The hospital can be considered a success in that it has met this goal. According to several hospital publications, by 2002, TCHSA in Riyadh was a 650-bed tertiary-care hospital admitting 212,000 patients a year, supporting 592,000 outpatient visits, and performing 1,400 open-heart surgeries, 130 bone marrow transplants, and 60 kidney transplants. The patient visits included 51,000 dental visits, 47,000 emergency department visits, and 90,000 oncology clinic visits. The hospital had 720 physicians and 1,940 nurses with a total staff of 7,150 composed of sixty-three different nationalities (hospital publications).

This success is the result of transnational partnerships interlinked into complex adaptive systems that have succeeded against all odds. Meschi (1997) has commented that individuals often have a hard time articulating their own culture, as it is in the nature of culture that one is unaware of one's own. At TCHSA, cultural differences were so stark that there was no way to be unaware of them. This may have worked to help traverse the cultural minefields and the resulting operational difficulties. In all transnational partnerships, culture is an issue but sometimes an ignored one. At TCHSA, no one could ignore the fact that culture was an issue. Yet, despite the extreme differences in culture of staff from over sixty countries, the partnerships have been a success in that they have helped achieve the goal of creating a world-class tertiary-care facility in the Middle East and of providing much needed health care to Saudi citizens. The ongoing transnational context of medicine practiced at the hospital is an effort to continue this world-class quality and requires continued participation in global complex adaptive systems.

Chapter 7
Rapid Rate of Change

On a camping trip with my sons in the desert south of Riyadh in 2002, I first encountered the white bedu tents, water trucks, and herds of sheep and goats that are typical of pastoralism in Saudi Arabia today. In talking with the bedu families living there, I found that they were as curious about me and my sons as we were about them. First of all, they assumed we were with the US Central Intelligence Agency. Who else would be crazy enough to go driving through this punishing desert where gasoline was unavailable (we carried extra cans of gas), tires were frequently punctured by sharp rocks (we carried extra tires), and we were always in danger of getting stuck in a sand dune (we carried equipment for digging the car out of the sand). From the perspective of the bedu, our interest in simply seeing the country and meeting people was folly; surely there must be some other purpose to our visit, like espionage. Given the punishing impact the terrain had on our automobiles, I could understand their views. I, however, wondered about these people who were wondering about us. I had read about traditional bedu life and this looked different. Vehicles, white cloth tents, and a preference for sheep herds over camel herds did not figure into my picture of bedu life. I had also heard the rumors that desert families of the twenty-first century were there by choice and probably had family members working in banks and law offices in the major cities of the Kingdom. At the same time, the women were traditionally attired, and the traditional desert hospitality was as prevalent as I had expected. So, I was curious about just how much had changed beyond the obvious characteristics that I could see.

Previous chapters in this book developed an understanding of the ways of life in the Arabian Peninsula in the early twentieth century and then focused on the modernization process used to enact change and the more recent economic goals of KSA. To summarize from earlier discussions, the two factors most significant in effecting change were the following:

1. ***State Formation:*** Ibn Saud and his sons employed several techniques to unify a previously politically fractured peninsula that included replacing

111

old, autonomous political entities with new local government structures that reported to the state and replacing old, tribal land-ownership policies with new state land ownership. Such strategic moves wrought substantial changes in traditional lifeways.

2. **Formal Development Strategies:** The effort to bring modern education, health care, industry, and business, which began in earnest with the five-year plans initiated in 1970 and continues to the present, has brought vast changes to the Kingdom in the last forty years through the modernization process described in the previous two chapters.

This chapter describes the resulting changes for pastoralists, villagers, city dwellers, and Saudi youth. First, let's return to the bedu.

The Bedu

A significant strategy of state formation was the weakening of tribal independence. Necessary to this goal were: (1) wresting control of lands from the pastoralist tribes and (2) subduing their mobile and warlike ways. In 1953 the government issued the Public Land Decree, which ended tribal rights over their traditional lands, making these traditional lands of the tribes now common property that could be used by all. The government took several steps to provide for the bedu. As mentioned in chapter 3, it relocated many of them to permanent settlements, encouraged many to take up agriculture, and employed others in the National Guard. These and other government strategies led to a changed but still unique bedu way of life.

While specific numbers are hard to find, bedu following a nomadic way of life were the majority of the population in the early twentieth century but were reduced to between 5 and 25 percent of the population by 1993 (Moaddel 2006:81; Champion 2003:111). The Public Land Decree of 1953 had an immediate impact. F. S. Vidal describes what happened in 1956 at Aramco's pipeline pump stations in northern KSA and at its gas-oil separator plants in eastern KSA. Attracted by a stable water supply when other parts of Arabia were experiencing drought, numerous bedu gathered at these locations. At Ghawar oilfield in eastern Saudi Arabia, twenty-five tribes with 2,901 tents in forty-seven sites were counted (Vidal 1975; Cole 2003:243). Prior to the land act and the automobile, a gathering of this many tribes in a single area would have been unlikely.

A study of bedu life conducted in the Al-Taysiyah area of north central Saudi Arabia during the late 1990s describes the changes in the bedu economic strategies after the land act (Finan and Al-Haratani 1998; Gardner 2003). One focus of this research was the pasturelands around the village of Al-Zabiran. This area is within the traditional lands of several clans of the Harb tribe. While members of the Otaybah, Mutair, and Dawassir tribes used the lands during the winter and spring, during the summer of 1995 only the Harb lived there. Of eighty-four families interviewed, three were nomadic, in that they moved to the north in the winter to pasture their animals elsewhere, and three were sedentary, living in the village of Al-Zabiran and going out daily to work with the herds. The remaining seventy-eight families were considered by the researchers to be seminomadic as they moved only within the tribal pasture-lands never going more than short distances (Finan and Al-Haratani 1998). A related study conducted in 1999 in the northern deserts included twenty-seven interviews with bedu members of seven tribes as well as health administrators, doctors, veterinarians, and other officials (Gardner 2003).

The researchers conducting these studies chronicle how the state efforts at unification and modernization changed the economic strategies of this group. The Public Land Decree of 1953 ended tribal management of the lands. No longer did tribal leaders with their complex alliances of clans and subclans control and manage the use of their traditional lands. Now, when the rains came to an area, no one had to ask permission of a traditional tribal leader to graze their herds in his lands. Bedu from all over the Kingdom could descend on a particular luxuriously green pasture area, and they routinely did, so that these areas quickly became overgrazed, resulting in degraded land that could not replenish easily or at all in future years. The automobile contributed to this overgrazing. Previously, travel to distant pastures might have taken months; now, herds could be moved quickly in transport trucks to greener pastures that would have been too distant to even consider before motor vehicles. One bedu herder explained:

> I hear about other places from other Bedouin. We always see each other and we talk. We are Bedouin, and we're always looking for good range-land. If it rains anywhere in the kingdom, people start to move, and we are always asking each other about the land. When I get there, even if it's crowded, I take my place among the others. (Gardner 2003:7)

During the rainy season of 1995, the researchers found not only local tribes grazing their animals around Al-Taysiyah but also nomadic tribes from south and southwest of the area as well as merchants from Riyadh (Finan and Al-Haratani 1998). In addition to the traditional bedu, middle-class townspeople were raising small herds as a strategy to increase their income while the wealthy from the cities kept herds to connect with the romance of the bedu past, so that herds grazing in the northern desert were owned by non-bedu as well as by bedu from distant regions (Gardner 2003:267). The traditional owners of the land were now only one group among the many herders using its resources. International politics also played a role in who grazed their animals in the northern deserts. In their 1999 study in the northern deserts, Gardner, Finan, and the other researchers found that since the Gulf War of 1991, bedu from Kuwait and Iraq were pasturing their animals in the northern deserts of the Kingdom because the stable Saudi government made the area safe, adding even more pressure on the land (Gardner 2003). "This is the dirah [tribal territory] of the Harb, but many tribes come here now . . . in the old times, you couldn't just go anywhere you wanted," said one of the tribesmen (Gardner 2003:7).

Further changes for the bedu resulted from other government actions that were aimed at pacifying the bedu raiding tendencies and reducing their mobility so that they could be more easily incorporated into the state system. The government encouraged settlement, provided access to health services and education, subsidized (after 1979) the price of barley, provided employment in the National Guard, and increased the numbers of roads and water wells. The new roads and water wells allowed bedu to continue to pasture herds but not move as far. The subsidized barley allowed them to buy this grain so cheaply they could afford to supplement their animals' diet of pasture grasses with barley when the pastures became too bare, again reducing the need to travel with their herds. One bedu commented, "There was no time this year I went without barley. The rangeland was bad all year, and if there's no food, the animals die. Barley goes for SAR 27 (just over $7.00) a bag, and I feed my animals 26 bags every other day" (Gardner 2003:267).

Roads allowed easier movement in vehicles between a sedentary residence and the herd grazing at a distance. Vehicles started appearing in the area in 1964, and by the time of the study, all families had at least one pickup truck, which allowed them to move easily from home to animal pasture to school for the children and then to the markets and then back home. New wells meant they did not have to move as far to find water for their herds. Of the eighty-four families in the study, all also had water tankers for taking water from the well in the village to their herds, and about half of them also had transport trucks for moving the animals to better pastures. Education

Modern transportation has changed the economic strategies of bedu and hadar alike.

and health care were additional reasons to become relatively sedentary. Valuing the health services and the education opportunities for their children, bedu moved to urban areas to reduce the distance of their travel to these services. While the older family members grew up in the days prior to the advent of the modern education system and were illiterate, the families valued education for their children, believing that it would allow them to find paying jobs, and 60 percent said their children were or had been in school. A primary reason for not sending children to school was that the family needed the children to help tend the livestock.

Another change was in the composition and size of herds. Today in Saudi, camels are kept for their symbolic importance, much like the longhorn steers in my home state of Texas. The steer of the Texas cattle drives, which gave Texas its economic independence and forged the state's identity, is no longer marketed for human beef consumption. Its beef does not measure up to the flavor and tenderness of other breeds; yet, many a Texas rancher still raises longhorns, demonstrating their symbolic importance in the state. The camel has a similar importance in Saudi Arabia. Today's economically important herds are 90 percent sheep, a valuable animal at market sold for its meat, and 10 percent goats, raised for their milk. Of the families in the Al-Zabirah study, 40 percent still had camels, with an average camel herd being thirty-six animals. Today, bedu pastoralists are raising animals for the cash market, as they must purchase barley, pay vet bills, and in some cases pay herders who are not family members. The bedu have moved from a barter system to a cash economy.

Many bedu are no longer engaged in their traditional occupation with animals. The importance of the National Guard as paid employment has already been mentioned. Many families had a son or brother in the National Guard whose paycheck benefited the family economically. In addition to the National Guard, young bedu were taking jobs in many sectors of the economy. Education was opening new doors. Now, the bedu camp is likely to be housing women, children, and possibly elderly men while the rest of the family lives in the urban areas working in the cash economy. Of the eighty-four families in the study, the average age of the head of a camp was fifty-eight years old, with the oldest being ninety and the youngest being nineteen. The average size of the camps was eight people, while the largest was seventeen people and the smallest was a single person. The median herd size was 450 total sheep and goats. This is substantially larger than the size of a traditional herd, which, as mentioned in chapter 4, would have been made up of roughly 100 camels and a few sheep and goats. The camps averaged about 30 kilometers (18.6 miles) from the village of Al-Zabirah. Al-Zabirah was the center of activities because it had a water well used to fill the tanker trucks for the animals, as well as schools and a market.

Approximately half of the families hired an expatriate as a herder and these families were more likely to send their children to school (Finan and Al-Haratani 1998:354–359). Expatriate herders were from foreign regions with herding economies and had prior herding knowledge. For sheep, most were from India, and for camels they came from Sudan. They were in the country on multiyear contracts, and like all expatriate workers, they had to be sponsored by their employers to enter the country. They lived in separate tents near the herds (Finan and Al-Haratani 1998). The availability of these expatriate herders was a factor in the decisions of non-bedu village and city dwellers to keep a herd. By hiring an expatriate with herding knowledge, those with no personal experience of herding and with jobs that prevented them from spending time herding the animals themselves could invest in a herd to increase their economic resources. Additionally, the availability of expatriate labor meant bedu families could increase their herd size beyond the size they were able to manage with family labor (Gardner 2003:6). These new strategies as part of the cash market economy have proven successful for the bedu of the Al-Taysiyah area, but the barley subsidy provided by the government is crucial for economic survival. Without it, the herding lifeway would die, and thus the bedu are dependent on the government for the continuation of their ways.

Another concern for the bedu is disease. The eighty-four families interviewed told the researchers that 20 percent of the camel herders lost an animal to disease in the previous year while some 85 percent of camps with sheep lost animals to disease. Many forces contributed to this disease problem, including (1) herds being grazed in the area by bedu from other parts of the Kingdom and indeed from other countries, like Kuwait and Iraq, and by non-bedu from urban areas, and (2) that the traditional land users had increased the size of their herds with the assistance of expatriate herders. These factors caused overcrowding and an increase in communicable diseases. Epidemic disease in sheep was causing more economic uncertainty (Finan and Al-Haratani 1998:365; Gardner 2003:5). As one bedu commented, "There are lots more animals on the range now because people have more money, and there's barley, and it's easy and affordable to bring in someone to care for the animals" (Gardner 2003:6).

The switch to a cash economy and a market orientation has impacted the traditional bedu communication system as well. While bedu hospitality continues intact, meetings with visitors over coffee and food in the leader's tent are no longer the primary way of sharing information. Now information is gleaned at the markets where one goes to buy barley and to sell animals because there one can find a much wider pool of knowledge since people from all over the Kingdom and beyond are likely to be trading there (Gardner 2003:8). The herdsman can learn about animal prices, good pasture locations, predictions of rain, and even the soccer scores while buying barley.

T. J. Finan and E. R. Al-Haratani conclude that

> public policy and the impacts of modernization have protected their
> [bedu] livelihood from extinction, and they are able to survive at reason-
> able levels of economic well-being. . . . In many ways, modernization has
> transformed the Bedouin into a tent-dwelling rancher, with a capital-

intensive enterprise that hires outside labour and depends critically on market conditions, as much as on range conditions. . . . Herd management strategies and grazing practices reflect the demands of short-term economic maximization, rather than long-term conservation. (Finan and Al-Haratani 1998:366–367)

In summary, all of the factors mentioned above are intertwined in a web of changes. The Public Land Decree of 1953 that ended tribal land ownership was a strategy designed to assist in national unification, but it also ended tribal management of the land, and, by permitting anyone to graze where they wished, led to (1) overcrowding on choice pasturelands and then to (2) land degradation. The coming of the automobile led to (1) the loss of economic importance for the camel and the resulting increase in herds of sheep for sale at market, rather than for barter with villagers, and (2) the availability of water trucks and transport trucks, allowing herds to be grazed in a vastly expanded geographic area of pastureland. The availability of expatriate herders led to (1) increased herd size for the bedu who could now graze more animals than their family had the manpower to watch and (2) the addition of herds by non-bedu who had no indigenous knowledge of herding or of the terrain but understood the advantage of adding a herd to supplement income from their wage-labor jobs, market stalls, and other village and urban economic strategies. The global price for barley subsidized by the government in order to provide the bedu with an economic cushion led to (1) bedu increasing the size of their herds because the herd size was no longer dependent on amount of pastureland and (2) non-bedu getting into the herding business because of the protection that the barley provided against failure in years of drought. Thus, global commodity prices, international politics, and the global movement of technology all have played a part in the changed lifeway of the bedu.

To be bedu no longer refers to following a specific way of life. Bedu city dwellers who might be accountants for international accounting firms or professors at public universities are no longer in the herding business, yet they remain bedu. The traditional bedu way of life, altered as described above by the forces of state formation, modernization, and globalization, is still revered in the Kingdom. Ibn Saud so valued it that he sent his older sons to live in bedu camps during their youth to learn the self-sufficiency, survival strategies, and value system important to Arabic culture. Today, bedu still identify with that culture, and I agree with Donald Cole (2003) who suggests that bedu today means not a particular subsistence strategy but an identity grounded in a cultural way of life.

Cole describes the move to town that occurred among bedu throughout the Kingdom. He explains that bedu began moving to the urban areas in the 1950s, but they came in greater numbers in the 1960s and in the largest numbers in the 1970s and 1980s. Those who came in the 1950s included many young men who had few livestock and were looking for another source of income. They did manual labor and lived in work camps at first. Some gained technical skills, others became taxi drivers, and as their own livelihoods in the cities stabilized, they moved their families to town. In the meantime, new communities, each composed of a gas station, a café, and a mosque, were appearing in the desert, and in the 1970s a school likely was added to the mix. At first, housing was likely to have been makeshift, but with the oil boom of the 1970s and 1980s, the government provided these communities with financial help for constructing permanent housing.

Donald Cole (2003:252) noticed another example of change in that tribal names were now being used as surnames. "Telephone books, for example, now list hundreds of subscribers under their tribal names." Traditionally, one used a lineage name to identify oneself. I found that use of these names today identifies one as tribal and bedu, an important distinction in modern Saudi Arabia. In addition, festivities have developed that honor the bedu past. Since the 1960s, horse and camel races are held in cities like Riyadh; these formalized races were never a part of traditional bedu culture, but their modern development is popular as a nostalgic remembrance of the past. Fine breeds of camels and horses are highly valued and seen as a symbol of the expertise of the bedu who bred them into existence. In Riyadh, the National Museum has a prominent display of a bedu tent and artifacts exhibiting a traditional bedu way of life; each year the government hosts the Jenadria festival, which celebrates the traditional regional dress, architecture, and lifeways of the country; markets in Riyadh sell bedu goods to tourists; and traditional bedu oral poetry is revered throughout the Kingdom. As a visitor to the Kingdom, I heard many stories about the valiant deeds of the ancestors of my bedu companions; these stories stressed the value system that they feel still underlies behavior in the Kingdom.

Today, bedu is an identity, which those who can claim it are proud to display. Beyond identity, however, I felt that even non-bedu Saudis were willing to point to the bedu way of life to explain to me the cultural values that undergird the modern Kingdom. This is because these values were shared by non-bedu. All valued honor, hospitality, honesty, and protection of the weak and felt I needed to understand these values in order to understand them.

The Hadar

It is not only the bedu who have experienced such changes in the last few decades; villagers have too.

'Unayzah

Remember the city of 'Unayzah studied by Altorki and Cole described in chapter 4 on traditional culture? Altorki and Cole describe its change in the twentieth century as occurring in two phases: the first phase was due to unification under Ibn Saud, and they date this phase from the 1920s to the 1970s. The second phase was due to the state modernization plans put in place beginning in the 1970s and lasting until their fieldwork in 1987 and, in fact, is ongoing today. They point out that central Arabia had experienced state formation repeatedly during the centuries preceding Ibn Saud's unification in the twentieth century. The emirs acted as "heads of de facto political formations" (Altorki and Cole 1989:233). Islam had for centuries served to bind the Arabian Peninsula together through religious beliefs and related rules of behavior. The first phase of change (1920s–1970s), is signified by four factors: (1) the establishment of a state system with its accompanying bureaucracy; (2) the beginning of a national education system that would train the city's population in new skills; (3) the establishment of the oil industry, which introduced contracts, new forms of wage and salaried labor, and new forms of business organization; and (4) the resulting switch to a cash economy from a barter system. The second phase is signified by the series of five-year plans that the government began in the 1970s and included interest-free government loans that encouraged the building of new housing and the development of local agricultural business. At the time of their study, Altorki and Cole characterized most Saudis in 'Unayzah as middle class (1989:243).

State formation and bureaucracy led to significant change in the position of the emirs, who previously had autonomy. Under the new system, emirs were appointed by the Ministry of Interior and were provided a budget by the Ministry. Thus, the emir is a government employee who reports to the district emirate in a nearby city. The modern education system has helped to create a national identity in that the curriculum is standardized across KSA, and just as with the bedu, it helped to move the town to a cash economy as students were trained not for the old jobs in the small-scale agriculture of the barter economy but in the new jobs of the cash economy. While 'Unayzah had some schools prior to the national development, there were more educational opportunities for boys than for girls, and whether one received an education depended on one's family's financial situation and inclination toward education. Not all families valued educating their children, especially their girls. The following comment describes schooling for one young girl:

> My father was poor and did many different kinds of jobs. He had one camel which he used to carry firewood and *'ushb* [a desert grass used for fodder] for others. As the eldest child, I helped my father in looking after the camel when it was not being used and I sometimes spent several months a year gathering *'ushb* in the desert. On days when I had to take the camel to the desert to graze, I would dash to the home of the teacher and ask her to write the verses I was supposed to learn on my board. I would then run to take the camel and would study my lesson while I was following it in the *barr* [wilderness]. On other days, I stayed longer in the school. But I did not learn to read and write, although I know enough of the holy Qur'an to pray. (Altorki and Cole 1989:96)

Agriculture changed in 'Unayzah with the introduction of mechanized water wells. Ibn Saud gave three pumps to the emir in 1925, and at the time of Altorki and Cole's fieldwork in 1987, people still marked the arrival of those first pumps as a time of agricultural change. The previous system used camels to pump the water and was labor- and time-intensive and consequently expensive. The new mechanized pumps decreased the cost of irrigation and allowed community members to increase the size of their agricultural plots and introduce new crops like oranges, apples, tomatoes, lettuce, and potatoes. Farmers began to grow crops for the cash market, and after 1975, expatriate workers predominated in the fields (1989:98–101).

In the 1940s and 1950s, old occupations disappeared and new ones developed; for example, the men who worked in the camel caravans were without a job. "We hated the trucks because they took our livelihood away from us," one of them stated (1989:101). By the 1950s, a network of roads connected 'Unayzah to neighboring locales, and by the 1960s, important roads were paved. Construction work building roads is an example of a new job area. In the 1950s and 1960s, the state was the primary employer in the city, and since the jobs provided were wage and salary jobs, they contributed to transforming the economy into a cash economy from a barter one.

Altorki and Cole estimate that the main occupations for locals in 'Unayzah in 1986 were in agriculture, commerce, and the government. The growing expatriate population worked in agriculture, commerce, construction, and domestic service. Expatriates who made up over half of the workforce held the lower-paying and manual labor jobs (1989:125). The markets, now in new buildings, were full of imported merchandise rather than locally made wares, and the purchase of this merchandise was made possible by the change to a cash economy. Patterns of food consumption had changed from dates, wheat, and milk, with occasional inclusion of vegetables and meat, to rice and meat as staples and new varieties of fruits and vegetables. With the help of government subsidies and loans, new farms were larger and more mechanized, used expatriate labor, grew new varieties of produce for the cash market, and used chemicals and fertilizers to increase yield. Some were large farms owned by entrepreneurs with no previous knowledge of farming.

Inventorying the businesses in 'Unayzah in 1987, Altorki and Cole found car repair shops, butchers, grocery stores, bakeries, pharmacies, several restaurants, and two hotels, as well as other specialty shops. These were owned by local individuals, but the salespersons were expatriates. Hiring expatriate labor is cheaper than hiring Saudis, and Saudis have transitioned from the traditional jobs that required manual labor to office work and professional callings. Previously, one did not work for a wage; work was cooperative and the result produced food or items to be bartered for food (1989:198–199). Altorki and Cole explain that in 1987, locals preferred positions in government and trade and managerial work rather than manual labor and semiskilled work. Traditionally, most work done by 'Unayzah natives was either manual labor or semiskilled, but in the new economy and with the availability of expatriate workers driving down the wages in manual labor, it is economically more advantageous for local workers to seek the higher-paying managerial jobs or secure work with the government. Additionally, they have obtained the education necessary to fill these jobs, thanks to the free state

Irrigation in the desert outside Riyadh in 2002.

education system. Expatriate workers are willing to work for lower wages because the cost of living in their home countries is lower. The high pay in KSA relative to the pay they would receive in their home countries is the driver causing them to seek employment in the Kingdom in the first place.

Another aspect of the changes since 1970 is new construction of homes and commercial buildings made possible by government loans. The old city neighborhoods were physically compact and socially close-knit with narrow streets and alleyways where children ran and played. Neighbors were close at hand and women could walk to the nearby homes of friends and relatives to visit. Neighborhoods were inhabited by a mixture of rich and poor, and a home was usually occupied by a patrilineal extended family, with rooms added as the family increased. The new homes have been built on the outskirts of the old city and are more geographically dispersed. Frequently, homes now are occupied by nuclear families instead of extended ones, and distances between the homes of friends and relatives are too great for women to traverse on foot. Children, now separated from other children, are sent to school earlier in order to give them access to socialization among other children. While people still value the old neighborhood ties and the time with extended family, the new living conditions have isolated women, children, and the old. New mechanisms of socialization are developing (Altorki and Cole 1989:231).

Thus, life in 'Unayzah has changed since state formation and particularly since the introduction of the five-year development plans in the 1970s. People in the community now live in new homes, have a new mosque and new markets, and eat more varied foods. Community members have changed occupations almost entirely, with the modern jobs being in government, managerial, and entrepreneurial areas. Agriculture continues to be of great importance, but the small plots irrigated with water pumped out of wells using camel energy have been replaced by larger, mechanized farms growing a greater variety of crops and using chemicals and fertilizers and irrigated by machinery. 'Unayzah's citizens now participate in a cash economy, and imported products are sold in the markets. While the extended family is still highly valued, many live in nuclear family residences.

Asir Region Towns

Mohammed Abdullah Eben Saleh at King Saud University in Riyadh has studied the physical transformation of settlements in the Asir region of southwest KSA (1998, 2000). He describes the compact traditional settlements with a Friday mosque, multiple daily mosques, watchtowers, a cemetery, residential areas, open meeting spaces, and in some cases a market. The building materials in each settlement depended on climatic factors and resource availability, so that in some villages, buildings were primarily of stone and in others they were adobe and stone. In contrast to most of the country, the southwest region has more rainfall and the villages are surrounded by flat or terraced agricultural fields. The inhabitants of each settlement were from a single tribe and neighborhoods were kin-based. Several of the characteristics of the village plan were necessary for purposes of defense from raiding tribes. The towers served for defense and warning, and the maze of pathways through the residential areas served to confuse invaders.

Citing many of the same forces for change that Altorki and Cole found in the central Arabian city of 'Unayzah, Saleh describes the changes in the village after the 1975 second development plan. The old village could not accommodate the new lifestyle of the villagers. The pathways were too narrow for cars, and the drainage system could not handle the new, greater water consumption.

New houses in Dammam.

As part of a now peaceful Saudi state, there was no longer a need for defense and no new towers were built, even as the old ones fell into disrepair. New homes were laid out in a grid pattern; this was very different from the organic growth of the old community where new rooms were added as needed and homes were bordered by winding, narrow paths. The old construction materials were also abandoned in favor of steel and concrete. Saleh concludes that the modern architecture is foreign in style and demonstrates no continuity with the patterns of the past. The new village and home designs changed behavior patterns in the same ways Altorki and Cole describe.

Riyadh

A 2001 study of change in Riyadh by Waleed Kassab Al-Hemaidi (2001) demonstrates the importance of considering cultural and environmental factors in change. Riyadh was a traditional adobe town of 83,000 in 1950, and by the turn of the century it had become the thriving national capital with a large international contingent and a population of 2.5 million. The government moved its offices from Makkah to Riyadh in 1953, causing a population growth spurt in Riyadh. In order to accommodate the population growth and the advent of the automobile, the government developed new housing. For example, it created a new neighborhood, Al-Malaz, for government workers. Lacking indigenous experts in urban planning, KSA hired expatriate urban planners and architects to design the new city additions. Their designs were not attuned to the culture and the climate of Riyadh.

The Al-Malaz neighborhood was designed in a grid pattern with wide streets and square lots. The homes built there were of a new architectural style. The old homes tended to have central courtyards; house walls were located at the edge of the streets with windows facing in. This style allowed for family privacy in the internal courtyards. Women could be out of doors, unveiled, and out of view of nonrelatives. Just as in 'Unayzah, the streets, which were for foot traffic, were the public spaces in which children played. The new house type, called the villa style, followed foreign design elements. It was set back from the street with no interior courtyard and had windows facing out. This left no private outside space for women to enjoy. The streets, now wide avenues for car use, were too dangerous for children to play. While this house type has become common in Saudi Arabia, it is not as functional as the old type, and some new housing developments, like the Ministry of Foreign Affairs Staff Housing complex built in the 1980s, have attempted to return to some of the important characteristics of the old structures while accommodating modern needs like transportation and sewage. The use of cul-de-sacs to bring back safer streets for children's play and of exterior walls and interior courtyards to provide privacy are some of the changes in this neighborhood that make it more amenable to Saudi cultural values. Changes in house type as new construction accompanied the oil boom occurred throughout the Gulf states; Nagy (2010) described the transition in Qatar.

Saudi Youth: Identity and Change

Next we look at Saudi youth at the end of the twentieth century to learn about their lives and concerns, as they are the third generation since unification of the Kingdom. Mai Yamani, a Saudi anthropologist, spent two years, 1997–1999, observing and interviewing Saudi youth aged fifteen to thirty about education, vocational aspirations, exposure to different cultural influences, access to information, values, generational differences, and the future. The youth interviewed came from a wide range of categories of Saudi society and she lists these categories as follows: (1) the royal family; (2) politically powerful families containing high-ranking state officials; (3) key trading and business families; (4) the intellectual or "educated class" composed of teachers, journalists, poets, and authors; (5) the new middle class, which was the largest single population segment and who primarily work for the government; (6) groups of recent migrants to the urban areas whose literacy and standard of living are below the national average; and (7) circles of religious activists and graduates of the religious universities.

Yamani (2000) describes her subjects as the third generation of KSA. In their grandparents' generation, grandmother and grandfather were probably not only from the same patrilineage but from the same extended family and were born in the 1930s around the time of the final unification of the modern Saudi state. As adults they experienced the first oil profits, but they also remember pre-oil life. They were the first Saudis to encounter non-Muslim foreigners, who would have been the expatriates working in the oil business.

The first generation's children, the second generation, were born in the 1950s and lived their adult lives in a Kingdom with substantial oil revenues. They lived in a country unified by a national education system, national dress, a single religious doctrine of Wahhabi Hanbalism, and a bureaucratic infrastructure. They traveled throughout the Kingdom, something their parents might not have done, and they even were likely to move to another region of the Kingdom for employment. The economic and political structures of the Kingdom were rapidly expanding, and most found it easy to find jobs, most likely working for the government. The Saudi state was legitimated through distribution of wealth, and these Saudis generally viewed the state positively since it distributed wealth.

The third generation, the one that makes up Yamani's study, was born in the 1970s and 1980s, mostly during the oil boom, which ended in 1984. They do not remember the pre-oil days and only know about it from their family stories. They live in a world of mass education, travel abroad, radio and television, and probably expatriate servants. At the time of interviews, however, they also lived in a world of greater financial insecurity than either of the preceding two generations. The rapid economic expansion was over, and while they were well educated in government schools, jobs were scarce and their economic future was uncertain (Yamani 2000:4–9).

Boys playing in a Riyadh park. (Josie Falletta)

Throughout the interviews, Yamani found that the predominant theme of this generation was identity. Rapid change and the continued importance of traditions based in a past they never experienced caused people in this generation to search for identity. Their Islamic and Arab heritage was the most important influence on their lives, but they were subject to additional influences. Some of these influences were traditional, tribal, and regional while others were new, national, global, professional, and educational. Sorting out these identities in the context of the country's new economic insecurities was a central theme of the interviews. Yamani states that the three constants providing this generation with stability are family, Islam, and nation. They do not view the Saudi state in as positive a light at their parents do because it is no longer able to provide for them the way it did for their parents' generation. They realize the KSA's limitations (Yamani 2000:146–148).

Salem Aleid explains that Yamani's third generation has been called the "Real-Estate Bank Generation" because they were born at a time when the government was providing interest-free loans to families who built new houses. While their grandparents were most comfortable in traditional dwellings and were likely to sleep in tents warmed by an open fire pitched in the yard of the new family home rather than deal with Western-style furniture, modern electrical appliances, and air conditioning, the generation born in the 1970s and 1980s wanted to live in contemporary houses and high-rise apartments (Aleid 1994:81). The following quote summarizes the drastic changes Saudis have experienced in three generations: "Less than 30 years ago, my peers and I did not own shoes. Now, we must own a luxury car to look modern and important" (Aleid 1994:80).

Conclusion

This chapter has presented a window into the changes in KSA over the last century, especially the last forty years. The government imposed changes, some economic and technological, that affected the daily lives of the bedu. This once transient group switched from a barter system to a cash economy, became more sedentary, moved to urban areas and hired others to tend their herds. Despite these changes, however, the high value they have always placed on hospitality, honesty, and protection of the weak has not changed. The transformation of villages and cities with new housing, buildings, and roads also impacted the traditional way of life for villagers—the Hadar. As education and jobs became available to Saudis, unskilled labor needs were filled by expatriates. As cities were redesigned, city dwellers had to let go of many of their past habits and behavior patterns. The new generation of Saudis born in the 1970s and 1980s, are figuring out their own identity, which is different from that of their parents and grandparents. The next chapter describes norms of daily life in today's Kingdom.

Chapter 8

Experiencing Life in the Modern Kingdom

 $\mathcal{E}$ very time I make a trip to Riyadh, it strikes me as a city under construction. There are new skyscrapers in the city center and new houses under construction in the suburbs. Much of the compact, old mud-brick city that one could easily walk through is gone, replaced by a new city of spread-out, marble and concrete buildings and wide streets requiring vehicle transportation. Only a few of the historic buildings in the heart of the old city still exist. As mentioned earlier, the old city of Ad-Dir'iyah, the early home of the Al Sauds and the seat of the first Saudi state, lies in disrepair beside modern Riyadh.

To wander the streets of the abandoned and unrestored sections of Ad-Dir'iyah is to gain a sense of the Saudi Arabia of old. The top sections of the mud-brick buildings are now washed away by the weather since mud brick must be regularly maintained or it quickly returns to the earth. The streets are narrow footpaths, and painted wooden doors still hang at the entrances to rooms where built-in shelves would previously have held the coffee and tea serving pieces. At one home, a door hung at an angle at the entrance; the door was sky blue with hints of turquoise still visible in a design involving triangles. In many places, the bottom five or so rows of the buildings are blocks of stone with the walls of mud brick built on top of them. Many buildings were several stories high with still-visible patterns created by geometric shapes like triangles and dots incised into the walls. To walk the streets is to feel the power of past lives and experience a sense of life fewer than 100 years ago, when animals were led through the streets and families slept on the roofs to keep cool. I once talked with a forty-something businessman, a computer and software specialist, who told me of the two years of his childhood spent in Ad-Dir'iyah with his grandparents. He told how he used to fight with his cousins over the best place to sleep on the roof at night. The wall around the roof protected one spot from the sun longer than the remainder and allowed the lucky child sleeping there to sleep later than his cousins before being roused by the hot morning sun. This now-eroding village is full of such stories.

Since most of the current city was built after 1970, the time when women scurried a few yards down a footpath to visit the homes of friends is gone. Now, foot traffic occurs primarily in the suq areas and in the modern, enclosed shopping malls. There are numerous shopping areas in the modern city divided by type of ware. For example, there are special areas with shops for selling cloth, musical instruments, meat, vegetables, electronics, and women's clothing respectively. The spice suq is a treat for the senses. Upon entering, one is accosted with the strong smell of freshly ground coffee mixed with the smell of curry. One shop holds an oil press where a machine drives an arm that moves round and round in a circle, crushing sesame seeds to extract their oil. Previously, a camel would have walked around in a circle to power the arm. Salespeople are male with a few exceptions, like the female salespeople on the women's floor at the Kingdom Mall and the bedu women's suq. At the latter location, women sit under tents and sell jewelry, baskets, and spices. Shopping areas, whether a traditional suq or a modern shopping mall, are centers of pedestrian activity in Riyadh, but for most of the city, one sees cars and traffic jams rather than pedestrians. Like Houston or Atlanta, modern Riyadh was built after the coming of the automobile and is not a walking city. To further describe life today, let me discuss Saudi values and public behavior.

Saudi Values and Behavioral Norms

Many foreigners come to Saudi Arabia every year. Some 25 percent of the population is foreign and the annual pilgrimage to Makkah draws some 2.5 million people, many of them from outside the country. Tourism, other than to Muslim sites, is a minor industry. To come to the Kingdom, one must have a sponsor. A check on the KSA Embassy website will show you that visas are required to enter the Kingdom; yet, no tourist visa is listed. One cannot visit the Kingdom even as a tourist without an official invitation from a sponsor in the Kingdom. KSA takes seriously its role as the home of the two holiest sites in Islam and its acceptance of the Wahhabi movement as the legal form of Sunni Islam in the country. Consequently, there are expectations that all visitors will follow KSA's official rules of behavior while in the Kingdom. Below are examples of these values and behavioral norms.

Modesty and Respect

Saudi norms center on modesty and respect. While the history of the veil and women in the Middle East is ancient—for example, AlMunajjed (1997:52) tells us that face veiling is recorded as long ago as 1250 BCE when the Assyrians practiced it during the Babylonia period—it is the mention of modesty in the Qur'an that is used as justification for the current practices of veiling and of separation of the sexes. For instance, one of the passages in the Qur'an is as follows:

> And say to the believing women that they should lower their gaze and guard their modesty; that they should not display their beauty and orna- ments except what (must ordinarily) appear thereof; that they should draw their veils over their bosoms and not display their beauty except to their husbands, their fathers, their husbands' fathers, their sons, their hus- bands' sons, their brothers or their brothers' sons or their sisters' sons, or their women, or the slaves whom their right hands possess, or male ser- vants free of physical needs. (Ali translation 34:30–31)

While the public expectation regarding the degree to which women should veil in the Arabian Peninsula has varied over time and depending on region, today one is required to dress modestly; in Riyadh this means men do not wear shorts in public. It is not intended that a Western male should wear the Saudi dress of thobe and ghutra, but he should dress in long pants in pub- lic. Sandals and short sleeve shirts are acceptable. Western women should wear the abaya when in public. Covering the hair and face are options, depending on one's religion and personal preference. Some Western and non- Muslim women, for example, do not always cover their hair; Muslim women are expected to cover their hair and most choose to cover their faces. Some Muslim women also cover their hands in black gloves and their feet in black socks to ensure that no skin shows. Are these state rules, family dictates, or personal preference? They are a bit of all three.

The mutawa'a who are the members of the Committee for the Order of the Good and the Forbidding of Evil are representatives of the state, paid by the government and with their own jail system separate from the police. A mutawa' who is on duty is accompanied by a policeman. In a discussion with a mutawa' and a policeman on their rounds, they make clear that issues of modesty and respect of religion are the area of the mutawa'a; the policeman is called into action when the offense is a criminal act like stealing.

A woman might cover her face at the request of a mutawa', at the request of her family, or at her own discretion because she feels it is proper in her home region or she is most comfortable with this modest behavior and con- siders it the proper religious gesture. Another Muslim woman might keep her face uncovered. Many women with whom I spoke prefer to cover their hair and faces as a sign of religious modesty. Even female doctors in the hospitals cover their faces if they wish; it is required that their eyes be uncovered while examining a patient, but otherwise they may cover as they choose. The norm of female modesty extends to the print media. Western magazines for sale in the Kingdom have pictures that have been altered so as to not show models in clothing that would be considered either too low cut or too short by Saudi standards. In 2001, I found most of the alteration to the pictures was done by hand with a felt-tip pen that colored over bare arms, chests, and legs. By 2009, the alteration was done digitally before printing by coloring the inappropriate skin in white.

Hospitality

This value of traditional Middle Eastern culture has been discussed in previous chapters. Today, most entertaining in the Kingdom continues to be done at home, and gracious hospitality toward visitors continues to be the norm. Many a majlis at an Arabian home still includes a coffee hearth where the host roasts the coffee beans, pounds them fine, pours them into a coffee pot along with water, and sets the pot to boil. After the requisite amount of time, he removes the pot from the fire and allows it to sit so that the grounds can settle. Then, he pours the coffee into another pot, and adds saffron, cloves, and ground cardamom seeds. The coffee is served in small, thimble-shaped cups. The host pours the coffee in a high, thin stream into the cup. He pours only a little in each cup, a sign that the visitor is expected to stay and drink many cups. The most honored guest is the first served and in true Saudi style; there is sometimes a deferring among guests as they try to decline this honor in protest that another guest is actually the most honored. The host continues to offer coffee until the guest holds out his cup and shakes it from side to side signaling that he has had enough. (My students had fun learning how to manage this ritual.)

In today's home, dates are offered with the coffee and afterwards one is served tea. This is likely to be followed by juices of several types, like orange, strawberry, and mango, and also by chocolates. All of this is served before the meal. The meal itself will contain so many dishes in such large quantities that the guests will be able to eat only a portion of the provided food. At one such meal in a rural village, I expressed dismay to my hostess at our inability to eat all the food as I feared it would be wasted. She explained that her relatives in the village could see the lights and knew she was having guests. The rest of the food would be taken to relatives and other villagers.

Dates, that staple of the bedu diet, continue to be a highly valued food. They are always served to visitors, are frequently given as gifts, especially during Ramadan, and are considered a nutritious and important part of the diet. I have even heard of individuals who went on a weight-loss regimen that consisted of eating only dates. Today, there are lavish stores that sell only dates. Different varieties of dates have different and well-recognized tastes, and a single variety of date will taste quite different depending on whether the date is freshly picked or has been allowed to cure. Dates are made into candy, much the way chocolate is in the West. For example, they are covered in powdered sugar or chocolate and filled with nuts or orange sections; date paste is used to make many types of desserts, and dates and date paste are mixed into other types of foods.

Separation of the Sexes

Public spaces allow for the separation of the sexes. There are no bars serving alcoholic beverages, as alcohol (and also pork) are prohibited under Islamic law. Restaurants often have two sections: one for men and the other for families; women eat in the family section, whether eating with their families or with female friends. In McDonald's, for example, each table in the family section is curtained off. This allows women to remove their face veils when dining, without concern that men who are not close relatives will see them.

As previously mentioned, women should not be in the company of men to whom they are not closely related. This means that male and female friends and colleagues should not appear together in public, whether shopping or having coffee. Many work environments are separated into male and female sections. The public library, King Abdul Aziz Public Library, in Riyadh, has male and

Sign indicating the family section of a restaurant.

female sections, for example. Except for the new King Abdullah University for Science and Technology, universities have separate campuses with separate administrations, classes, and faculty for male and female students. Any classes available to both sexes are conducted by video hookup so that the female students do not sit with male students. Classes at one of the more conservative women's colleges were described to me this way. Courses for women were sometimes taught by male faculty by closed-circuit TV. The students can see the teacher but he cannot see them. If the students are doing experiments, for example, the camera will focus on their hands so that the instructor can see if they are performing the experiment correctly. It is the student's decision whether she wishes to allow the camera to focus on her face.

Banks have separate branches for male and female patrons staffed respectively by only male or only female employees. In Riyadh, I visited a jewelry factory where the sexes were separated. Men and women work in separate buildings, although they do many of the same jobs in the jewelry-making process. Women workers were provided transportation by bus to and from work, since women are not allowed to drive in the city. On Saudia Airline flights in the Kingdom, it is common for women to ask for changes in passenger seating before the plane departs. A woman who does not wish to sit next to a man who is not her male relative may ask and will have seating changed so that she is seated next to another woman. On occasion, I have accommodated a Saudi female passenger by volunteering to exchange seats with her male seat mate so that the woman is now sitting next to another woman, me. There are some notable exceptions to this rule of separation of the sexes. One of the exceptions is medical facilities where the staff is composed of both male and female medical professionals, as discussed in chapter 6.

From the street, one can spot establishments like hair salons or clothing stores that are for women only by the characteristic appearance of the buildings. If there is glass on the front windows, it will be opaque, preventing anyone from being able to see in from the street. There will also be some sort of screen at the front door so that, when the door is open, people passing in the street cannot see into the entryway where women might be present without abaya coverings.

As a female, I am not allowed to drive in any cities or in parts of the countryside. In 2009 during my most recent visit, this was not actually a law but a very carefully held custom. Women do drive in the desert, however, where they have special permits to do so. Since women do not drive in the city, I must have a male driver or hire a taxi. The consequences of women not driving are significant for men as well as women. Women have active, busy lives despite not driving. Either women must hire drivers or the men in their families must drive them around. Both options have serious economic implications for families. The hiring of drivers adds to the family's expenses. Men are responsible for their wives, mothers, and sisters, and if the family does not have access to a driver, male family members must drive the women. This is a time-consuming enterprise for men. Once, a friend was visiting me, and after about an hour and a half she got up to leave, stating that her husband had

Men at a café in the old section of Jiddah.

been waiting in the car. It was inappropriate for him to come in with her to an all-female gathering, and so, as her source of transportation, he waited for her in the car for one and one-half hours.

The Importance of Family

Descent in the Kingdom continues to be reckoned through the male line. Women retain the names of their fathers, never taking their husband's name at marriage. Generations of marrying within the patrilineage means many marriages are between men and women who are related to each other through more than one connecting relationship. While I met many individuals who chose their own marriage partner, arranged marriages are still common. This is a matter of tradition and of family importance, but it is also a matter of practicality. If women are always covered in public and if young men and women are not allowed to interact, how would you decide upon a mate? It is the responsibility of mothers, aunts, and sisters to help a young man in this matter because they can see and talk to the young women who are potential brides. Young men and women must depend on their relatives to help them pick a mate.

While of course the mother's lineage is recognized and individuals understand the genealogical significance of that lineage, culturally, family is recognized as one's father's lineage. At a gathering of women I attended in Riyadh, the hostess commented that the mother of one of the guests was related to the prophet Mohammed. The guest in question agreed that this was true but added that of course the prophet was not in *her* family but the family of her mother. This was because her family was the family of her father. Families are close, and it is not uncommon for a family gathering with 300 attendees to occur at least monthly. The following examples of two family parties I attended exemplify the rapid changes in the Kingdom and the importance of family. Both parties were for women only.

A women's dinner I attended in northern Saudi Arabia was a dinner of multigenerational women in a bedu family that had moved into the urban community decades before. As we entered the walled gate of the family home, we were greeted by women of all ages from very old to girls of five or six. As this was a women-only gathering, all faces were uncovered. We were escorted across the yard, into the house, and into a room with traditional seating. This means we sat on the floor on low cushions with thicker cushions at our backs and cushion armrests spaced about every third person or so. Napkins and plastic bottles of water rested on small, cylindrical tables about 12 inches in diameter and 18-inches high and placed as frequently as the armrests. Oriental rugs covered the floor. This style of seating is the furniture style in a bedu tent and continues to be used in some modern houses. I was invited to this dinner by a Saudi woman who grew up next door to this family. The old women in the room were asking her about her grandmother.

Present were five or six women probably ranging in age from fifty to eighty who were dressed in the traditional bedu style. Their hair was parted down the middle and fixed in a knot at the nape of the neck. Over their heads, they wore thin black veils that fitted across the forehead below the hairline. The veils were then pulled back over the head, tied, and allowed to flow down their shoulders. Over these they wore heavier veils, and their dresses were loose-fitting revealing no body shape. Some wore abayas as well.

At least one of the older women had hennaed hands. Her fingers looked as if they had been dipped in dark henna up to the cuticle and the palm side of her hands was colored a lighter shade. To create this pattern on the hands, one makes a paste of henna and rolls it into a ball. Then, once the ball is placed in one's palm, the hand is closed so that the fingers rest in the henna with the tips of the fingers covered with henna up to the first knuckle. It takes thirty minutes to six hours for this to stain the hands. The palm of the hand is stained because one is holding the ball of henna in the hand. Today, some women put plastic bags on their hands in order to sleep during the procedure. When I asked an elderly woman why she went to all this trouble to henna her hands, she said, "Do you want my hands to look like a man's hands?" It is popular among young women to paint elaborate designs on their hands and bodies with henna.

Also at the dinner were some fifteen young women in their twenties and teens wearing contemporary makeup, modern hairstyles and clothing, and high-heeled shoes. The contrast in the dress and appearance of the young and old women exemplifies the dramatic culture change in the country. We were served coffee, tea, and a regional specialty made from date paste and a wheat-like plant that grows wild in this part of the desert. After visiting, we moved for dinner into a smaller room that was carpeted but had no furniture. A huge cloth was spread in the center of the room and on it were two huge, oval-shaped platters piled high with rice and a whole roasted lamb. Other foods in smaller containers were placed around these. Foods were hummus, tabbouleh, and buttermilk soup. Bread was flatbread some 18 inches in diameter folded into fourths. We sat around the edges of this cloth where the hostesses had set out plates, silverware, a bottle of water, and a can of Pepsi-Cola at each place. The room was of a size that we could sit with our backs against the wall and partake of this lavish feast.

In another instance, I was invited by a friend to a party at her sister's home. The dinner was attended by some thirty women and children, with most attendees all in the same family; they ranged in age from her ninety-something aunt to the newest infant. There were five generations of women in the room, and learning about the lives of the women present was like walking thorough time in Saudi Arabia. My friend's ninety-year-old aunt was married at the age of nine and her seventy-year-old daughter was married at the age of thirteen. They were young wives in the days of camel transportation, while my much younger friend went to university in the West and married in her twenties. I looked across the room and saw two old women sitting side by side on a sofa. Their movements seemed synchronized as their heads moved in unison while they talked and their gestures seemed part of the same dance. I asked my hostess who they were. She explained that they were not twins or even sisters, as I had suspected, but were instead co-wives who had

Women's dinner in northern Saudi Arabia.

been married to the same man since their teens. He died and the two wives continued to live together. Through some sixty years of living and working in such close proximity, they had taken on each other's mannerisms.

It seemed to me that there was a break in the generations between the very old who dressed in traditional dresses and had their heads covered and their hands hennaed in the traditional way (fingertips and palms) and then the middle-aged and younger women who were dressed and coiffed in the latest international fashions in velvet and satin and the little children who dressed and acted like kids. Everyone was busy talking; young children were weaving in and out among the chairs, being caught in a grandmother's hug or given a piece of candy by an aunt, as they darted in and out of the room. The dinner was a celebration of family and a reaffirmation of the importance of family as a cultural value.

The importance of family in Saudi Arabia cannot be overstated. It is the reason one goes to work with little sleep because of responsibilities to attend family gatherings during Ramadan. It is the reason many Saudis prefer the traditional Saudi work hours, which end the day at afternoon prayers and give people time to fulfill their responsibilities to family members. It keeps men behind the wheel of the automobile in order to see that their wives and mothers have transportation. It causes stress, but it also provides valuable support.

Islamic Time

There are several ways in which Islamic time differs from the Western time I experience in the States. First, the Islamic calendar reckons the years beginning with Muhammad's migration from Makkah to Madinah in the year CE 622 (Common Era based on the Christian calendar). Additionally, the Islamic calendar is divided into lunar months, and thus the named months do not fall at the same time each year so that Ramadan, for example, is some years in the Saudi winter and others in the Saudi summer in accordance with the lunar calendar. The first day of the first month of the Islamic calendar corresponds to CE July 16, 622.

As a Texan, I am used to "clock time." Offices in my university are open from eight to five; shops in the United States usually open at nine or ten in the morning and remain open until five or six or maybe even nine at night. These time frames are so common in the United States that one does not even notice them. In the Kingdom, one's day is marked by the five calls to prayer. Prayer is one of the pillars of the Islamic faith and the five prayer times are before dawn, noon, afternoon, sunset, and evening. They are set based on the movements of the sun, and thus the times change by a few minutes each day. The rhythm of life in KSA is created by the five daily prayer times, and stores open in the morning and close with the noontime prayer.

When out shopping, one hears the call to prayer from nearby mosques; in a city the size of Riyadh, one is likely to hear the call to prayer from several if not dozens of mosques. Shopkeepers close their shops when they hear the noon call to prayer and keep the shops closed during the afternoon. Remember this is a desert where temperatures may reach 54° Celsius (130° Fahrenheit) in the afternoon. Then shops open up again about 4:00 PM, which will be after the afternoon prayer time, and remain open until nine or ten at night. Their evening hours encompass the two final prayer times of the day. For each of these, the shops close for thirty minutes or so in order that shopkeepers and customers may go to pray. Any shoppers who wish to continue shopping must step out of the shops and wait for them to reopen after prayer time. Restaurants also close during these times and while many will allow seated patrons to remain inside during the prayer time, the doors will be closed to new customers until the prayers are over.

Many businesses close their business day before mid-afternoon prayer, meaning they close around 3:30 PM. Others follow Western hours and work an eight-to-five workday. Aramco, with its strong US influence, is one of the companies that adhere to a Western work schedule. Hospitals also typically run work shifts similar to the ones in the West. In all cases, however, the weekend is Thursday and Friday, as Friday is the holy day in Islam.

This rhythm of Islamic time is experienced all over the Kingdom, and it is the rhythm by which people measure their lives. For example, it was common for friends to say to me, "Let's meet after *Maghrib*" (the fourth prayer of the day just after sunset), demonstrating how prayer times divide up the day.

At my university in the United States, campus life is tuned to the chiming of the carillon in the bell tower of the administration building. It tells me I am late for class or that the department office is about to close. Off campus, however, I hear no similar sounds marking the passing hours of my day. In all urban areas of the Kingdom, one will never be far from a mosque, and one's day is measured by the sounds of the call to prayer. In Jiddah, on more than one occasion, I have been escorted to the rooftop of an old home at sunset. From this location I could hear the call to prayer from dozens of mosques as I watched the sun set over the city. This experience rarely fails to impress the non-Muslim with its spiritual beauty.

During Ramadan, the rhythm of the day changes again. Since Muslims fast during daylight during Ramadan, they have a light meal after sunset to break the fast and a larger one later in the night. Restaurants are closed during daylight hours. Stores are closed during their regular morning hours but are open in the evenings and until two or four in the morning. Ramadan is a time for religious observance and for celebration with family. One woman described for me the spiritual experience of Ramadan by explaining, "If you go to Makkah or Madinah during Ramadan, it is like being cleaned from the inside." As much as their work schedules will permit, people sleep during the day and stay up at night celebrating with their family. While family obligations are always taken seriously, they are especially important during Ramadan. A medical doctor commented that the daytime fasting was not difficult for her during Ramadan; it was the lack of sleep from being up all night at family gatherings, a family obligation, that was difficult since she must continue her work in medical research during the day. Another woman explained to me that she wakes her children at 4:30 AM during Ramadan so that they can eat before sunrise; then they go back to sleep for two hours before getting up for school. Otherwise, they would be in school all day with empty stomachs.

Orientalism and the Western View of the Kingdom

In chapter 2, I introduced the concept of Orientalism, which is the Western bias of viewing people of the Middle East as the exotic "other," so different from the West that they are an object of study. In this chapter, I have described some experiences in and characteristics of Saudi culture that mark it as different from that in the West. It is important to move past simple description that makes a people seem exotic and use that description to better understand culture.

Here is a modern world that is based on traditional Islamic and Middle Eastern values as described in other sections of this book. It is a world of rapid change in which people are almost dizzy with the pace of movement from old to new and one in which people are carefully considering what features of the old culture they want to keep and what they want to give up. It seems that many have decided to give up the traditional mud-brick homes in preference for modern ones of concrete and marble; however, they are reluctant to give up the traditional values. The Islamic religion continues to be of vital importance. There is no talk of giving up the religious rules of Ramadan and the requisite fasting during daylight. This puts a burden on the family that has also chosen modern ways, such as school for children and daytime jobs for adults, but the burden is managed by feeding children a meal at 4:30 AM. There is no talk of giving up the strong traditional family, which can be a burden as well as a strong support and blessing. Just as the modern mixes with the traditional in the dress of the women at a family gathering, so the modern mixes with the traditional in all aspects of Saudi life.

While to a Westerner like me, at first some aspects of Saudi life seem very different, one finds oneself adjusting to those as one experiences the life in context. The abaya, for example, is a symbol in the West of Saudi women's oppression and frequently discussed when news media present programs on the Kingdom. While the dress seems unusual to a Westerner, I found myself attracted to the beauty of women's abayas after only a few short months in the Kingdom. Abayas are fashion statements in Saudi Arabia, just like any other item of women's clothing. They come in different styles, and each time I returned to the Kingdom, I discovered that abaya styles had changed since my previous visit. In fact, in wearing abayas from my previous visit, I was always hopelessly out of fashion. Abayas can be plain or a beautifully decorated expression of femininity. I also found that I became accustomed to the modesty of the abaya in its cultural context. In an occasion in KSA where I happened to be in public without an abaya, I still remember how uncomfortable I felt, as if I were only partially dressed. On that occasion, I worked to keep my arms covered by my shawl and to keep the slit in my long skirt closed as I walked in order to avoid exposing my leg.

The Saudi women with whom I spoke consider the West's preoccupation with the abaya ridiculous. None consider the wearing of an abaya to be an important social issue. There are many more important social issues they are interested in seeing their country solve and all are concerned about the rapid rate of change as they appreciate the value of some change, like improved education and medical facilities, but fear the loss of important traditional values, like the focus on the close-knit family. One Saudi woman who had lived in the States for a few years previously commented to me that there is now a generation in Saudi that is not "pre-oil," meaning they do not remember what life was like in the Kingdom before the oil money started to come in. This concerned her, as she felt they did not understand the old values and would consider money too easy to come by.

Conclusion

In the end, I experienced KSA as full of people just like me; they were working to make a living, concerned about their families, and striving to give their children the best possible start in life while taking care of their elder relatives. Thus their contemporary variant of modernity, to use once again Ferguson's terms from chapter 2, does not have to be characterized by the unitary set of social and cultural forms devised in the West. Saudis have characterized modernity in an Arab and Muslim way. But, in helping outsiders understand KSA, it is this outsider's (i.e., my) opinion that some issues must be discussed head-on. In the next chapter, I will tackle some of these.

Chapter 9
Saudi Arabia in the Global Spotlight

$\mathcal{W}$hile Saudi Arabia is closed to the random visitor and requires that one have a sponsor to enter the country, it is squarely in the global spotlight due to its strategic importance as a stable nation-state in the heart of the Middle East that happens to possess 25 percent of the world's oil supply. Its global virtual image is seen through multiple lenses that interlock and overlap each other and depict the country alternatively or simultaneously as terrorist and dangerous, corrupt and backward, modern and international, and religiously devout. The media, including print media, television, radio, the Internet, cell phones, and audio and video tapes passed hand to hand, provide an up-to-the-second source of images by Saudis and about Saudis. This book becomes one more of those interlocked lenses through which to view this subject. This chapter discusses three issues frequently at the center of global discussions of Saudi's image: religion, resistance and terrorism, and women. After a discussion of each of these, I end the chapter with a reflection on the media itself.

Religion

According to a demographic study by the Pew Foundation, 1.57 billion (23 percent) of the world's 6.8 billion people are Muslim, with 20 percent of that Muslim population living in the Middle East and North Africa (Pew Forum on Religion and Public Life 2009). To explain religion in the Kingdom requires, first, more information on Islam. The life of the prophet Muhammad and the early expansion of a Muslim empire were described briefly in chapter 3. Here, I begin with the fracturing of Islam into different divisions and then describe the five pillars of Islamic faith and the basis of Islamic law. With that as background, I then turn to the impact of Islam in Saudi Arabia today.

The Branches of Islam

Islam, like Christianity, Judaism, Hinduism, and the other major world religions, contains numerous branches whose interpretations of the religion diverge. The first of these divergences occurred shortly after Muhammad's death, because he had not appointed a successor and his followers were left to decide who should take up leadership. The majority of his most devoted followers believed that Abu Bakr, one of Muhammad's first converts, should hold this post of *khalifa,* or caliph, but a minority thought the leadership should go to one of Muhammad's kinsmen so that leadership would remain in Muhammad's family. This minority, who supported 'Ali, Muhammad's son-in-law and first cousin, for this position, was called the *Shi'at 'Ali,* or those favoring 'Ali. This caused the birth of the deepest and oldest schism in Islam, the one between those Muslims known as the Sunni, who favored Abu Bakr as successor, and those known as the Shi'a, who favored 'Ali (Bates and Rassam 2001:42).

Abu Bakr was elected caliph and was followed in this position by others who were chosen by the Sunni. Eventually, 'Ali, the original choice of the Shi'a, was elected as the fourth caliph by the Sunni majority, but his election resulted in a civil war between the two divisions, Sunni and Shi'i, and 'Ali was quickly deposed. By this time, the supporters of 'Ali, the Shi'a, were beginning to spread through the Middle East. For example, a group of Shi'a had settled in southern Iraq and were the beginnings of what would become Iraq's Shi'i majority today. (As an example of the importance of this early Islamic history in today's world, the differences of opinion and loyalty between the Shi'i majority in the south, the Sunni minority in the center, and the Kurds in the north of the country form a basis for much of the internal strife in Iraq now.) Eventually Shi'a spread through Persia (modern-day Iran), southern Iraq, eastern Saudi Arabia, and parts of Turkey, Syria, and Lebanon, forming a belt of devout Muslims who opposed Sunni rule and considered Sunni-chosen leaders to be impostors because they were not direct descendents of Muhammad. Shi'a believe in an additional pillar of faith not accepted by the Sunni, which is that the imam, the single leader of their faith who is a descendant of Muhammad, has the ability to experience divine revelations and his word is infallible. This is in contrast to the Sunni Muslims who assign no leader such power and, in fact, use the title of imam for many religious scholars. Among the Shi'a, however, there are again numerous branches, and not all agree on which descendent of Muhammad is the imam, although for the Shi'a, all the descendents of 'Ali have special status; 'Ali's descendents are known as *sayyid* and practice patrilineal endogamy (marrying within the patrilineage) in order to keep the bloodline of 'Ali pure.

Out of this political situation of dispute over leadership emerged the most important rituals specific to the Shi'a. 'Ali was the first Shi'i imam and he was succeeded by two of his sons in the order of their birth. The second son, Imam Hussein, and his family were murdered near Karbala, Iraq, in CE 680. This violent act has been recast as a ritual of martyrdom that is reenacted today by Shi'a around the world on the tenth day ('Ashura') of the month of Muharram. As an example of how events hundreds of years ago in the early days of Islam have religious importance reverberating into the twenty-first century, in Iraq while Saddam Hussein, the former ruler of Iraq, enforced Sunni rule, the majority population of Shi'a was not allowed to publicly practice this ritual of martyrdom or to make a pilgrimage to Karbala where Imam Hussein is entombed. The removal of Saddam Hussein from power has meant Iraqi Shi'a are once again publicly participating in 'Ashura' and the pilgrimage to Karbala. The tomb of 'Ali is located in another Iraqi city, Najaf, and it also has become a pilgrimage site once again. The ritual commemorating the death of Imam Hussein demonstrates the importance of martyrdom in the Shi'i religion and the conflation of the political and the religious. This ritual may be accompanied by self-flagellation and political discourse against oppression by illegitimate leaders. In many different time periods and geographic places, the Shi'a have been subjected to leaders who were either Sunni or secular and have been prevented from practicing their own religious/political way of life.

The Kharijites, or "seceders," are another important division. This branch developed when a group of followers of 'Ali who wished to reconstruct the characteristics of the original Muslim community in Madinah split with 'Ali. Descendants of this group are found today in Oman, Zanzibar, and East and North Africa. The importance of this group is that they established a principle that has been adopted by other branches of Islam since. They labeled Muslims who did not agree with them as "apostates," which redefined what it means to be a Muslim community. Today, when Muslims fight and kill other Muslims, it is based on the logic that one's own beliefs are the true Islam and that Muslims who do not subscribe to the same beliefs are not truly in the Muslim community, and thus it can be acceptable to fight against them in the name of Islam.

The Pillars of Faith

Muslims all believe in and follow a basic set of tenets of Islam. First and foremost is the belief that there is but one god, Allah, and that Muhammad was a prophet but was not divine. Muslims are "people of the book" as they also consider Jews and Christians to be; they recognize Abraham as the first prophet, the Torah as the book God gave the Jews, and the Gospels as the book God gave the Christians, although they do not recognize Jesus as divine. The Qur'an is the book God gave the Muslims. Human behavior is either *halal*, lawful, or haram, forbidden, the former meaning "right" and "pure" and the latter meaning "polluted." The most important acts of a believer are encompassed in the Five Pillars of Islam, which are as follows:

1. *The Profession of Faith:* "I profess that there is no god but God; Muhammad is his messenger" is frequently repeated by followers and signifies one's conversion to Islam.

2. *Prayer:* Muslims face Makkah and pray five times a day (at dawn, noon, mid-afternoon, sunset, and nightfall).

3. *Almsgiving:* This requirement has traditionally taken two forms, the zakat, which in some locales is a tax of 2.5 percent of one's worth collected by the government and then redistributed according to community need, and the *sadaqat*, a charitable contribution to those in need. Devout Muslims consider almsgiving to be a religious duty.

4. *Fasting:* The month of Ramadan in the Muslim calendar represents the month when Mohammad first received revelations for the Qur'an. It is a special month of spiritual observance when believers are required to fast during the daytime.

5. *Hajj, the pilgrimage to Makkah:* All Muslims are expected to make the pilgrimage to Makkah once in their lifetimes if they are able. There is a special time of year during the twelfth lunar month when all who are able perform a ritual together in Makkah and the surrounding area. First, they all ritually wash and shave and men dress in two white pieces of cloth. This dress unifies all Muslim males no matter their standing or wealth. In Makkah, the pilgrims take a ritual walk around the shrine, attend sermons in the Great Mosque, and then travel to Mount 'Arafa, the site where Mohammed had revelations. After more ritual acts, the pilgrimage concludes on the tenth day with the sacrifice of an animal. While the hajj can only be performed in the twelfth lunar month, Muslims make pilgrimage to Makkah all year-round. These smaller pilgrimages are called *umra* (Bates and Rassam 2001:44–50).

In Islam there are other restrictions and behaviors important for the faithful to follow. Dietary restrictions include the forbidding of pork, blood, and alcohol. Animals must be appropriately slaughtered by having their throats cut. The dead are to be buried on the same day that they die in a grave that allows the body to face Makkah. Graves are unadorned, as elaborate gravestones could encourage ancestor worship, which is unacceptable in the strict monotheism of Islam.

Islamic Law

The Qur'an is of unparalleled importance to Islam. It is the literal word of God as revealed to Muhammad. Only in the original Arabic does the Qur'an have its divine validity. It cannot be altered and is the ultimate source of information about right behavior. Second in importance is the Hadith, a compilation of stories about the words and activities of Muhammad, the prophet. Together, the Qur'an and the Hadith form the basis for the law of Islam. These books tie all Muslims together, no matter the branch of Islam to which they belong. These books of course do not provide direct answers to all questions relevant to the religious today. Thus, the 'ulama', the theologians and religious scholars, have the task of interpreting the Qur'an and the Hadith. A great

Pilgrims in Makkah.

body of legal opinion has grown up as a result of centuries of interpretation by the 'ulama'. The body of knowledge developed by the 'ulama' makes up the shari'a, or religious law. Among the Sunni Muslims, four different schools of interpretation developed. They are the Hanafi, the Maliki, the Shafi'i, and the Hanbali. All four are recognized as orthodox schools of interpretation (Bates and Rassam 2001:54) The Wahhabi doctrine adhered to in Saudi Arabia is of the Sunni Hanbali school. Much like the Supreme Court in the United States, today the 'ulama' continue to issue opinions on questions not explicitly addressed in the previous body of religious knowledge. An opinion of this sort is called a *fatwa*.

Islam has no ruling bureaucracy and no leader who can tell all followers what is right and wrong. Thus, different 'ulama' can issue contradictory and controversial fatwas that are accepted by some and repudiated by others. There is no individual in the position of being final arbitrator for the whole of the faith of Islam. This is similar in most of the world's religions with large numbers of followers. For example, in Christianity the Pope is the final arbitrator of what is right and wrong for the Roman Catholic branch of Christianity, but his word does not carry the same gravitas with members of other branches of Christianity, like the Southern Baptist Convention or the Church of Jesus Christ of Latter-day Saints. Likewise, Islam has many branches and these branches share a belief in the Qur'an, the Hadith, and the shari'a and in the five pillars of faith, but they differ in many other details of their beliefs.

The Importance of Islam in Saudi Arabia

It is impossible to overstate the importance of Islam in Saudi Arabia, and to begin to understand the Saudi culture, one needs to understand the rudiments of the Islamic faith as described above. First, consider that the country includes the city where Muhammad was born, Makkah, and the one in which his early religious organization coalesced, Madinah. It is thus home to the two holiest sites in Islam. This gives it a religious importance for Muslims unlike that of any other nation-state in the world. Ibn Saud justified his consolidation of much of Arabia based on the need to protect these holy sites, and modern-day dissenters to the Saudi government also justify their dissent on the need to protect these holy sites. For the Muslim world, Saudi Arabia is more important for these holy sites than for its oil, and control of these two cities is contested and co-opted. It is these holy sites that make proper religious behavior in the Kingdom so important.

Second, understand the importance of Ibn Saud's selection of the views of al-Wahhab as the official doctrine of KSA. This is part of the Sunni Hanbali division of Islam, and the adherents of al-Wahhab's doctrines consider their beliefs and practices to be the single correct version of Islam to the exclusion of all other schools of Islam. It is important for the reader to appreciate that Islam as a whole is not represented by the Wahhabi movement but rather that this movement is only one branch of a whole that is millions of followers strong. However, it determines behavioral norms in the Kingdom. Thus, while Islam is a religion with millions of followers, worldwide, most Muslims are not followers of al-Wahhab and many are not Sunni. When they come to visit the sacred sites of Makkah and Madinah and their surroundings, Muslims must adhere to Islamic rules of behavior as taught by al-Wahhab because these sites are in KSA.

Furthermore, not all Saudis accept the teachings of al-Wahhab. Saudi Arabia includes not only a large Shi'i minority in the Eastern Province but also established Shi'i communities in some Hijazi cities like Madinah (Ende 1997). Because these populations were not members of the Sunni Wahhabi doctrine, official KSA history has either ignored the Shi'i population or described them as foreigners or Iranians, and they were economically and politically disenfranchised. In 1979, encouraged by the Shi'i Islamic revolution that had just occurred in Iran, during *'Ashura'*, the ritual for the mourning of Imam Hussein, Shi'a in the Eastern Province moved out into the streets. Public display of this ritual had been banned by the Saudi government, as had all public display of religious rituals not belonging to the Wahhabi tradition. The Saudi government sent the National Guard to stop this public demonstration. A year later, on the anniversary of the Iranian takeover by Imam Khomeini, Shi'a demonstrated again in the Eastern Province, and the demonstration was once again stopped by the National Guard and deaths occurred. After these violent events, Saudi government officials visited the area and agreed to improve the economic, education, and health situation in Shi'i towns. The Shi'i leadership was pleased with this response, but many young Shi'i activists were not satisfied and some left the country. London became a seat of the new Shi'i resistance. In the 1990s, this resistance shifted from public demonstrations to print and Web-based media campaigns. The thrust of much of this work was to reframe Saudi history so as to demonstrate that the Shi'a were an ancient population in the Peninsula rather than foreign interlopers, thus providing them with an identity that would be legitimate within the Saudi framework of history and inclusion (Al-Rasheed 1998:123). Additionally, not all Sunni Saudis are followers of the Wahhabi doctrine; some of them chafe at the controls of a branch of Sunni Islam with which they do not agree.

On the whole, Saudis are devout followers of Islam. When there, although I heard comments of opposition to the practices of the royal family and of Wahhabi doctrine, I never heard comments opposing Islam in general. In a 2003 survey of 1,026 Saudis, conducted by Mansoor Moaddel, 99 percent identified themselves as Muslim, 90 percent stated religion was very important in their lives, and 87 percent stated that they prayed five times a day as prescribed in Islam. When asked what the most important element of their identity was, 75 percent stated they considered themselves Muslim first and foremost, while only 17 percent stated that their most important facet of identity was being Saudi. These survey results suggest that Saudi religious identity is much stronger than national identity and that most Saudis take their religion seriously (Moaddel 2006:82). My own experience in KSA supports Moaddel's conclusion.

View from a rooftop in old section of Jiddah with mosques prominent in the picture.

The five pillars of faith form the basis for everyday actions in the King-dom. One hears the profession of faith in multiple contexts and so frequently that it almost becomes the background music of Saudi life. As described in a previous chapter, the five calls to prayer create the rhythm of daily life with work hours, shopping hours, and social commitments organized around them. Almsgiving is also taken seriously as a requirement of faith. It is not unusual for Saudis to give substantial charitable contributions to complete strangers and ask for no accounting regarding the use of the funds. This is the Islamic way. Ramadan, the holy month of fasting, brings normal life in the Kingdom to a halt. No one eats in public during daylight hours, including non-Muslims. On a trip to the grocery store during Ramadan, I had to care-fully remind myself not to sample any of the fruit on display, as this would be offensive to my Muslim colleagues since I would be eating during daylight. As a non-Muslim, I was not expected to fast during the day, but I was expected to respect their requirements when in public. Since it was impossi-ble to order a coffee or a sandwich during the day during Ramadan, this was not too difficult to accomplish.

Other than Ramadan, the most important month of the year is that of hajj. While most Saudis do not participate every year, they follow the events closely as they watch it on television and talk about its progress. The hajj brings 2.5 million people to the Makkah area, and many of them travel through the spe-cial hajj terminal at the Jiddah airport, the largest international airport close to the holy cities. The dangers of sickness, overcrowding, and even death, when 2.5 million people are crowded into very small spaces, are great. To the extent it is possible without disturbing the religious sites, the Saudi government has spent millions to reconfigure the spaces to accommodate such crowds. In 2009, there was much talk preceding the event of the dangers of H1N1 virus, and the Saudi government was hoping to inoculate pilgrims against the virus when they entered the country in order to prevent an outbreak. Hajj offers a unique opportunity to spread a pandemic worldwide. If some pilgrims bring the virus to the holy sites and millions are exposed, the millions then take the virus back to their homes and literally spread it around the world.

The success of the annual hajj is a source of pride to Saudis; it shows the world their rather incredible ability at crowd control and organization. In the same way that the 2008 Olympics promoted China's image to the world, the hajj promotes the image of Saudi Arabia. Additionally, the Saudi govern-ment, which is legitimized by its ability to protect the two holy sites, is able to reinforce its legitimation by successfully hosting the hajj. It is not only in the month of hajj that pilgrimages take place, however. All year round Muslims go to Makkah on umra. On air flights into Jiddah, it is common any time of the year to be seated next to a man wearing only two white strips of cloth; he is going on the pilgrimage.

Funerals follow Muslim dictates. The burial itself is a quick and simple affair, and burial sites do not exhibit elaborate markers. One reason for this is to discourage reverence for the dead that could become worship. Only God is to be worshiped. Instead there is a three-day period in which mourners can visit the homes of the bereaved family to express their sympathy and sadness. The mourning observances I attended were solemn affairs for women only. Chairs were lined up along all the walls of the reception room, and at one end of the room the female relatives of the deceased sat together. Upon entering the room, one went immediately to these women and expressed one's condolences and then proceeded around the room greeting all the women present and then took an open seat along the wall. All women, most wearing their black abayas, were seated in the chairs along the wall. Coffee was served by attendants. It was appropriate to stay thirty minutes or so, as a Westerner, and then depart. The tone of the room was somber; the black-clad women talked in hushed voices.

In Saudi Arabia, the constitution is the Qur'an, the revelations God gave to his prophet Mohammad four hundred years ago. As a constitution, this document of course does not discuss branches of government and the formation of the state; it does provide wisdom on which to base rules of behavior. In addition to the Qur'an, Saudi Arabia is governed by the Hadith, the stories about Mohammad's words and deeds; and the shari'a interpretations of Muslim scholars, especially those of the Hanbali school of Sunni Islam. From this basis, the Saudi 'ulama', who are state employees, issue fatwas that clarify and proclaim what the government should do. Rules for the people emanate from this base. The rules of public behavior described in chapter 8 are legitimized on religious grounds by the 'ulama', who issue statements defining and clarifying the rules, and by the mutawa'a, who enforce them. In actuality, the basis of behavioral norms is more complex, combining religion, tradition, economics, politics, and power in response to both historical and recent events. With this background on religion in Saudi Arabia, I turn to the topic of political/religious resistance.

Dissent

Recent events have fueled global speculation that KSA is a country filled with violent radicals determined to bring harm to the West. While I cannot claim to be a specialist on violent dissent, I can state, from time spent in the Kingdom, that this speculation is incorrect, bred from xenophobia, and promotes dangerous stereotyping and divisiveness. Given the prevalence of these ideas, however, I consider a discussion of Saudi resistance to be a valuable addition to this book. First of all, I do not plan to use the words "terrorism" and "terrorist," as use of them has become so politically charged and their definitions so varied and contextual that the words mean nothing and everything. They mean nothing because one can never know just what definition is in use when they are uttered. They mean everything in that they are always used to signify dangerous radicalism and opposition and to evoke fear and anxiety. Anthropologically, they are multivocal. Thus, I will use words like "dissent" and "resistance" instead, as these are words that are not so loaded with fear and xenophobia. Further, I distinguish between resistance to the Saudi government and resistance to Western power and ideology. This section focuses on resistance to the Saudi government, but that will involve understanding the role of resistance to Western power and ideology.

Partial Overview of Resistance to Saudi Government

Religion, politics, and power are interconnected in the resistance movements against the Saudi government. There are almost as many different opinions of the Saudi government as there are Saudi citizens. Some are conservative, yet conservatives can hold many different views; others are liberal, but liberals are not in agreement about what they believe. Others are moderate, holding an equally disparate group of opinions. Dissenters make up only a portion of the Saudi populace, and violent dissenters make up only a fraction of the dissenters. This last point bears repeating. In a world quick to essentialize, Saudi Arabia is typically stereotyped as a backward country full of violent militants. This stereotype is far from the truth. What follows is a partial overview of Saudi resistance in order to provide some context. I will look at nonviolent dissenters as well as violent ones and place both in a larger historical, political, and global context.

The first well-known example of dissent against the Saudi government is the ikhwān rebellion in 1929 when the ikhwān fighting forces rose up in opposition to Ibn Saud. Scholars suggest several possible causes for this rebellion, including (1) ikhwān frustration that Ibn Saud had ceased attempts to conquer additional territories leaving the ikhwān fighting force with no cause for which to fight and (2) ikhwān frustration that with unification the tribes were losing their autonomy and the ikhwān were consequently losing power. Whatever the cause of the rebellion, Ibn Saud's forces fought the rebels militarily, destroyed their camps, and stripped them of authority at the same time that he pardoned some of the leaders, giving them positions of importance in his government, and made the loyal ikhwān into military units that would eventually become the National Guard.

Other well-known acts of resistance include the 1979 takeover of the Grand Mosque in Makkah by Juhaiman al-'Utaibi and his Sunni followers. They proceeded to control the Mosque for three weeks before the Al-Saud regained control. This was the same year as the Shi'i riot against discriminatory treatment in the Eastern Province discussed in the above section on religion. More recently, attacks against Western facilities in the Kingdom have occurred. The 1996 bombing of the Khobar Towers, residence to members of the US military, and the 2003 bombings at three Western housing compounds in Riyadh are examples. As a result of these and other incidents, the Saudi government faced not only the obvious dangers of violent militancy in the Kingdom and its own decision whether to violently respond but also the problem of the Kingdom's global virtual image, especially when the US tragedy of September 11, 2001, is included in the list of violent events involving the Kingdom. These events lead one to question: Who were these militants and what was the reasoning behind these violent acts?

The Importance of Afghani Politics and the First Gulf War in Developing Saudi Resistance

Afghanistan is at the center of several decades of events resulting in the development of a small group of Saudi militant resistance fighters. In the 1980s, with the consent and support of the Saudi government and the religious establishment, young Saudis went to Afghanistan to fight against the Russian invasion there. Osama bin Laden, a nontribal Saudi from a successful and wealthy Saudi business family with Yemeni roots, was able to rise to prominence in this environment. In 1989, the Russians withdrew from Afghanistan, and the Saudis who had been fighting against them returned to the Kingdom.

In 1990, Saddam Hussein of Iraq invaded Kuwait, which is KSA's neighbor and one of its close allies. Saudis feared Saddam Hussein would march through Kuwait and invade KSA. Reports state that Osama bin Laden offered to fight Saddam Hussein, but this was rejected by the Saudi government. Instead, the Council of Senior 'Ulama' issued a fatwa authorizing the Saudi government to invite an international coalition of foreign armies into KSA to stop the Iraqi invasion. Some of the Kingdom's religious conservatives disliked this solution as this meant non-Muslim, Western troops would be defending KSA and resolving a conflict between Muslims (Al-Rasheed 2007:113). During this first Gulf War, the streets of Riyadh and other Saudi cities were awash in American soldiers. Some conservative Saudis were dismayed at so much Western (US) presence. Saudi dissent against the Saudi government was fueled by this situation. Saudis wondered, why could not the Saudi forces do it themselves? Had their government failed them? Again, it is important to avoid stereotypes and to stress the variety of responses among Saudis. Given the diversity of opinion among the Saudi populace, many other Saudis were pleased by the Western influence and wanted to explore ways the country could liberalize its rules but in an Islamic way.

Meanwhile bin Laden had been marginalized, put under house arrest, and eventually left the country; in 1994, the Saudi government revoked his citizenship. He set up a base in Sudan and some of the Saudi youth who fought in Afghanistan followed him there. When he was expelled from Sudan, he moved back to Afghanistan where the Taliban were now in control. Bin Laden made clear his opposition to the Saudi government and worked to build his forces in Afghanistan. Among his recruits to his Afghanistan training camps were a new generation of young Saudis who had not fought the Russians in Afghanistan a decade before. The Saudi government cut off diplomatic recognition of the Taliban in early 2001; months later, the tragic bombings of September 11 occurred. The subsequent US invasion of Afghanistan caused many of these militant Saudis to leave Afghanistan and return to Saudi (Hegghammer 2006:41).

Several scholars have suggested that many Saudi militants involved in incidents in KSA since 1990 had in common previous experience in Afghanistan. Mamoun Fandy (1999:3–5) researched the backgrounds of the four men who conducted the bombing of the al-'Uliyya US military mission in Riyadh; three had fought in Afghanistan. It is Fandy's conclusion that they were radicalized by the Afghanistan experience, which brought them to accept violence as an acceptable means of resistance.

During research trips to KSA in 2004 and 2005, Thomas Hegghammer studied the biographies of 240 individuals involved in militant activity in Saudi Arabia since 2002. With relatively extensive biographies on seventy of them, he provides a picture of violent militants in the Kingdom. All were male; most were Saudi nationals in their late twenties and were middle class or lower middle class with a high school education or less; many were urban. The common denominator among them was that most of them had previous experience in combat or training camps, usually in Afghanistan, where Hegghammer asserts they received violence acculturation, indoctrination, and training (2006:46). He is quick to point out that young Saudis who went to Afghanistan in the late 1990s were not going there to join al-Qa'ida, as there was little awareness of the al-Qa'ida organization before 2001. Most who went were recruited through personal connections; of those who returned to Saudi after the US invasion of Afghanistan, some then joined the local al-Qa'ida organization in KSA. The Saudi government's response to the May 2003 bombings in Riyadh led to the capture and death of militants and the extreme weakening of the al-Qa'ida organization in the Kingdom.

The government drive to root out violent militants in KSA continues today. One measure of the success of that drive is that it has pushed al-Qa'ida operatives out of KSA and into Yemen, one of Saudi's neighbors to the south. The Yemeni central government has not been as successful as the Al Saud in pacifying its tribes and unifying its country, and in 2009 the government was fighting insurgents on several fronts, making Yemen a safer home for al-Qa'ida operatives due to the lack of central controls. Yemen is now the base for al-Qa'ida in the Arabian Peninsula, and the Saudi government continues its efforts to root out militants. For example, a Saudi intelligence tip in October 2010 resulted in the interception in Dubai and Britain of package bombs on cargo planes from Yemen (Shane and Worth 2010).

Globalization of Resistance

Meanwhile, the resistance movements had globalized. London became one of the important centers of Saudi dissent. Islamic dissidents facing prison in their own countries moved to London in the 1990s. Others came to London considering it a safe base from which to launch a media campaign. Bin Laden sent followers there in 1994 to establish the Advice and Reform Committee, which never succeeded in having much influence and whose leader was eventually imprisoned in Britain. Most dissidents in London were not violent, however, and they worked for a more peaceful change in Saudi government using the weapons of the print media and the Internet. It is not only dissenters who use London as a base; it is also the home of pro-Saudi government publications like the *al-Sharq al-Awsat* newspaper and the *al-Majalla* magazine, as well as the Middle East Broadcasting Corporation (MBC), which are at least partially owned by members of the Saudi royal family (Fandy 1999:11).

Among both peaceful and violent dissenters, while their reasons varied, their opposition was typically religiously based and frequently accepting of the original Wahhabi doctrine that the Saudi royal family had adopted from the beginning. They opposed the royal family and the establishment religious leaders in the Kingdom for not following original Wahhabi doctrine. Al-Rasheed explains that there are multiple Wahhabi discourses: the official one espoused by the Saudi state and multiple others that contest the official version and use Wahhabi doctrine to explain why the Saudi government is not fulfilling its duties. These arguments usually revolve around the royal family's alliance with non-Muslim states and the presence of hundreds of thousands of non-Muslims in the Kingdom. They contend that the King, the custodian of the two holy mosques in Makkah and Madinah, is not protecting the religious purity of these mosques or the religious values of the Saudi state. The Saudi 'ulama' are paid by the government and thus are seen as corrupt, too, in that they issue proclamations in support of the Saudi rulers. The 'ulama' proclaim that to follow the ruler is to follow God. If a devout Muslim accepts this premise, it leaves no room for opposition to the Saudi government (Al-Rasheed 2007:256).

Fandy explains how dissenting groups in Saudi Arabia that were marginal and contained in a Saudi Arabia that had little contact with the outside world have now reached a worldwide audience. With the coming of satellite television, the Internet, and the 1991 Gulf War, Saudi Arabia became globally connected, and previously marginalized and local pockets of resistance were able to take on new power. Spreading their messages on the Internet gave them a new audience and a new legitimacy. Resistance groups became virtual, and those participating through social networking websites and e-mail do not know whether they are in a virtual group composed of five individuals or five thousand. Thus, the resistance movements live no longer just in local space where individuals meet face to face; they now live in virtual space where communications can move back and forth in a split second and where followers of a particular movement or leader live in distant corners of the world. At the same time, political forces external to the Kingdom, whether from Egypt, Syria, or London, have influenced Saudi radicals (Fandy 1999:3–5). Thus the modern age of dissent is a global phenomenon not possible prior to global mass communication. Resistance is not confined within Saudi's borders, taking place in secret in the narrow pathways of old sections of Saudi villages and cities, but in the open, on the Internet and cable television. Nevertheless, at the same time, pockets of resistance are also a local phenomenon reacting to issues at home in KSA. Al-Rasheed purports that

> Jihadis combine a longing for a return to the authentic tradition with ultra-modern concerns. Jihadi rhetoric is very traditional, yet the messages reflect issues that are a product of modernity. Jihadis are concerned with the question of loss of identity, hardly an issue in traditional societies. Their messages tended to be global, yet they are fully immersed in the politics of the locality. (2007:259)

A comprehensive explanation of dissent in Saudi Arabia and dissent by Saudi Arabians globally is a complex undertaking. I have given only a brief introduction to the topic here.

Women

In my first week after arriving in Saudi Arabia in 2002, I was excited to be invited to a dinner of Saudi women. This was a dinner of eight female professionals and would be my first opportunity to learn about the individuals hidden behind those black coverings. I arrived at the gathering and watched as six other women arrived and removed their hair and face coverings and abayas. We were all introduced and served Arabic coffee. No sooner had the first sips of coffee been taken than they all looked pointedly at me and began. They wanted to know about US policy in the Middle East, and they grilled me in angry voices about how my country could be, as they perceived it, supporting the violence of the Israelis against the Palestinians. At the time, the Saudi newspapers were full of pictures of violence in Palestine, including many pictures of bloodied bodies and death. This discussion of US policy continued for a full hour before we moved on to other, less volatile topics.

Later, back in my room, I sat stunned at the evening's events, thinking through what had happened. It was not the grilling about US policy that surprised me, as this has happened to me numerous times; it was the force of their personalities. While I had not known what to expect when meeting the women under those veils for the first time, it certainly was not this. Like many Westerners, I equated the wearing of the veil with meekness and lack of worldly knowledge. Instead, I found I was dealing with women who were forceful, dynamic, articulate, and more knowledgeable than I was on many international events. Without realizing it, I had been ethnocentric in my assumptions about the meaning of the veil and had equated the wearing of the veil with certain personality characteristics (meek and mild) and a specific level of knowledge of international affairs (minimal). This was obviously wrong.

A few months later, I had the opportunity to attend a Saudi wedding celebration. These events are much talked about, and I looked forward to the opportunity to experience one. Wedding celebrations are segregated events, which means the men celebrate in one location and the women in another. In this case, the two celebrations were in a large wedding hall, which was a rectangular building split in the middle so that it had two large, separate reception areas. To reach the separated celebration rooms, the men entered the entrances on one end of the building and the women entered the entrances on the other end. My hostess instructed me to arrive around 11:00 PM, as celebrations in Saudi begin late and continue well into the night.

Upon my arrival at the hall, I entered a foyer and heard the sounds of high-pitched, vocal tremolos as several women located in the foyer registered the arrival of each guest with these loud, vocal greetings. Entering the large hall, I faced a sea of tables seating some 300 women and scanned the room looking for my hostess, who was a relative of the bride. She spotted me and I was promptly seated at her table. Looking around, I saw that the women were dressed in evening dresses of all colors and styles. In the front right corner, there was an all-female band playing Arabic music and in the front of the room there was a stage. Women were moving about visiting and dancing. Some ten of them were up on the stage dancing to the music and others were dancing in the aisles. While I sipped fruit juice and ate hors d'oeuvres at the table, I watched the activity. I was mesmerized by the dancing. In my opinion, the Saudi female dancing style is stately, graceful, and slightly sensuous in nature.

At some point later in the evening, the band broke into a song with a different tempo and two guests in their fifties, clad in beautiful evening dresses, walked up on the stage, tied their long, black headscarves around their hips, and, smiling broadly, began to belly dance. Other guests joined them. The music was an Egyptian belly dance, and the guests clearly enjoyed participating. The women at this gathering were having fun.

Around 2:30 AM, the energy in the room changed. With great commotion, most women donned their abayas and head coverings. I learned that the bride and groom were about to enter and consequently all women who were not closely related to the groom put on their coverings. From the back of the room, the bride, dressed in a white traditional Western-style wedding dress, and the groom made their way slowly down the central aisle to the cheers of the crowd and with the assistance of the women in their families. They walked up on stage in the front of the room and sat on a small sofa center stage. At this point, women greeted them and there were more celebratory cheers. At some weddings, other male relatives accompany the groom, but on this occasion, only the groom braved the women's celebration. After an interval of some thirty minutes to an hour, the couple got up and found their way back out of the celebration. At that point, doors to another room were thrown open and all the women moved to the other room to have dinner. After dinner, they began to depart for home in the early morning hours. Women repeatedly told me that they had it on good authority from their husbands and brothers that the men's celebration was not nearly so much fun and that the men went home early.

The women at that first dinner and at the wedding exemplify the direct, forceful, strong, and fun-loving characteristics of Saudi women that were so different from those ethnocentric assumptions held by me and many other

Westerners. With regard to the rules they follow in their country, women had much to say. Below are a few of their comments.

- We like wearing the abaya; it is our national dress.
- When reporters come here from the US, all they ask us about is the abaya and driving; all they want to know about is the abaya and driving; the abaya and driving are nothing; we have many more important issues for women. Why don't the Western reporters ever want to talk about those?
- I want to see things change for women in my country, but I love my country; there are many good things here that I don't want to change.
- We will be driving in a few years.
- We don't want to be like the West.
- You in the West think we are sexual objects here with our rules about covering and driving; you women in the West are sexual objects. We don't want to become like you.

The statements above are from Saudi women living in Saudi Arabia who were my friends and colleagues while I lived in the Kingdom. For the most part, they are members of the professional and intellectual middle class, have traveled extensively internationally, and by choice live in their native country and submit to the rules for women as required. What is to be made of their comments and of the "plight" of women in the Kingdom? To answer that question, I start with the recent research on women, most of it by Middle Eastern female anthropologists.

To place the position of Saudi women in a longitudinal context, I start with the work of Soraya Altorki (1986), who was raised in a Saudi family but spent much of her life outside the Kingdom and who researched continuity and change for three generations of women in elite Jiddah families. At the time of her study, the three generations were (1) women aged fifty to eighty whose first children were born after Ibn Saud unified the Kingdom, (2) women whose first children were born during and just after World War II, and (3) women who were themselves those postwar children who became of marriage age from the mid-1960s to the mid-1980s. By documenting the life histories of these women, she was able to identify trends of change.

One trend was the shift from (1) viripatrilocal residence (newly married couple moved into the home of the groom's father) to (2) semineolocal residence (newly married couple moved into the groom's father's home but had their own separate entrance to their separate wing of the house) to (3) neolocal residence (newly married couple lived in a different house from groom's father's home). Thus, she documented a trend away from extended family living arrangements to nuclear family living arrangements. Imagine for yourself the difference in living as a married adult in the home of your in-laws versus living in your own home; some of you have probably experienced these differences. In Saudi Arabia, where the practice of viripatrilocality was the norm, this change in residence pattern had long-range implications. The physical distance from the mother-in-law gave the young wife a level of autonomy that her older female relatives never had. Younger women were living lives of less seclusion than did their grandmothers at the same age.

Another trend Altorki identified was that, while marriages were still arranged and patrilateral cousin marriage (marriage to the paternal uncle's son) continued to be the norm, women in the younger generation were gaining more say in marriage arrangements, with the power to refuse an arranged marriage, whereas their grandmothers may not have known they were about to be married until the marriage contract was to be signed. Women in the younger generation were also getting more control over their own wealth; the bride was likely to know the amount of the customary payment the groom's family made to the bride's family, and, what is more, the money went into a bank account for her; young women in the grandmother's generation were not likely to know the amount of the dowry, as this would have been their fathers' business to arrange, not theirs. Younger generations of married women had certain rights unknown to older generations, like the right to spend the household budget and participate in decisions about their children's future (1986:13, 21, 95).

Altorki pointed out that in Jiddah society, religious dogma and social norms were fused, and in matters of marriage, women had always played an important role. Marriages were arranged and the arrangement was between families, not between the two individuals, the bride and groom. For the older generation, while the bride agreed to the marriage contract, it was arranged by her male relatives and she was expected to and did sign it without any knowledge of the groom. It was not necessary or desirable and was in fact scandalous for the bride and groom to spend time together prior to the wedding. Even getting a look at the prospective groom was done surreptitiously. Mothers played an important role in the arrangements of their sons' marriages; they were able to see, talk with, and get to know prospective brides and report back to the male members of the family on the attributes of these young women. Among the older generation, an eligible young woman did not attend large social gatherings of women, like weddings, as this would appear as if the family was trying to find a husband for her and indicated that the family was not able to care for her itself. By the time of Altorki's study, eligible young women were allowed to attend large female gatherings, like marriage ceremonies, in the company of their mothers, and the female members of families of eligible young men were likely to be present (1986:95,135).

In Altorki's research, an unmarried woman of marriage age was more thoroughly veiled because to be improperly covered would damage her reputation and that of her family at a time when her good personal reputation and that of her family was crucial to success in marriage arrangements. While covering the body and the hair was appropriate for all, veiling was culturally negotiable; norms about covering the face have changed over the generations and have often depended on the woman's marital status. Some of the factors involved in these changes were foreign travel, made possible by oil wealth, and education. After education for women was introduced in the 1960s, the difference in education levels of the three generations of women was vast, with some of the oldest being illiterate and the some of the youngest holding advanced graduate degrees. Their education gave the younger women more power in dealing with their male relatives. Altorki suggested that while behaviors had changed gradually over the three generations she studied, the principles had not; life was still predicated on the seclusion of women and the asymmetrical power distribution between males and females and between old and young (1986:36–37, 154, 157).

Almost two decades later, at the time of my work, I found large gatherings, like weddings, to hold the same function of allowing the female relatives of eligible young men the opportunity to observe and evaluate unmarried young women. In a society as segregated as Saudi Arabia, it is still not possible for young people to develop open friendships; arranged marriages are still a common practice, although some young people do chose their own mates. Modern technology has allowed young people to develop ways of communicating with each other, by cell phone and e-mail, for example, which changes the dynamics. In addition, I experienced some liberal Saudi families encouraging open contact among their children and friends of both sexes, while conservative families followed strict practices of segregation of the sexes. I understood degree and type of veiling expected of a woman to be more complex than Altorki described. It depended on one's region and family and the rules that were the norm for both of these. It also depended on politics. For

Women shopping.

example, many women told me that the public expectation of covering conservatively had increased since the first Gulf War, and this was a reaction by the 'ulama' to the strong Western presence in the Kingdom during that war and to the presence of unveiled, uniformed US female soldiers walking the streets.

Saddeka Arebi (1994), an anthropologist of Libyan descent, received her anthropological training in the United States and knows what it is like to negotiate between two worlds, Arabic and English, Islamic and Western. She conducted a study of nine contemporary Saudi women writers and provides an anthropological analysis of their work and its meaning for contemporary society. Their voices, as Arebi presents them, reflect many of the voices I heard while in the Kingdom. She concludes that these women are writing about their own identity—an identity that distinguishes (1) the present from the past, (2) their civilization from that of the West, (3) themselves as "real" rather than as symbols, and (4) women as different from but not in opposition to men.

The "woman" is exploited as a symbol at multiple levels in Saudi and Western discourse. The Saudi government protects women, which symbolizes protecting Islam. The Saudi 'ulama' suggest that changes in the rules for women, like lifting the veil, are Western ideas; thus, rules for women must stay the same in order to avoid Westernization of this Islamic culture. For the 'ulama' the struggle between Islamic and Western values is played out symbolically through women. Meanwhile, Western governments, like that of the United States, cite the seclusion of women in Saudi Arabia as evidence of human rights abuse because they view human rights through a Western lens; therefore, for the West, Saudi treatment of women symbolizes abuse and backwardness. Arebi explains that the nine women writers she worked with are countering the view of women as symbol by telling their own stories and those of other real women. Real women are not the symbolic woman.

Additionally, these writers speak powerfully of the value of some of the norms of their society, for example, the value placed on family and its importance as an institution. They do not denigrate men but instead stress their difference from men. Further, they tend not to denigrate the veil or their own segregation, both of which are seen as symbols of distance from the West. The veil can actually represent freedom that allows them to move in the public sphere. I have experienced this myself. When veiled in Saudi, I have great freedom of movement; in fact, in some situations, I have felt more freedom of movement than I would unveiled in the West. In walking in public when wearing an abaya and a headscarf, I find that, even though my face is exposed, no one seems to notice me. I can move in public as if I were invisible. Longva (1997:194) commented that her Kuwaiti female informants similarly described the anonymity of the hijab and abaya, which allowed a woman "to go about her business without being readily recognized."

Arebi makes the important point that the discourse of these Saudi women writers is "neither a reaction to Western discourse nor to the local discourses but rather an autonomous enterprise readily distinguishable from both." I experienced women making this point many times during my stay in KSA.

While Westerners, including Western feminists, perceive Saudi women to be oppressed as compared to women in the West and want to free them from this oppression, Saudi women think that position says more about the West than it does about Saudi Arabia; Saudi women are not in a dialogue with the West; they are in a dialogue with their own country's norms and laws.

The Western emphasis on unveiling focuses on women as sexual objects and physical beings who must be physically exposed to be free. Arebi points out that the power of the issue of the veil is that the West advocates lifting it and this poses Islam against the West where Islam and male power are viewed as negative. Saudi women writers disempower the Western argument and take charge of their own future by supporting both Islam and males and providing their own interpretation of female freedom. Similarly, the Saudi government discourse touts the freedom of modern women compared to their more restricted, uneducated, unemployed female ancestors, while the Saudi 'ulama' compare the women of today with an idealized version of the women of early Islam. The women writers, however, also speak to the discourse of both the government and the 'ulama' by visioning history in a way that redeems their past and informs their present; that is, they take charge of the present through a visioning of the past (1994:285–86). By telling the stories of Islamic women of the past, they again dissociate themselves from the West and instead draw from their own history (1994:281, 285–86).

I find that Arebi's critique of contemporary female voices resonates with my own experiences listening to Saudi women's voices in the Kingdom. They made many of these same points to me. It is not that they don't recognize the impact of the West on their society. They frequently wear Western-style clothing, use technology developed in the West, and so on. They do not, however, equate the use of material culture and even some ideology and behavior from the West with accepting Western modernization in its entirety. They instead reinterpret what is borrowed and place it in a Saudi context. They want to choose from social and cultural forms that comprise modernity in the West only those that they can shape to fit in their society, like Western clothing and technology, but reject others, like the Western emphasis on exposing female bodies in public, in order to fashion a Saudi way of being modern.

Lila Abu-Lughod (2002) has written a much-cited reflection on Muslim women. Reflecting on the media treatment of Muslim women in the aftermath of the 9/11 tragedy, she comments that Western media were asking questions about Islam and the treatment of women that artificially divide the world into separate spheres of East versus West rather than asking questions that explore our global connections. In response to the interest in veiling, she points out that Muslim women cover by preference in many circumstances; the veil "must not be confused with, or made to stand for, women's lack of agency," and it should not be equated with women's lack of freedom, nor should the diversity of attitudes, life situations, and cultural affiliations of Muslim women worldwide be represented by a single form of dress. She describes the all-covering garments of Afghan women as "mobile homes," allowing a woman to travel publicly while observing the rules of separation of the sexes, for example (2002:786). She implores us to do the hard work of acknowledging different histories and respecting different ways of life.

Abu-Lughod states that Western feminism should be viewed as just that—*Western* feminism—and we must recognize that Western feminism is a product of particular historical and cultural forces; feminism in other parts of the world is likely to look different, as it is the product of different historical and cultural forces. To force Western feminist views on Islamic women is not freedom but is, instead, neocolonial repression. She quotes Saba Mahmood, who states with regard to Egyptian women, "The desire for freedom and liberation is a historically situated desire. . . ." (2002:788). While she does not discuss Saudi Arabia specifically, Abu-Lughod's points are appropriate to their concerns. Women in KSA are a product of Arab and Islamic historical and cultural forces; their views of women's freedom and power are the product of their backgrounds and will consequently be different than those of Western women. Just as modernity in Saudi Arabia grew out of Arab and Muslim traditions rather than Western ones and consequently looks different than Western modernity, women's freedom and power in Saudi Arabia grew out of Arab and Muslim traditions and consequently look different than Western women's freedom and power.

Almohsen (2000), a Saudi male sociologist, states that in 2000, 55 percent of Saudi university graduates were women, although they were excluded from studying some subjects like engineering, journalism, and architecture. Women made up only 5 percent of the workforce and held jobs primarily in education and health care, with smaller numbers working in business, philanthropy, banking, retail sales, and media. My experience in 2002 was that women were expanding their work arena and beginning to move into new fields, like law. By the time of my 2009 work in the Kingdom, the first women members of both the Jiddah and the Riyadh Chambers of Commerce had been elected and the Majlis al-Shūrā had female advisors. More than freedom from the abaya, Saudi women desire more access to job opportunities and government decision making.

In conclusion, I will risk repeating a point I may have made one too many times but feel is essential to understanding KSA and the position of its women. Their positions on the rules, restrictions, and freedoms they experience in their country are as varied as the number of women holding them. Their views on this matter cannot be essentialized; their views are mixed and complex. There is a strong theme in their thoughts, however, which is that it is the business of Saudis to decide what those rules, restrictions, and freedoms should be in the future and that those decisions will be made from within a Muslim and Arab framework; consequently, their decisions will be different from those made by the West. Just as modernity can take different forms in the West and the East, so can feminism.

Conclusion

With the movement of media flows around the world, text, images, and sounds travel instantaneously to disparate parts of the globe. The stereotyping of Saudi Arabia common in written works focuses on its conservative version of Islam, its connection to "terrorism" and known "terrorists," and its rules for women. But these are often partial representations that reflect more about their presenters than about their subjects. While the representations in this chapter also reflect on the presenter, they are intended to counter this simplified global virtual image of KSA by providing a more historical, contextual, and nuanced presentation of these topics, thereby painting a more complex picture of the culture of KSA today.

Chapter 10

Essential Concepts for Reflection

9 have come to the end of the story I planned to tell and I return to the beginning. Specifically, in order to summarize my findings I return to goals of this book as I listed them in chapter 1.

Goals of This Book

Goal 1: to describe a process of globalization: specifically, how complex organizations (supranational institutions, transnational corporations, national governments, local businesses, and others) join into complex adaptive systems that form, change, dissolve, divide, and recombine to satisfy the goals of the various participating organizations.

Using Daniel Falvo's definition of a complex adaptive system as a collection of agents that are involved in a process of co-adaptation that can result in the formation of ordered networks of agents from disordered collections (Falvo 2000:641), I suggest that nation-state governments, transnational businesses, and supranational regulatory bodies are all complex organizations important not just for their economic might and consequent political power but also for the ways in which they couple, intertwine, divide, and recombine through partnerships, contracts, treaties, joint ventures, and other intraorganizational arrangements. These organizations form complex adaptive systems, and in this book I have given multiple examples of how this phenomenon has worked in KSA.

In KSA, a five-step process was one of the methods of modernization. Those five steps administered by the government are summarized as follows:

1. Enter into a foreign partnership, to include foreign management of the necessary companies, with a complex organization like a transnational business to bring needed expertise into the Kingdom.

2. Set up foreign-led training programs in KSA for Saudis and send Saudi students abroad for further education.

3. Train Saudis in all areas of expertise needed to execute the desired business.

4. Saudization: Slowly replace foreign experts with Saudi experts until all the enterprise has been Saudized.

5. Dissolve foreign partnership.

Using this process, KSA participated and continues to participate in multiple complex systems. For example, in the 1930s the government of the nation-state of Saudi Arabia and Standard Oil Company of California partnered to form California Arabian Standard Oil Company creating a complex adaptive network in which the interests of each of the partners as well as the interests of the network were satisfied through the discovery and extraction of oil in KSA's Eastern Province. Later, this adaptive network combined with other oil companies—Texaco, Exxon, and Mobil—to form a different but equally adaptive network for the same purpose. Other related combinations of organizations were those involving Japanese and French oil companies in the 1950s. All of these networks intertwined, divided, and recombined to produce a network of complex systems that were adaptive from the perspective of the organizations. For the oil companies, successful adaptation to their environment meant maintaining economic viability.

Other examples of this process are found in chapter 6 on the Tertiary Care Hospital of Saudi Arabia. Here, the complex organization of the Saudi government partnered with that of Hospital Corporation of America (HCA) to set up and run a third complex organization, the Tertiary Care Hospital of Saudi Arabia (TCHSA), and then added to that partnership the other complex organizations that provided services for the hospital, like Baylor College of Medicine in Houston, Texas, which performed cardiac surgery; WorldCare, an organization that connects TCHSA with specialists around the world for second opinions on patient health care issues; and CBAY, an organization that provides medical transcription electronically by beaming digital data from Saudi Arabia to the United States to India and back within twenty-four hours. All of these form complex systems of organizations that are adaptive from the perspective of the organizations as long as they are economically viable and contribute to bringing state-of-the-art health care to the Kingdom.

Another example of complex adaptive systems is the offset company of Advanced Electronics Company (AEC) begun in 1988 as a joint venture with Boeing, Arabic Computer Systems, National Commercial Bank, National Industrialization Company, and Saudi Arabian Airlines (Saudia)

(Ramady 2005:74). AEC has built electronic components for Boeing for F-15 airplanes and for Lockheed Martin for F-16 airplanes. Other customers include the Saudi Armed Forces; the US Army, Navy, and Air Force; Saudi Aramco; Lucent Technologies; Siemens; Nokia; and Raytheon. AEC partners with international companies like Cisco that are seeking to increase their market share in the Kingdom, creating even more complex adaptive networks. Another example is the government of KSA's participation in the complex adaptive system created by the World Trade Organization.

All of these examples demonstrate how the individual organization and the network formed by two or more of these organizations are adapting to their environments. Successful adaptation here means successful from the participants' point of view. This can mean economic success, as for Aramco, or success in bringing biomedical health care to KSA for Tertiary Care Hospital. So, a successful network combines with more organizations and creates more networks so that what we experience is a web of interconnected organizations, each acting in its own interest but achieving its self-interest through partnerships with other organizations and other networks and through adaptations that appear beneficial to all network partners. From the perspective of the KSA government, the adaptive advantage is to increase the economic success of the Kingdom and to bring state-of-the-art knowledge and technology to be used for solving social problems in the Kingdom. When viewed in a larger context, we can see their actions as a case study of the use of complex adaptive systems as one of the processes of globalization active in the world today.

Goal 2: to provide an example of an emerging economy that was never colonized and also possesses significant resources allowing it to negotiate with world powers from a position of strength. This makes it a valuable anthropological contribution, as most anthropological studies of emerging economies are of countries colonized by the West and/or with little economic wealth and few bargaining chips with which to negotiate with the global power brokers.

A reason for telling the history of the Arabian Peninsula before describing the modern Saudi state is to demonstrate that the area was never successfully colonized. Although at times the Ottoman Turks and the British attempted to exert control over the Peninsula, they never succeeded, and the land was continuously ruled by traditional Arab forms of government and culture. Thus, the Saudi state is an indigenous state developed from indigenous religious and political systems. Its constitution is the Qur'an, it measures time according to the Islamic calendar and the daily calls to prayer, and its public norms of behavior are based on the Islamic teachings of al-Wahhab. Also, the story of the oil industry, of KSA's rapid economic growth, and the building of the physical structures of a wealthy society with well-maintained highways, proliferating shopping malls, and the general embrace of consumerism is the story of a developing nation with the resources to enter the world stage with vast economic wealth. Anthropology has few detailed studies like this.

Goal 3: to describe KSA culture change over the last one hundred years, especially the rapid change at the end of the twentieth century.

The development of the current Saudi state and of the cultural lifeway of its inhabitants in the early and mid-twentieth century is described in order to provide a baseline for understanding how much has changed in the Kingdom since the purposeful modernization process began around 1970. Another reason for describing this traditional cultural life is to help the reader understand the basis for modern Saudi culture, which is rooted in traditional values like hospitality, generosity, honor, closeness of family, and tribal identity. The two factors most significant in effecting change were the following:

1. *State Formation:* Ibn Saud and his sons employed several techniques to unify a previously politically fractured peninsula. Ibn Saud unified a peninsula of disparate and politically autonomous tribes and towns through the use of traditional cultural behaviors like hospitality, marriage ties, the majlis, and redistribution of wealth. He also imposed cultural unification through a variety of means, including requiring Nejdi traditional dress in all regions of the Kingdom, supplanting old political entities with new local government structures reporting to the state, and replacing old tribal ownership policies with new state land ownership. Such strategic moves wrought substantial changes in traditional lifeways.

2. *Formal Development Strategies:* The effort to bring modern education, health care, industry, and business to the Kingdom began in earnest in 1970 with the five-year plans; they brought vast changes to the Kingdom through the end of the twentieth century and into the twenty-first century. These changes have had significant ramifications for traditional life.

For the bedu, the Public Land Decree of 1953 ended tribal control and management of traditional lands as the government encouraged abandonment of the mobile lifestyle and settlement into permanent towns. In addition, the government provided access to health services and education, subsidized the price of barley for animal feed, provided employment in the National Guard, and increased the numbers of roads and water wells. The automobile made camels less economically important, and the introduction of the cash market made sheep and goats more valuable, and bedu changed from raising camels to raising sheep and goats. Just as many bedu moved into the cities for salaried jobs, many urbanites purchased small herds and paid an expatriate herder to tend them. Both of these strategies increased the family's income streams and thus its economic strategies for survival. All moved to a cash economy. Small towns sprang up in the desert, each with a gas station, a mosque, and a school. So while most bedu have become sedentary, the bedu way of life is still much celebrated and the values it embodies are still popularly held.

For the hadar, changes were wrought by (1) the establishment of a state system with its accompanying bureaucracy; (2) the beginning of a national education system that would train the city's population in new skills; (3) the establishment of the oil industry, which introduced contracts, new forms of wage and salaried labor, and new forms of business organization; and (4) the resulting switch to a cash economy from a barter system (Altorki and Cole 1989). Emirs were no longer the de facto heads of political entities but were now appointed by the Ministry of Interior and operated not with monies they acquired independently from tax and tribute but instead using a budget provided by a government ministry. As modern education helped to create national identity through its standardized curriculum and to prepare the youth for jobs in a cash economy, agriculturalists turned to new crops in order to exploit the new diversified cash market.

For all Saudis, villages and towns took on a new look as people moved out of traditional mud-brick homes and into new ones of steel, concrete, and marble. The new homes separated previously united extended families and disrupted the organic expansion of villages that had progressed for hundreds of years. With no need for defense against raiding, villages took on a different plan. Electricity became widely available, and automobiles and roads appeared throughout the country. Saudis born in the 1970s and since do not remember the pre-oil days. They live in a world of mass education, travel abroad, radio and television, and possibly expatriate servants. Saudi Arabia today strikes the foreigner as a country under construction, with new skyscrapers in Riyadh, new cities growing up on the Red Sea, and new housing developments everywhere. Using the oil wealth that emerged in the 1970s, the sons of Ibn Saud set the Kingdom on this path of modernization at the same time that they created two lines of tension still evident today: (1) one between Islam and the new consumerism and technology transfer that the oil wealth allowed, and (2) the other between Islam and a reliance on US technology and military expertise.

Goal 4: to acquaint readers who have no experience in KSA with the country, its people, and their ways of life through a more complex and nuanced understanding than the understanding available through the popular press.

It is to satisfy this goal that I tell the tale of (1) the actual creation of the Arabian Peninsula and describe the many climates it has endured and geological features it has developed over its 600-million-year history; (2) the early humans who settled on this land from Paleolithic hunters and gatherers to the first agropastoralists, the domestication of the camel, the development of towns and trade routes, and then complex kingdoms like that of the Nabateans; (3) the life of Muhammad and the coming of Islam and the resulting Islamic Empire; and (4) the eventual development of the three Saudi states, the last of which is the current Kingdom. This long timeline of understanding helps one see that the modern Saudi government grew out of the emirate form of government common in the Peninsula in pre-Saudi state times and that the cultural norms like hospitality and honor came from the traditional cultural norms of the bedu and hadar. The modern state of KSA is tied to Islamic teachings of al-Wahhab because the preceding two Saudi states had been linked to these teachings in a successful attempt to legitimate their rule. Being aware of the land helps one to see that the beautiful but harsh land has played a role in developing those cultural norms for a society that, until recently, lived directly off the land through its camel herds and oasis agricultural plots. Understanding that Arabia is home to the birthplace of Islam and its two holiest religious sites is to see why Islam holds such importance in the modern Kingdom.

"Modern" Reconsidered

So, what does "modern" mean anyway? That is a question I asked at the beginning of this book and I return to it now. For KSA, "modern" means choosing to accept the technology and other material goods, from cell phones to designer clothing to advanced medical equipment, that are available throughout the world and make use of them in Saudi society in order to improve health care, education, and economic well-being. It also means retaining important traditional cultural values like modesty, separation of the sexes, hospitality, honor, and importance of the family. It means placing religion at the center of life with the Qur'an as the constitution and the call to prayer creating the rhythm of daily life. Just as Saudi women let me know that it is the business of Saudis to decide what the rules, restrictions, and freedoms for women should be in the future, that those decisions will be made from within a Muslim and Arab framework, and that consequently their decisions will be different from those made by the West, all Saudis I spoke with let me know that they will determine how modernity is developed in their country.

Issues and Strengths in the Twenty-First-Century Kingdom

In conclusion, I describe what I see as a series of issues the Kingdom faces in the twenty-first century and correspondingly what I see as its strengths.

Issues

The Need for Economic Diversification and Development: While Saudi is a wealthy country, that wealth is oil dependent and the government recognizes the need to diversify the economy. While the oil supply is so vast that is should sustain the economy for many years to come, the world is fast developing alternative sources of energy. In the future, the oil supply is not likely to provide as much economic security or to provide the government as much power on the political world stage. Consequently, new sources of economic livelihood need to be developed. This is the reason for the current building of investment cities and the push to bring investment to the country.

The Problems of Saudization and a Sizeable Population of Unemployed Youth: Saudis under the age of eleven make up 38 percent of the population and the Saudi government is concerned about finding jobs for this large group of youth as they mature (Rugh 2002:53). This population group is facing the prospect of unemployment while also searching for identity, as young people are *too young* to remember the days before the oil boom and thus to have experienced KSA in its traditional world. Saudization has been only partially effective. The youth are uninterested in the menial jobs now performed in KSA by foreigners. The young are the face of the twenty-first-century Kingdom, accustomed to modern life and consumerism and in danger of not having the jobs to support that life. Thus, one of the reasons for KSA's aggressive plan to bring business to the country is to provide jobs for this large cohort of youth in danger of becoming disillusioned with the Saudi state.

The Tensions of Islam as Preached by Al-Wahhab: While al-Wahhab's version of Islam is the official doctrine of the Saudi state and serves to legitimize the Saudi royal family's rule, it also creates tension. First, not all Saudis agree with al-Wahhab's teachings. Certainly the Shi'a population disagrees, as the Wahhabi teachings in Islam are a Sunni doctrine not a Shi'i one, and, as a second example, many Sunnis, in the Hijaz area especially, disagree with the doctrines of al-Wahhab and consider this the religion of the people of Nejd and consequently as foreign to Hijazi ways of practicing Islam. Thus, it creates some tension within the country for al-Wahhab's teaching of Islam to be the official religion of the state. Also, since it is a conservative form of Islam, many of its believers dislike change that they think goes against the doctrines of al-Wahhab. The towns and villages of the countryside are populated with conservative Saudis for whom change has been rapid, and they question further change. Remember that many Saudis over the age of fifty did not attend school. Consequently, as Saudis told me, change in the Kingdom must come slowly. They understand that outsiders are frustrated by the slow pace of change in what is perceived as a backward state, but those outsiders do not understand the social dynamics in KSA where pushing for change could cause a backlash.

Internal Tension and Dissatisfaction with the Royal Family: In an earlier section, I discussed resistance movements. There is dissatisfaction with the royal family and the current Saudi government among groups of Saudis inside the country and outside as well. These tensions need to be managed in order for the current government structure to remain or even for the current structure to change, slowly, into another form. In the last few years the government has been allowing limited local elections. This could be a possible first step toward wider use of elections. The Majlis al-Shūrā is currently an advisory body but could be reshaped into a national, elected, legislative body with the power to make law. The 2011 demonstrations for democracy in other Middle Eastern states have not, as of this writing, spilled over into Saudi Arabia where the popularity of King Abdullah and his recent declaration of substantial additional dollars for social programs are likely to ward off serious calls for government change in the near future. However, some Saudis discuss a future in which KSA might become a democracy, and they study the existing forms of democracies to determine what form might fit them best.

Negative Image in the World: There is no question that Saudi Arabia has an image problem. This results from the fact that Osama bin Laden and fifteen of the nineteen hijackers on September 11, 2001, were Saudi and from the continued perceived threat that many in the West see in the spread of the Wahhabi version of Islam around the world. While KSA has been tackling this image problem by sending its citizens abroad to tell its story and by creating media campaigns to spread its message, the message is not reaching the international community. This problem will continue to plague the country well into the twenty-first century. The image problem is fueled by what are perceived as human right violations in the treatment of women and the closed nature of the society.

Strengths

Intact Social Fabric: In KSA, a base of cultural norms exists to which most in the society subscribe, and as a consequence, there is little socially deviant behavior. For example, compared to my home in the United States, there is relatively little theft and individuals leave rooms in their homes unlocked and available to visitors. Saudis continue to follow the social rules of hospitality and protection for guests. This social fabric is a strength—one the Saudis do not wish to lose as their country changes.

Lack of Colonialism: There are no structures of colonialism to unravel in KSA. It is an Arab and Islamic state developed on an Arab and Islamic cultural and religious base.

Ample Available Resources: Obviously, the resources that KSA is able to amass and enjoy as a result of its oil reserves is an advantage few other nation-states in the world experience. The difficulty for the Saudi government and the Saudi royal family is to determine how to use these resources wisely.

Economic and Political Stability: KSA is a large nation-state in a central, strategic location in the Middle East, and its ability to remain politically moderate and economically stable since the 1930s is an advantage many other states do not enjoy. This increases its value on the world stage and allows it to develop programs at home.

Importance in the Middle East and the World: As a consequence of its oil resources and its stability, it is an exceedingly important ally in the Middle East for many Western powers.

In this book, I have woven together personal reflection, research by other anthropologists, and my own anthropological analysis in order to tell the story of a modern Kingdom in its historical context and its ongoing cultural complexity with the intention of providing a nuanced and detailed view of Saudi Arabia as well as of some of the mechanisms of globalization. How will KSA handle change in the twenty-first century? KSA has entered this century with a clear set of strengths with which to tackle its corresponding issues. Anthropologists possess no crystal ball that allows them to predict the future, but it is my hope that the future will be bright for the Kingdom of Saudi Arabia, the Middle East, and the interconnected world of which they are a part.

References

Abram, Simone. 2003. "Anthropologies in Policies, Anthropologies in Places: Reflections on Fieldwork 'In' Documents and Policies." In *Globalisation: Studies in Anthropology*, edited by T. H. Eriksen, 138–157. London: Pluto Press.

Abu-Lughod, Lila. 1989. "Zones of Theory in the Anthropology of the Arab World." *Annual Review of Anthropology* 18:267–306.

———. 2002. "Do Muslim Women Really Need Saving? Anthropological Reflections on Cultural Relativism and Its Others." *American Anthropologist* 104 (3): 783–790.

Akers, Deborah Sue. 2001. "The Tribal Concept in Urban Saudi Arabia." PhD Dissertation, Ohio State University.

Al-Dosary, Adel S., and Syed Masiur Rahman. 2005. "Saudization (Localization)—A Critical Review." *Human Resource Development International* 8 (4): 495–502.

Al-Enazy, Askar Halwan. 2002. "The International Boundary Treaty" (Treaty of Jeddah) Concluded between the Kingdom of Saudi Arabia and the Yemeni Republic on June 12, 2000. *The American Journal of International Law* 96 (1): 161–173.

Al-Farsy, Fouad. 1982. *Saudi Arabia: A Case Study in Development*. London: Kegan Paul International.

———. 1990. *Modernity and Tradition: The Saudi Equation*. London: Knight Communications.

Al-Hariri-Rifai, Wahbe, and Mokhless Al-Hariri-Rifai. 1990. *The Heritage of the Kingdom of Saudi Arabia*. Washington, DC: GCG Publications.

Al-Hemaidi, Waleed Kassab. 2001. "The Metamorphosis of the Urban Fabric in an Arab-Muslim City: Riyadh, Saudi Arabia." *Journal of Housing and the Built Environment* 16 (2): 179–201.

Al-Rasheed, Madawi. 1991. *Politics in an Arabian Oasis: The Rashidis of Saudi Arabia*. London, New York: I. B. Tauris.

———. 1998. "The Shi'a of Saudi Arabia: A Minority in Search of Cultural Authenticity." *British Journal of Middle Eastern Studies* 25 (1): 121–138.

———. 2002. *A History of Saudi Arabia*. Cambridge, UK: Cambridge University Press.

———. 2007. *Contesting the Saudi State: Islamic Voices from a New Generation*. Cambridge, UK: Cambridge University Press.

Al-Sharideh, Khalid A. 1999. "Modernization and Socio-Cultural Transformation in Saudi Arabia: An Evaluation." PhD dissertation, Kansas State University.

al-Zirkili, K. 1972. *al-Wajiz fi sirat al-makil 'abd al-'aziz* [A short account of the life of King Abd al-Aziz], Beirut: Dar al-Ilm.

Aleid, Salem E. A. 1994. "The Role of Traditional Material Culture in Contemporary Saudi Arabia: The Traditional Courtyard House as Exemplar." PhD dissertation, Department of Art Education, Ohio State University.

Ali, Abdullah Yusuf, trans. and comm. n.d. *The Meaning of the Glorious Quran*, vol. 2. Cairo: Dar Al-Kitab Al-Masri.

Almohsen, Mohsen A. 2000. "An Exploratory Study of the Views of Modernization of Educated Saudi Women." University of Pittsburgh.

AlMunajjed, Mona. 1997. *Women in Saudi Arabia Today.* London: Macmillan.

Alsharekh, Abdullah M. 2002. "An Archaeological Study of Stone Structures in Northeast Riyadh, Saudi Arabia." *Adumatu* 5 (January): 35–68.

Altorki, Soraya. 1986. *Women in Saudi Arabia: Ideology and Behavior among the Elite.* New York: Columbia University Press.

Altorki, Soraya, and Donald P. Cole. 1989. *Arabian Oasis City: The Transformation of Unayzah.* Austin: University of Texas Press.

Andreosso-O'Callaghan, Bernadette, and Wei Qian. 1999. Technology Transfer: A Mode of Collaboration between the European Union and China. Europe-Asia Studies 51(1): 123–142.

Appadurai, Arjun. 1996. *Modernity at Large: Cultural Dimensions of Globalization.* Minneapolis: University of Minnesota Press.

———. 2001. "Grassroots Globalization and the Research Imagination." In *Globalization,* edited by A. Appadurai, 1–21. Durham, NC: Duke University.

Arab Law Quarterly. 2001. "The Endeavours of Gulf Countries to Meet WTO Requirements." *Arab Law Quarterly* 16:49–54.

Arebi, Saddeka. 1994. *Women and Words in Saudi Arabia: the Politics of Literary Discourse.* New York: Columbia University Press.

Asad, T. 1986. *The Idea of an Anthropology of Islam.* Washington, DC: Georgetown University Press.

Baer, Robert. 2003. *Sleeping with the Devil.* New York: Crown.

Bahgat, Gawdat. 1999. "Education in the Gulf Monarchies: Retrospect and Prospect." *International Review of Education* 45 (2): 127–136.

Bates, Daniel G., and Amal Rassam. 2001. *Peoples and Cultures of the Middle East.* Upper Saddle River, NJ: Prentice Hall.

Business Monitor National. 1997. *Saudi Arabia.*

Buyandelgeriyn, Manduhai. 2008. "Post-Post-Transition Theories: Walking on Multiple Paths." *Annual Review of Anthropology* 37:235–250.

Champion, Daryl. 1999. "The Kingdom of Saudi Arabia: Elements of Instability within Stability." *Middle East Review of International Affairs* 3 (4) 49–73.

———. 2003. *The Paradoxical Kingdom: Saudi Arabia and the Momentum of Reform.* New York: Columbia University Press.

Clark, Arthur P., and Muhammad A. Tahlawi, eds. 2006. *A Land Transformed: The Arabian Peninsula, Saudi Arabia and Saudi Aramco.* Dahran, Saudi Arabia: The Saudi Arabian Oil Company (Saudi Aramco).

Cole, Donald Powell. 1975. *Nomads of the Nomads: The Al Murrah Bedouin of the Empty Quarter.* Chicago: Aldine.

———. 2003. "Where Have the Bedouin Gone?" *Anthropological Quarterly* 76 (2): 235–267.

Comaroff, Jean, and John Comaroff. 2001. *Millennial Capitalism and the Culture of Neoliberalism.* Durham, NC: Duke University Press.

Comaroff, John. 1996. "Ethnicity, Nationalism, and the Politics of Difference in an Age of Revolution." In *Politics of Difference: Ethnic Premises in a World of Power*, edited by Edwin N. Wilmsen and Patrick McAllister, 162–183. Chicago: University of Chicago Press.

Council on Foreign Relations. 2008. "Gaining on Competitiveness." *Foreign Affairs* 87 (3): Special Section 1, p.2.

Library of Congress. 2007. "Library of Congress Country Studies: Saudi Arabia." In *Library of Congress Country Studies.* Washington, DC: Library of Congress.

Dent, Christopher M. 2003. "Transnational Capital, the State and Foreign Economic Policy: Singapore, South Korea and Taiwan." *Review of International Political Economy* 10 (2): 246–277.

Edelman, Marc, and Angelique Haugerud, eds. 2005a. *The Anthropology of Development and Globalization: From Classical Political Economy to Contemporary Neoliberalism.* Malden, MA: Blackwell.

———. 2005b. "Introduction: The Anthropology of Development and Globalization." In *The Anthropology of Development and Globalization*, edited by Marc Edelman and Angelique Haugerud, 1–74. Malden, MA: Blackwell.

Ende, Werner. 1997. "The Nakhawila, a Shite Community in Medina Past and Present." *Die Welt des Islams* 37 (3): 263–348.

Erikson, Thomas Hylland. 2003. *Globalisation: Studies in Anthropology.* London and Sterling, VA: Pluto Press.

Escobar, Arturo. 1991. "Anthropology and the Development Encounter: The Making and Marketing of Development Anthropology." *American Ethnologist* 18 (4): 658–682.

Esteva, Gustavo. 1992. "Development." In *The Development Dictionary: A Guide to Knowledge as Power*, edited by W. Sachs. London: Zed Books.

Evans, Peter. 1997. "The Eclipse of the State? Reflection on Stateness in an Era of Globalization." *World Politics* 50 (Oct.): 67–87.

Falvo, Daniel J. 2000. "On Modeling Balinese Water Temple Networks as Complex Adaptive Systems." *Human Ecology* 28 (4): 641–649.

Fandy, Mamoun. 1999. *Saudi Arabia and the Politics of Dissent.* New York: Palgrave.

Ferguson, James. 1999. *Expectations of Modernity: Myths and Meanings of Urban Life on the Sambian Copperbelt.* Berkeley: University of California Press.

———. 2002 (originally published in 1999). "Global Disconnect: Abjection and the Aftermath of Modernism." In *The Anthropology of Globalization*, edited by Jonathan X. Inda and Renato Rosaldo, 135–153. Malden, MA: Blackwell.

Finan, T. J., and E. R. Al-Haratani. 1998. "Modern Bedouins: The Transformation of Traditional Nomad Society in Al-Taysiyah Region of Saudi Arabia." In *Drylands: Sustainable Use of Rangelands into the Twenty-First Century*, edited by. Victor R. Squires and Ahmed E. Sidahmed, 345–368. Rome, Italy: International Fund for Agricultural Development.

Fischer, Michael M. J. 2007. "Culture and Cultural Analysis as Experimental Systems." *Cultural Anthropology* 22 (1): 1–65.

Foucault, Michel. 1972. *The Archaeology of Knowledge and The Discourse on Language.* New York: Pantheon.

Friedman, Jonathan, ed. 2003. *Globalization, the State, and Violence.* Walnut Creek, CA: Alta Mira Press.

Gardner, Andrew. 2003. "The New Calculus of Bedouin Pastoralism in the Kingdom of Saudi Arabia." *Human Organization* 62 (3): 267ff.

———. 2005. *City of Strangers: The Transnational Indian Community in Manama, Bahrain.* PhD Dissertation. University of Arizona.

Gogte, Vishwas. 2000. "Indo-Arabian Maritime Contacts during the Bronze Age: Scientific Study of Pottery from Ras al-Junayz (Oman)." *Adumatu* 2 (July): 7–14.

Grace, Robert. 2007. "Saudis Seek Investors for 'Plastic Valley.'" *Plastic News* 19 (19).

Graeber, David. 2002. "The Anthropology of Globalization (with notes on neomedievalism, and the end of the Chinese model of the nation-state)." *American Anthropologist* 104 (4): 1222–1227.

Habib, John. 1978. *Ikhwān, Ibn Sa'ud's Warriors of Islam: The Ikhwān of Najd and Their Role in the Creation of the Sa'udi Kingdom, 1910–1930.* Leiden: Brill.

Halliday, Terrance C., and Bruce G. Carruthers. 2007. "The Recursivity of Law: Global Norm Making and National Lawmaking in the Globalization of Corporate Insolvency Regimes." *American Journal of Sociology* 112 (4): 1135–1202.

Hannerz, Ulf. 2002 (originally published 1989). "Notes on the Global Ecumene." In *The Anthropology of Globalization*, edited by Jonathan X. Inda and Renato Rosaldo, 37–45. Malden, MA: Blackwell.

Harvey, David. 2000. *Spaces of Hope.* Berkeley: University of California Press.

———. 2005. *A Brief History of Neoliberalism.* Oxford: Oxford University Press.

Hassan, Fekri A. 2000. "Holocene Environmental Change and the Origins and Spread of Food Production in the Middle East." *Adumatu* 1:7–28.

Heady, H. F. 1972. Ecological Consequences of Bedouin Settlement in Saudi Arabia. In *The Careless Technology: Ecology in International Development*, edited by M. T. Farvar and John P. Milton. Garden City, NY: The Natural History Press.

Hegghammer, Thomas. 2006. "Terrorist Recruitment and Radicalization in Saudi Arabia." *Middle East Policy* 13 (4): 39–60.

Hertog, Steffen. 2007. "Shaping the Saudi State: Human Agency's Shifting Role in Rentier-State Formation. *International Journal of Middle East Studies* 39:539–563.

———. 2008. "Petromin: The Slow Death of Statist Oil Development in Saudi Arabia." *Business History* 50 (5): 645–667.

———. 2009. "A Rentier Social Contract: The Saudi Political Economy since 1979." *Middle East Institute Viewpoints: The Kingdom of Saudi Arabia, 1979–2009: Evolution of a Pivotal State.* www.mei.edu.

———. 2010. *Princes, Brokers and Bureaucrats: Oil and the State in Saudi Arabia.* Ithaca: Cornell University Press.

Heyman, Josiah McC., and Howard Campbell. 2009. "The Anthropology of Global Flows: A Critical Reading of Appadurai's 'Disjuncture and Difference in the Global Cultural Economy.'" *Anthropological Theory* 9:131–148.

Hoffman, Lisa, Monica DeHart, and Stephen J. Collier. 2006. "Notes on the Anthropology of Neoliberalism." *Anthropology News* 46 (September): 10–11.

Holland, J. H. 1993. *Adaptation in Natural and Artificial Systems.* Cambridge: MIT Press.

Humphrey, C. 2002. *The Unmaking of Soviet Life: Everyday Economies after Socialism.* Ithaca, NY: Cornell University Press.

Huntington, Samuel. 1996. *The Clash of Civilizations: Remaking the World Order.* New York: Simon and Schuster.

Inda, Jonathan Xavier, and Renato Rosaldo. 2002a. "Introduction: A World in Motion." In *The Anthropology of Globalization: A Reader*, edited by Jonathan X. Inda and Ronaldo Rosaldo, 1–34. Malden, MA: Blackwell.

———, eds. 2002b. *The Anthropology of Globalization: A Reader.* Malden, MA: Blackwell.

Inkpen, Andrew C., and Steven C. Carroll. 1998. "Trust, Control and Learning in Joint Ventures: A Theoretical Framework." *Journal of International Management* 4:1–20.

Jordan, Ann T. 2003. *Business Anthropology.* Long Grove, IL: Waveland Press.

Kapiszewski, Andrzej. 2001. *Nationals and Expatriates: Population and Labour Dilemmas of the Gulf Cooperation Council States.* Reading, UK: Ithaca Press.

Kauffman, S. 1993. *The Origins of Order: Self-Organization and Selection in Evolution.* Oxford: Oxford University Press.

Kennedy, David, and Hamed Qatamin. 2001. "Nabataean Archaeology from the Air." *Adumatu* 4 (July): 21–40.

Knauft, Bruce. 2002. "Critically Modern: An Introduction." In *Critically Modern: Alternatives, Alterities, Anthropologies,* edited by B. Knauft, 1–54. Bloomington: Indiana University Press.

Koraytem, Thabet. 2000. "The Islamic Nature of the Saudi Regulations for Companies." *Arab Law Quarterly* 15:63–69.

Kostiner, Joseph. 1993. *The Making of Saudi Arabia, 1916–1936.* Oxford: Oxford University Press.

Lancaster, William. 1997. *The Rwala Bedouin Today.* Long Grove, IL: Waveland Press.

Lauziere, Henri. 2000. "On the Origins of Arab Monarchy: Political Culture, Historiography, and the Emergence of the Modern Kingdoms in Morocco and Saudi Arabia." Ph D dissertation, Simon Fraser University.

Lewellen, Ted. 2002a. *The Anthropology of Globalization: Cultural Anthropology Enters the 21st Century.* Westport, CT: Bergin & Garvey.

———. 2002b. "Groping Toward Globalization: In Search of an Anthropology without Boundaries." *Reviews in Anthropology* 31: 73–89.

———. 2006. "The Anthropology of Development and Globalization: From Classical Political Economy to Contemporary Neoliberalism." *American Anthropologist* 108 (1): 240–242.

Louër, Laurence. 2008. "The Political Impact of Labor Migration in Bahrain." *City and Society.* 20 (1): 32–53.

Long, David E. 1997. *The Kingdom of Saudi Arabia.* Gainesville: University Press of Florida.

———. 2010. Oil and State in Saudi Arabia by Steffen Hertog, a Review. *Middle East Journal.* 672–673.

Longva, Anh Nga. 1997. *Walls Built on Sand.* Boulder, CO: Westview Press.

———. 2006. "Nationalism in Pre-Modern Guise: The Discourse on Hadhar and Badu in Kuwait." *International Journal of Middle Eastern Studies* 38:171–187.

Looney, R. 2004. "Can Saudi Arabia Reform its Economy in Time to Head Off Disaster?" *Strategic Insights* 3 (1). www.ccc.nps.navy.mil/si/2004.

Luciani, Giacomo. 1995. "Resources, Revenues, and Authoritarianism in the Arab World: Beyond the Rentier State?" In *Political Liberalization and Democratization in the Arab World: Theoretical Perspectives,* edited by Rex Brynen, Bahgat Korany and Paul Noble. Boulder, CO: Lynne Rienner.

Machado, Kit G. 1989–1990. "Japanese Transnational Corporations in Malaysia's State Sponsored Heavy Industrialization Drive: The HICOM Automobile and Steel Projects." *Pacific Affairs* 6 (4): 504–531.

Mansi, Ayman. 2009. "SAGIA Driving Saudi Arabia's Ambitious 10x10 Economic Development Strategy." *Dinar Standard* 30 (October). http://www.dinarstandard.com/intraoic/SAGIA030608.htm.

Masry, Abdullah Hassan. 1962. "The Ancient and Historic Legacies of Saudi Arabia." In *Saudi Arabia and Its Place in the World.* Riyadh, Kingdom of Saudi Arabia: Ministry of Information.

Mejcher, Helmut. 2004. "King Faisal Ibn Abdul Aziz Al Saud in the Arena of World Politics: A Glimpse from Washington, 1950–1971." *British Journal of Middle Eastern Studies* 31 (1): 5–23.

Meschi, Pierre-Xavier. 1997. "Longevity and Cultural Differences of International Joint Ventures: Toward Time-Based Cultural Management." *Human Relations* 50 (2): 211–228.

Middle East Policy. 2006. "Document: Terms of Saudi Arabia's Accession to the WTO." *Middle East Policy* 13 (1): 24–27.

Moaddel, Mansour. 2006. "The Saudi Public Speaks: Religion, Gender, and Politics." *International Journal of Middle Eastern Studies* 38:79–108.

Moore, Mick. 2004. "Revenues, State Formation, and the Quality of Governance in Developing Countries." *International Political Science Review* 25 (3): 297–319.

Musil, Alois. 1928. *The Manners and Customs of the Rwala Bedouins*. New York: Charles Crane.

Nagy, Sharon. 2000. "Dressing Up Downtown: Urban Development and Government Public Image in Qatar." *City and Society* 12 (1): 125–147.

———. 2006. "Making Room for Migrants, Making Sense of Difference: Spatial and Ideological Expressions of Social Diversity in Urban Qatar." *Urban Studies* 43 (1): 119–137.

———. 2010 "Social Diversity and Change in the Form and Appearance of the Qatari House." *Visual Anthropology* 10 (2): 281–304.

Nawwab, Ismail I., Peter C. Speers, and Paul F. Hoye (eds.). 1995. *Saudi Aramco and Its World: Arabia and the Middle East*. Dhahran, Saudi Arabia: The Saudi Arabian Oil Company.

Ong, Aihwa. 2006. *Neoliberalism as Exception: Mutations in Citizenship and Sovereignty*. Durham, NC: Duke University Press.

Onley, James. 2004. "Britain's Native Agents in Arabia and Persia in the Nineteenth Century." *Comparative Studies of South Asia, Africa and the Middle East* 24 (1): 129–137.

Okruhlik, Gwenn. 1999. "Rentier Wealth, Unruly Law, and the Rise of Opposition: The Political Economy of Oil States." *Comparative Politics* 31 (3): 295–315.

Pew Forum on Religion and Public Life. 2009. "Mapping the Global Muslim Population: A Report on the Size and Distribution of the World's Muslim Population." In *Pew Forum on Religion and Public Life Publication*, 202 ff. Washington, DC: Pew Charitable Trusts.

Philby, H. 1952. *Arabian Jubilee*. London: Hale.

Ramady, Mohamed A. 2005. "Components of Technology Transfer: A Comparative Analysis of Offset and Non-offset Companies in Saudi Arabia." *World Review of Science, Technology and Sustainable Development* 2 (1): 72–91.

Rashid, Nasser Ibrahim, and Esber Ibrahim Shaheen. 1987. *King Fahd and Saudi Arabia's Great Evolution*. Joplin, Missouri: International Institute of Technology, Inc.

Rostow, Walt Whitman. 1960. *The Stages of Economic Growth: A Non-Communist Manifesto*. Cambridge, UK: Cambridge University Press.

Ruggie, John. 1998. *Constructing the World Polity*. London: Routledge.

Rugh, William A. 2002. "Education in Saudi Arabia: Choices and Constraints." *Middle East Policy* 9 (2): 40–55.

SAGIA. 2009. "Saudi Raises the Standard." In *Think: Global Issues in Perspective*, vol. 11. The Heymersh, Britford, Salisbury SP5 4DU, UK: Camel Publishing Ltd.

———. 2009 Presentation. May, Riyadh, Saudi Arabia.

Said, Edward W. 1978. *Orientalism*. New York City: Vintage.

Saleh, Mohammed Abdullah Eben. 1998. "Transformation of the Traditional Settlements of Southwest Saudi Arabia." *Planning Perspectives* 13:195–215.

———. 2000. "Value Assessment of Cultural Landscape in Al 'Kas Settlement, Southwestern Saudi Arabia." *Ambio* 29 (2): 60–66.

Sassen, Saskia (ed.). 2002. *Global Networks Linked Cities.* New York City: Routledge.

Schuler, Randall S. 2001. "Human Resource Issues and Activities in International Joint Ventures." *International Journal of Human Resource Management* 12:1–52.

Schwab, Klaus, Michael E. Porter, and Sala-I- Xavier Martin. 2007. "Global Competitiveness Report 2007–2008." *World Economic Forum.* New York: Palgrave Macmillan.

Sernau, Scott. 2009. *Global Problems: The Search for Equity, Peace, and Sustainability.* Boston: Pearson Education Inc.

Shaker, Fatina Amin. 1972. "Modernization of the Developing Nations: The Case of Saudi Arabia." PhD dissertation, Purdue University.

Shane, Scott, and Robert F. Worth. 2010. "Earlier Flight May Have Been Dry Run for Plotters." *New York Times.* November 2.

Sowayan, Saas Abdullah. 1985. *Nabati Poetry: The Oral Poetry of Arabia.* Doha-Qatar: The Arab Gulf States Folklore Centre.

Tabutin, Dominique, Bruno Schoumaker, Godfrey Rogers, Jonathan Mandelbaum, and Catriona Dutreuilh. 2005. "The Demography of the Arab World and the Middle East from the 1950s to the 2000s: A Survey of Changes and a Statistical Assessment." *Population* 60 (5/6): 505–615.

Taecher, K. R. 2003. "Myths and Realities about Unemployment in Saudi Arabia." *Saudi-American Forum,* 30 March. www.saudi-american-forum.org/newsletters.

Teitelbaum, Joshua. 2005. "Terrorist Challenges to Saudi Arabian Internal Security." *The Middle East Review of International Affairs* 9 (3) Article 1. http://meria.idc.ac.il/journal.

Thompson, Andrew. 2000. *Origins of Arabia.* London: Stacey International.

Toth, Anthony B. 2005. "Tribes and Tribulations: Bedouin Losses in the Saudi and Iraqi Struggles over Kuwait's Frontiers, 1921–1943." *British Journal of Middle Eastern Studies* 32 (2): 145–167.

Tsing, Anna L. 2002. "The Global Situation." In *The Anthropology of Globalization,* edited by Jonathan X. Inda and Renato Rosaldo. Malden, MA: Blackwell.

Twal, Ghazi O. 2009. *Discover the Kingdom of Saudi Arabia.* Riyadh: King Abdulaziz Public Library.

Tylor, Edward B. 1871. *Primitive Culture.* London: Murray Press.

van der Meulen, D. 1957. *The Wells of Ibn Saud.* London: John Murray.

Vassiliev, A. 1998. *The History of Saudi Arabia.* London: Saqi Books.

Vidal, F. S. 1975. *Bedouin Migrations in the Ghawar Oil Field, Saudi Arabia.* Miami: Field Research Report: Aramco.

Yamani, Mai. 1997. "Changing the Habits of a Lifetime: The Adaptation of Hejazie Dress to the New Social Order." In *Languages of Dress in the Middle East,* edited by N. Lindisfarne-Tapper, 55–66. Richmond, UK: Curzon in association with School of Oriental and African Studies.

———. 2000. Changed Identities: *The Challenge of the New Generation in Saudi Arabia.* London: The Royal Institute of International Affairs.

Yavas, Ugur, Dogan Eroğlu, and Sevgin Eroğlu. 1994. "Sources and Management of Conflict: The Case of the Saudi-U.S. Joint Ventures." *Journal of International Marketing* 2 (3): 61–82.

Index

Abaya, 1, 139, 156
  at TCHSA, 104–105
  Western women in, 129
'Abd (slave) affiliation, of
  hadar, 71
Abd al-Wahhab, Muham-
  mad ibn, 41
Abdul Aziz Al Saud. *See* Ibn
  Saud
Abdullah (King), 39, 47–48
Abha, 41
Abram, Simone, 12
Abu Bakr, 37, 142
Abu-Lughod, Lila, 21–22,
  25, 160–161
Adaptive systems, 77,
  164–165
Ad-Dir'iyah, 127
Advanced Electronics Com-
  pany (AEC), 89, 90,
  164–165
Advice and Reform Com-
  mittee, 152
Afghanistan, impact of poli-
  tics in, 151–152
Agricultural city-states, 35
Agriculture
  of bedu, 61
  of hadar, 70, 72
  in 'Unayzah, 119
Air transportation, 75–76
Alcohol, serving of, 131
Al-Dosary, Adel, 79
Al-Haratani, E. R., 116–117
Al-Hasa, 41, 55

Al-Hemaidi, Waleed Kasab,
  123
'Ali, 142, 143
Al Jazeera, 26
Allah, 143
Allegiance Commission, 49
Alliances
  bedu movement and, 63
  marriage and, 43
Al-Malaz neighborhood, in
  Riyadh, 123
Al-Masari, Muhammad, 25
Almohsen, Moshen, 161
Almsgiving, 144
Al Murrah tribe, 56–57, 67
Al Oni, poem by, 67
al-Qa'ida, 152
Al-Rasheed, Madawi, 38,
  47, 56, 65, 67, 69, 70,
  153, 154
Al-Saud family, 38, 40, 43,
  150
al-Sharq al-Awsat, 25
Al-Shaykh family, 43
Al-Sudayri family, 47
Al-Taysiyah area, bedu life
  at, 112–113, 116
Alternative energy sources,
  78
Altorki, Soraya, 70, 71, 73,
  118, 119, 120, 122,
  123, 156–158
al-'Uliyya US military mis-
  sion, 152
Aluminum, 93

al-'Utaibi, Juhaiman, 150
al-Wahhab, Muhammad ibn
  Abd, 17, 38–39, 41, 46,
  49, 91, 146, 169
Al-Zabirah, 113, 115
Animals
  bedu, 56–58, 113–114,
  115
  domesticated, 35
  slaughter of, 144
Anthropology, Western context of, 21–22
Appadurai, Arjun, 13, 14,
  15, 16, 17, 18
  on area studies, 20–21
Arabia
  control of, 37–40
  creation of, 29–33
Arabian American Oil Com-
  pany. *See* Aramco
Arabian Gulf, 30, 50n
Arabian Peninsula
  ethnic groups in, 18
  formation of, 30
  lack of direct foreign control in, 37–38
  oil workers from, 87
Arabian people, Paleolithic
  to CE 600, 34–37
Arabian Shield, 29–30, 32
Arabic Computer Systems,
  89
Aramco, 24, 84–85, 86, 94
  in Al-Hasa, 55
  bedu and, 112

electricity provided by, 88
employees at, 87
Saudization of, 86–87
Area studies, 20–21
Arebi, Saddeka, 159
Arid climate, 34–35
Aristocratic families, bedu, 69
Arranged marriages, 157, 158
Art
bedu, 67
rock, 35
Artisans, hadar, 70
Ashair. *See* Ashira
Ashira, 66
Ashura, 143
Asia, oil workers from, 87
Asir region, 41, 55, 122–123

Bahrain
democracy in, 24–25
Ibn Saud in, 39
kingdoms in, 35
oil in, 83
Bani Khalid confederation, 40, 70
Banks, branches by gender, 132
Baylor College of Medicine, 99
Bedu (bedouin pastoralists), 3, 55–68, 112–118
hadar and, 68–69
land and, 67–68, 166
lifestyle of, 111–126
women of, 64, 134–135
Behavior
five pillars of faith and, 148
Qur'an-based, 149
for raiding, 59
of women, 158
Behavioral norms, 128–138
Beit (residential tent), 66
bin Laden, Osama, 25, 151, 152, 170
Biomedicine, 99–100. *See also* Health care; Tertiary Care Hospital of Saudi Arabia
Boeing, 89
Borders, 41
Branding, wasm, 35
Bretton Woods Agreement, 14–15, 16–17

Britain, 38, 40–41, 87, 89
Bronze Age, Indus Civilization of, 34
Bureaucracy, 45–46
fragmentation in, 24
in Islam, 145
Burials, 144, 148–149
Business
hours of, 137
personalization of relationships in, 91
Business laws, 91
Buyandelgeriyn, Manduhai, 10

Calendar, Islamic time and, 137
California Arabian Standard Oil Company (CASOC), 84, 94
Caliphs, 37, 142
Camels
bedu use of, 56–58
caravan trade, of 'Unayzah, 72–73
domestication of, 35
symbolic importance of, 115
Camps, bedu, 115
Capital, for business, 92
Capitalism, neoliberal, 14
Caravans, 56, 61, 62
Carroll, Steven, 78
Carruthers, Bruce, 16
CASOC. *See* California Arabian Standard Oil Company
Cash economy, bedu and, 116
CBAY, 101
Center-periphery models, 13
Chiefdoms, 38
Chinese investment, 93
Cisco, 89
Cities
bedu in, 117
economic, 92–94
City-states, agricultural, 35
Classes. *See* Social classes
Cleveland Clinic, 100
Climate, 30–31, 33–34, 54
Clothing, 1–2, 128–129
Coed university, 93
Coffee-making ceremony, 65

Cole, Donald, 56–57, 59, 67, 68–69, 70, 71, 73, 117, 118, 119, 120, 122, 123
College of Petroleum and Minerals (Dhahran), 85
Collier, Stephen J., 14
Colonization and colonialism, 38, 81, 165, 170
Commerce, 4
Commercial law, 91–92
Committee for the Order of the Good and the Forbidding of Evil, 42, 45
Communities, bedu, 117–118
Competitiveness measures, 90
Complex adaptive systems, 163–164. *See also* Transnational complex adaptive systems
Constitution, Qur'an, 149
Construct culture, viability of, 17–18
Consumerism, 47
Contract enforcement, 90
Core-periphery model of global development, 17
Criticism, 25
Crops, 120, 167
Cultural evolution, 13
Culture
bedu, 67–68, 69, 117–118
camel, 57
change in, 166–167
hadar, 118–123
national, 18
oil wealth in rentier theory and, 24
regional, 53–55
in Saudi Arabian state, 18
at TCHSA, 101–108
traditional Arabian, 38
traditional Saudi, 51–74
"Custodian of the Two Holy Mosques," Abdullah as, 48

Dammam, 55
Dedan Kingdom, 35
Defense, Ministry of, 46
DeHart, Monica, 14
Democracy, demonstrations for, 24–25, 169–170

Demonstrations
  for democracy, 24–25
  by Shi'a Muslims,
    146–147
Dependency theory, 13
Descent, 134
Deterritorialism, 17–18
Developing nations, transnational partnerships in,
    81
Development
  need for economic,
    168–169
  strategies for, 46, 112, 166
Development theory, 13
Dhahran, 55, 87
Diet, 130, 144
Diffusion, 13
Dilmun Kingdom, 35
Dissent, 25, 149–150,
    152–154
Diversification, need for
    economic, 168–169
Diversity
  regional, 53–55
  regional loyalties and,
    43
Divine revelations, to
    Muhammad, 37
Dollar (U.S.), Saudi currency tied to, 102
Domesticated animals, 35
Dowry, 157
Dress, 44–45
Dress code, at TCHSA,
    104–105
Driving, by women, 132–134,
    156

Ease of doing business,
    report on, 90
Eastern Province, 83, 88
Eastern region, 4
Economic activities, in
    world cities, 17
Economic cities, 49, 92–94
Economic development, offset investment and,
    88–90
Economic goals, 92–94
Economies
  of bedu and hadar, 68–69
  globalization and, 13

Economy, 47. *See also* Globalization
  of hadar cities, 70
  modernization process
    and, 77–78, 165
  stability of, 170
Edelman, Marc, 9
Edomites, 36
Education, 43, 167
  bedu, 114
  for girls, 47, 52, 82, 87
  improvement in, 90
  national identity and, 119
  of Saudi nationals in oil
    industry, 85–86
  transnational partnerships in, 81–83
  in 'Unayzah, 119
  for women, 158
Egyptians, 40, 82, 161
Electricity, 76
  Aramco provision of, 88
Electronics, 90
Elementary school, population in, 82
Emirates, 38
Emirates Aluminum, 93
Emirs, 37, 119
Employees. *See also* Jobs
  at Aramco, 87
  of oil industry, 84, 85
Employment, of bedu, 112,
    115
Empty Quarter. *See* Rub al-
    Khali
Energy sources, alternative,
    78
Engineering training, 90
England. *See* Britain
Environment, of bedu, 56,
    63–64
Eritrea, oil workers from, 87
Esteva, Gustavo, 10
Ethnocentric ideas, Orientalism and, 20
Evans, Peter, 16
Evolution theories, 13
Expatriates
  in Saudi Arabia, 79
  as workers, 79, 90, 116,
    120

Face covering, 129–130. *See
  also* Veiling

Fahd, 47–48
Faisal, 41, 46, 81
  assassination of, 47
  power struggle with
    Saud, 46–47
  Tertiary Care Hospital of
    Saudi Arabia and, 97
Faith, profession of, 143
Fakhd, 66
Falvo, Daniel, 163
Family
  in bedu camps, 115–116
  of hadar, 72
  importance of, 52,
    134–136
Fandy, Mamoun, 152, 153
al-Faqih, Saad, 25
Farmers. *See* Agriculture
Fasting, 138, 139, 144
Fatwa, 145
Feminism, Western and
    Saudi, 161
Ferguson, James, 10, 11
Finan, T. J., 116–117
Finances, traditional, 45–46
Financial sector, 90
First World War, Ibn Saud
    and, 40–41
Fischer, Michael, 18
Five Pillars of Islam,
    143–144, 148
Five-year plans, 46, 77, 78
Foreign Affairs, Ministry of,
    46
Foreign affairs directorate, 46
Foreign Capital Investment
    Law, 91
Foreign control, of Arabian
    Peninsula, 37–38
Foreign investment, attracting, 90–92
Foreign partnerships, 77, 164
  offset programs with,
    89–90
  in oil industry, 83–85
  Saudization and dissolving of, 86–87
  in training programs,
    85–86
Foreign population, 4
Foreign workforce, 78, 80
Foucault, Michel, 19
Fragmentation, in state
    bureaucracy, 24

France, 84, 89, 91
Free trade, 15
Fukhud (lineages), 66
Funerals, 148–149

Gabila (tribe), Shammar as, 65–66
GATT. *See* General Agreement on Tariffs and Trade
GCC. *See* Gulf Cooperative Council countries
GCI. *See* Global Competitiveness Index
Gender. *See also* Men; Women
separation of sexes and, 131–134, 154–155
General Agreement on Tariffs and Trade (GATT), 15
General Petroleum and Mineral Organization. *See* Petromin
Geographical area
scholarship based on, 20–21
study of subjects beyond, 17–18
Geography
climate and, 33–34
creation of Arabia, 29–33
creation of land, 32–33
Al Murrah knowledge of, 68
Geopolitical economy, TCHSA and, 108
Ghawar oilfield, bedu tribes at, 112
Gifts, 47
Girls, education for, 47, 82, 87
Glaciers, 30
Global Competitiveness Index (GCI), 90
Global development, core-periphery model of, 17
Globalization, 4, 11–18, 163–164
anthropological debate over, 15–18
defined, 12–14
of resistance, 152–154

Government, 23
Arabian traditional, 38
as complex organization, 19
resistance to, 25, 150–151
Graduated sovereignty, 16, 17
Graeber, David, 15, 16
Grand Mosque, takeover of, 150
Graves, 144
Grazing, bedu, 113–114
Great Britain. *See* Britain
Great Nefud, 33
Great Rift Valley, 30
Great Ulamas Committee, 91
Gulf Cooperative Council (GCC) countries, 88–89
Gulf of Aden, 30
Gulf states, nationalization of workforce in, 80
Gulf War, Saudi resistance and, 151–152

Hadar (settled peoples), 3, 56, 68–69, 70–73, 118–123, 167
Hail, 61, 69, 94
Hajj, 144, 148
Hajj terminal, at Jiddah international airport, 76
Halliday, Terrance, 16
Hamula, 66
Hanafi school of interpretation, 145
Hanbali Islamic school of thought, 91, 145
Haram, 106
Harb tribe (bedu), 112–113
Harem, use of term, 21–22
Harvey, David, 14
Hashemite rulers, in Hijaz region, 41, 54
Haugerud, Angelique, 9
Heady, Harold, 55
Health care
bedu, 115
for oil employees, 87
at Tertiary Care Hospital of Saudi Arabia, 97–110
transnational partnerships in, 99–100
Western standards in, 107

Healthgulf, 100
Hegghammer, Thomas, 152
Henna, women and, 135, 136
Herding
by bedu, 114, 116
of sheep, 57–58
Hertog, Steffen, 24
Higher education, 82
High school, population in, 82
Hijaz region, 37, 39, 40, 41, 54, 81–82, 146
Hoffman, Lisa, 14, 15
Hofuf, 33, 55
Holy sites, 146
Homes. *See* Housing
Homo erectus, 34
Horse, bedu use of, 58
Hospital Corporation of America (HCA), 98, 99
Hospitality, 45, 130
bedu, 64–65, 69
majlis and, 43–44
Housing
electricity and, 76
of hadar, 70–71
for oil employees, 87
in Riyadh, 123
for Saudi youth, 125–126
for TCHSA, 98, 104
in 'Unayzah, 121
Human rights, 48
Humans, Paleolithic to CE 600, 34–37
Humphrey, Caroline, 10
Husayn, Sharif, 38
Hussein, Imam, 142–143
Hussein, Saddam, 143, 151
Hybrid culture, at TCHSA, 101–108

Ibn amm (unit of cousins), 66
Ibn Saud (Abdul Aziz Al Saud), 3, 40–46, 49–50, 81
bedu and, 68
death of, 46
sons as Kings, 47
Ibn Saud, Muhammad, 38, 39, 41
Ibn Sbayyil, 62–63

Identity
    bedu, 118
    national, 119
    of Saudi youth, 124,
        125–126
    tribal, 67
Ikhwān (brotherhood), 42,
    68, 150
Illiteracy, 82
Image, of Saudi Arabia, 170
IMF. *See* International Mon-
    etary Fund
Immigration policies (KSA),
    17
Income, outflow of, 79
Inda, Johathan X., 12, 14
India, oil workers from, 87
Indus Civilization, 34
Industry. *See also* Oil industry
    offset programs in non-
        oil-related, 89
Inkpen, Andrew, 78
Institute for Management
    Development, 90
International human rights
    conference, 48
International Monetary
    Fund (IMF), 15, 90
Internet sites, for health
    care, 100
Investment
    Chinese, 93
    foreign ownership in, 92
    offset, 88–90
    in plastics, 93
Iranian revolution, 47
Iraq
    Saudi Arabia and, 26
    Saudis in, 39
    threat of invasion by, 151
Iraq War, 5, 26
Ireland, oil workers from, 87
Irrigation, ancient, 35
Islam, 39, 119
    bedu and, 68
    branches of, 142–143
    Faisal and, 47
    holy sites of, 4, 146
    Ibn Saud and, 41–42
    importance of, 146–149
    interpretation of, 144–145
    origins of, 37
    pillars of faith and,
        143–144

in Saudi Arabia, 146–149
    tensions of, 169
    use of term, 21–22
Islamic Empire, 37
Islamic law, 144–145
Islamic schools, 82
Islamic time, 137–138
Isthmus of Suez, 30
Italy, oil workers from, 87

Japan, oil partnerships with,
    84
Jiddah, 76, 156, 157, 161
Jizan Economic City, 93–94
Jobs. *See also* Employees
    from offset programs, 90
    for Saudis, 95
    Saudization for, 78
    willingness to undertake,
        79–80
Jubayl, 73
Judicial reforms, 91
Justice, Ministry of, 47

KAEC. *See* King Abdullah
    Economic City
Karbala, pilgrimage to, 143
Kelberer, John J., 86
Khadija, 37
Khadiri (nontribal) affiliation,
    of hadar, 71
Khalid, 47
Khalifa (caliph), 142
Kharijites, 143
al-Khobar, 55
Khobar Towers, bombing of,
    150
Khomeini, 146
Khuthayla, Majid bin, 42
Kilwa, 35
Kinda Kingdom, 35
King
    contact with, 44
    dissenter views of, 153
King Abdullah Economic
    City (KAEC), 17, 93
King Abdullah University
    for Science and Tech-
        nology, 90, 93
    campuses by gender and,
        132
Kingdom of Saudi Arabia
    (KSA), 3, 4–5, 42–43
Kingdoms, 35

King Fahd University of
    Petroleum and Miner-
        als, 85–86
King Faisal University Fac-
    ulty of Medicine and
    Medical Sciences
    (Dammam), 85
Kinship, 66
    bedu organization
        through, 65–67
    segmentary lineage as, 21
Knauft, Bruce, 12
Knowledge, modernization
    and, 77
Koraytem, Thabet, 91
KSA. *See* Kingdom of Saudi
    Arabia
Kuwait, hadar and bedu in,
    69
Kuwaitization, 80

Labor, of hadar, 72, 120–121
Lancaster, William, 21, 56
Land. *See also* Public Land
    Decree (1953)
    bedu and, 67–68, 112, 113
    creation of Arabia, 29–33
    tribal rights over, 112
Law of the Provinces, 48
Laws
    for business, 91
    Islamic, 144–145
Leadership, female, at
    TCHSA, 106
Legal system, moderniza-
    tion of, 90
Levant, 34
Lewellen, Ted, 13, 14
Lifestyle, 167–168
    adjustment to, 139
    bedu people, change
        and, 112–118
    in cities, 127–128
    hadar people, change
        and, 119
Lineage
    of mother and father, 134
    segmentary, 21
Literacy, 82
Literature, bedu poetry and,
    65
Lockheed Martin, 89
London, dissidents in,
    152–153

Long, David, 24
Lucent Technologies, 89
Luciani, Giacomo, 23, 24

Macroeconomic stability, of
    KSA, 90
Madinah, 4, 37, 39, 146
Madinah Economic City,
    93–94
Mahmood, Saba, 161
Mail rules, after September
    11 terrorist attacks, 108
Majlis, 43–45
Majlis al-ahli (council of the
    people), 41
Majlis al-Shūrā (consultative
    council), 41, 48, 169
Makkah, 4, 37, 39, 146
    caravan routes through,
        61
    pilgrimage to, 144, 148
    seizure of mosque at, 47
Male-female interaction, at
    TCHSA, 106
Maliki school of interpreta-
    tion, 145
Marriage
    arranged, 157, 158
    bedu, 69
    polygyny and, 43
    relationships of partners,
        134
Mars, 93
McDonald's, gender separa-
    tion in, 131
Medain Saleh, 36
Media treatment, of Mus-
    lim women, 160–161
Medical facilities. See also
    Tertiary Care Hospital
    of Saudi Arabia
    for oil employees, 87
Medical schools, 98–99
Medical system, creation of,
    97–110
Medunet, 100
Men
    clothing of, 2, 129
    gender separation and,
        131–132
    hadar, 72
MENA. See Middle East
    North Africa region

Menial jobs, lack of interest
    in, 79
Merchants
    contributions by, 45
    hadar, 70
Meschi, Pierre-Xavier, 109
Mesopotamia, Saudis in, 39
Metals, 34
Microsoft academy, 94
Middle East
    Muslims in, 141
    Saudi importance in, 170
    Western views of,
        138–139
Middle East North Africa
    region (MENA), 90
Midian Kingdom, 35
Migration, Paleolithic, 34
Militants, 151–152
Military, of Ibn Saud, 41
Military academies, 81–82
Ministry of Defense, 46
Ministry of Finance, 45–46
Ministry of Foreign Affairs,
    46
Ministry of Justice, 47
Ministry of Planning, 46
Modernization, 3, 4–5
    defined, 9, 11, 168
    under Faisal, 46–47
    five steps of, 163–164
    rate of, 75–83
Modernization theory, 9–11
Modesty, in clothing,
    128–129, 139
Monotheism, 39
Morgan, Lewis H., 13
Mosques, at TCHSA, 104
Movement
    annual cycle of, 61–64
    by Al Murrah tribe, 56–57
Muhammad, 37
    branches of Islam after,
        142–143
Multicultural mix, at
    TCHSA, 102–108
    raiding vs. war by, 59
    skills of, 68
Musil, Alois, 60
Muslims, 37. See also Islam
    percentage of world pop-
        ulation as, 141
    Wahhabi Islam in Saudi
        Arabia and, 146

Mutawa'a, 42, 149

Nabataean Kingdom, 36
Nagy, Sharon, 80
Naif (Prince), 79–80
Naimi, Ali, 86
National Commercial Bank,
    89
National culture, unity of, 18
National Dialogue sessions,
    48
National Guard, bedu in,
    112, 115
National Human Rights
    Commission, 48
National identity, 119
National Industrialization
    Company, 89
Nationalization, of work-
    force in Gulf states, 80
Nation-state. See also State
    contemporary signifi-
        cance of, 16–17
    of Saudi Arabia, 21
Natural resources, 81. See
    also Resources
Neighborhoods, in
    'Unayzah, 121–122
Nejd, 41, 46, 49, 54
    clothing and, 45
    families, 43
    village life in, 70
Neoliberal capitalism, 14
Niqab, 1–2
Nokia, 89
Nomads, 61, 69, 112. See
    also Bedu
Norms, 128–138
    value to women, 159,
        160
North Africa, Muslims in,
    141
Northern Region, 55
Nursing shortage, after Sep-
    tember 11 attacks, 108

Oases, agriculture in, 61
Occupational groups, hadar,
    70
Occupations
    foreign, 37–38, 49
    hadar, 71, 120–122
Offset investment, 88–90
Oil embargo (1973), 46

Oil industry, 4. *See also*
  Aramco; Petromin
  complex adaptive sys-
    tems and, 83–88, 164
  economic diversification
    and, 168–169
  economic impact of,
    87–88
  Faisal and, 46
  foreign partnerships in,
    83–85
  Saudi oil business and, 84
  Saudization of, 86–87
  sources of workers for, 87
  wealth from, 167
  wealth in rentier theory,
    24
Oil resources, 76, 78
Okruhlik, Gwenn, 24
Omanization, 80
Ong, Aihwa, 16, 17
OPEC. *See* Organization of
  Petroleum Exporting
  Countries
Organization of Petroleum
  Exporting Countries
  (OPEC), 17
Organizations, suprana-
  tional, 14–15
Orientalism, 19–22
  in anthropology, 21–22
  Western view of King-
    dom and, 138–139
Orientalism (Said), 19
Orient/Oriental, use of
  terms, 19
Ottoman Empire, 37–38, 39

Paleolithic period, Arabians
  of, 34–35
Palestinians, as oil workers,
  87
Partnerships, 77–78
  in health care, 99–100
  oil, 83–85
  for TCHSA, 98
  transitional, 77
  transnational, 78
Pastoralists, 35, 111, 115.
  See also Bedu
Patient-care assistants, at
  TCHSA, 103
Patrilineage, 134

Patrilineal endogamy, of
  Shi'a, 142
Pay scales, by nationality, at
  TCHSA, 102–103
People, 3
  Paleolithic to CE 600,
    34–37
People of the book, 143
Periphery, new concept of, 17
Persian Gulf, 50n
Personalization, of business
  relationships, 91
Petromin, 24, 85
Philippines, oil workers
  from, 87
Pilgrimage, to Makkah, 144,
  148
Pillars of faith, 143–144
Planning, Ministry of, 46
Plastics, investment in, 93
"Plastics Valley," 93
Poetry
  by Al Oni, 67
  bedu, 60, 62–63, 65, 67
Political issues, rentier state
  theory and, 23–25
Politics
  dissent and, 149–150
  polygyny and, 43
  religion and, 39
  of research, 25–27
  stability of, 170
  women's behavior and,
    157–158
Polygyny, 43
Population
  of bedu, 55
  under eleven, 78
  foreign, 4
  peoples in, 3
  of Riyadh, 75
  urban, 76
Possessions, bedu, 67–68
Power struggle, between
  Saud and Faisal, 46–47
Prayer, 106, 137, 144
Prince Abdul Aziz bin Mousaed Economic City, 94
Private business develop-
  ment, 94. *See also* Business; Investment
Publications, pro-Saudi government, 153
Public behavior. *See* Behavior

Public education, for girls, 82
Public Land Decree (1953),
  112, 113, 117, 166
Pyxis, 101

Qabili (tribal) affiliation, of
  hadar, 71
Qatar
  bedu in, 69
  housing in, 123
  Ibn Saud in, 39
  nationalization of work-
    force in, 80
Qur'an, 143, 144–145

Radicals, 153
Rahman, Abdul, 40
Rahman, Syed, 79
Raiding
  by bedu, 58–60, 69, 114
  camels in, 57
  end of, 60
  poetry reflecting values
    of, 60
  timing of, 59
Rain, bedu and, 59
Ramadan, 138, 148
Ramady, Mohamed, 90
Rasheed family, of Sham-
  mar tribe, 61
Rashid, Muhammad ibn,
  40, 41
Rashidi emirate, 40
Rashidi family, 40, 69
Ras Tanura, 55
Raytheon, 89
Real estate, Saudi youth
  and, 125–126
Recreation, for oil employ-
  ees, 87
Redistribution of wealth, 44
Red Sea, 30, 32, 37
Reforms, by Fahd, 48
Regional diversity, 53–55
Regional dress, 44–45
Regulation, of international
  financial activities, 14
Religion, 141–149. *See also*
  Islam
  Ibn Saud and, 41
  politics and, 39
Relocation, of bedu, 112
Rentier state theory, 23–25
Research, politics of, 25–27

Reserve National Guard, 68
Residence patterns, 156–157
Resistance, 25, 150–151
    Afghani politics, first
        Gulf War, and,
        151–152
    globalization of, 152–154
Resources, 23, 42–43, 170
Revenues, 47
Rights, of married women,
    157
Rituals, of Shi'a, 142–143
Riyadh, 3, 26, 167
    changes in, 123
    lifestyle in, 127–128
    population of, 75
Riyadh Chamber of Com-
    merce, women in, 161
Roads, 75
Rocks, 31, 32–33, 35
Rosaldo, Renato, 12, 14
Royal family, dissatisfaction
    with, 169–170
Rub al-Khali (Empty Quar-
    ter), 33, 55, 56, 57
Ruggie, 16
Rwala Bedouins, 21

SAGIA. *See* Saudi Arabia
    General Investment
    Authority
Said, Edward, 19, 21, 22
Saleh, Mohammed Abdul-
    lah Eben, 122–123
Saline Water Conversion
    Corporation, 79
Salvation, 39
Sanitation, at TCHSA, 105
Saud, power struggle with
    Faisal, 46–47
Saudi Arabia. *See also* King-
    dom of Saudi Arabia
    first state of, 38–39
    second state of, 39–40
    third state of, 40–49
    in WTO, 15
Saudi Arabia General
    Investment Authority
    (SAGIA), 90
Saudi Arabian Airlines
    (Saudia), 89
Saudi Arabian National
    Guard, 42

Saudi Arabian Oil Company
    (Saudi Aramco),
    86–87, 89
Saudi Consolidated Electric
    Company, 88
Saudi Geology Survey
    Bureau, 79
Saudis, harassment after
    9/11, 25–26
Saudization, 77, 78–80, 94,
    169
    of oil industry, 86–87
    at TCHSA, 103, 107–108
Schedules, Islamic time and,
    137–138
Schools, 81–83, 87, 119. *See
    also* Education
Schuler, Randall, 78
Science training, 90
Second Women's Health
    Update Symposia,
    100–101
Secrecy, in rentier states, 23
Sedentary lifestyle, bedu
    and, 114, 115
Segmentary lineage, 21
Segregation of sexes, 158–159.
    See also Gender; Women
September 11, 2001, terror-
    ist attacks, 25, 151, 170
    media treatment of Mus-
        lim women after,
        160–161
    TCHSA and, 108
Settlement, by bedu, 68
Seventh Development Plan,
    94–95
Sexes, separation of, 131–134,
    154–155
Shafi'i school of interpreta-
    tion, 145
Shammar tribe, 43, 46, 61,
    65, 66–67
Shari'a, 42
    bedu and, 68
    Sunni interpretation of,
        145
Sharifian family, 37, 40
Shaykhs, 45
Sheep herding, automobile
    and, 57–58
Shi'a Muslims, 25, 55,
    142–143, 146
    riot by, 47

Shi'at 'Ali, 142
Shipping, in KAEC, 93
Shopping, for oil employees,
    87
Shopping centers, 1–3
Siemens, 89
Singapore, partnering with,
    93
Skills, bedu, 68
Slaves, hadar, 70
SOCAL, 83–84, 94
    training of Saudi nation-
        als by, 85–86
Social classes, of Hail, 69
Society, 3–4, 170
    bedu, 55–68
    hadar, 70
    Islam and technology
        and Islam vs. United
        States technology, 47
    pre-oil, 139
Southeast Asia, graduated
    sovereignty in, 16
Sowayan, Saad Abdullah,
    59, 65
Sri Lanka, oil workers from,
    87
Standard Oil Company of
    California. *See* SOCAL
State. *See also* Nation-state
    first Saudi, 38–39
    second Saudi, 39–40
    third Saudi, 40–49
State formation, 111–112,
    166
State owned oil company,
    Aramco as, 85
State system
    bedu and, 68
    move from tribal system,
        42
Stone carvings, 35
Subay' tribe, 70
Subsidies, in rentier states,
    23–24
Subsistence strategy, bedu
    culture and, 117
Succession, future, 49
Sudan, oil workers from, 87
Suez, Isthmus of, 30
Sunni Muslims, 24–25, 55,
    142, 143
    interpretation of reli-
        gious law by, 145

Wahhabi doctrine and, 147
in western region, 4
Supranational organizations, 14–15, 16–17
Supreme Council of Petroleum and Minerals Affairs, 87
Suq (market), 72, 79
Syria, Saudis in, 39

Taliban, 151
Taurus Mountains, 30
Taxation, rentier state theory and, 23
TCHSA. *See* Tertiary Care Hospital of Saudi Arabia
Teachers, Egyptians as, 82
Technology, 47
Technology transfer, modernization and, 77
Tectonic plates, movement of, 29–30
Television service, 47
Tents, bedu, 64
Terrorist attacks, in United States, 25, 151
Tertiary Care Hospital of Saudi Arabia (TCHSA), 5, 7n, 79, 97–110, 164
Textuality, of Orientalism, 20
Thamuc Kingdom, 35
Time schedule
Islamic, 137–138
Muslim/Western at TCHSA, 106
Tombs, Nabataean, 36
Topography, 32
Tourism, 128
Towns, 35, 70, 167
Tracking, by Al Murrah tribesmen, 68
Trade, 4, 35
ancient, 34
in annual movement, 62
of bedu, 61
caravan, 56
neoliberal capitalism and, 14
Western-style, 11
Traditional lifestyles, bedu people and, 112–118

Training, 77, 164
for business, 77
of Saudi nationals in oil industry, 85–86
Transnational complex adaptive systems, 18–19, 163
in medical care, 97–110
nation-state in, 21
in oil industry, 94
Transnational partnerships, 77–78
in developing nations, 81
in education, 81–83
in health care, 99–101
Transportation, 43
bedu, 114
improvements in, 91
by men, 132–134, 136
modernization of, 75–76
seating by gender on, 132
Tribalism, 21, 49
move to state system, 42
Tribes, 38, 39
bedu, 63, 112–113, 166
kinship organization and, 65–67
land rights of, 112, 113
Al Murrah, 56–57
Truman, Harry, 10
Turki (son of Abdullah), 39–40
Tuwaiq Escarpment, 32
Tylor, Edward B., on culture, 13, 17

'Ulama', 48, 144–145
dissenters' views on, 153
Ottomans and, 39
Umra (pilgrimages), 144, 148
'Unayzah, 70, 72, 118–122
Underdeveloped, use of term, 10
Unemployment, 79, 169
Unification, strategies for, 43–45
United States
Aramco and, 84–85
Cold War alliance with, 49
as node rather than center of development, 17
offset programs with, 89
Saudi students in, 82

Saudi travel for medical care and, 108–109
TCHSA partnership with, 98
terrorist attacks in, 25, 151
Universities, 49, 82
campuses by gender, 132
King Abdullah University for Science and Technology, 90, 93
University of Petroleum and Minerals, 82
Unmarried women, veiling of, 157–158
Urban areas
animals from, 67–68
bedu in, 117–118
population of, 76
Urban settlements, in Al-Hasa, 55

Values
bedu, 69, 118
hadar, 70
pre-oil, 139
Saudi, 128–138
Veiling, 45, 128–129, 157–159
Vidal, F. S., 112
Villages, 167
Asir region towns and, 122–123
of hadar, 70
Violent militancy, 150–151
Viripatrilocality, 156–157
Volcanic activity, 30, 32

Wahba Crater, 32
Wahhabi Islam, 55, 124, 145, 146, 153
TCHSA culture and, 107
Warriors, raiding by, 60
Wasm marks, 35
Water
in Arabia, 29, 30
bedu and, 59, 62, 114–115
in 'Unayzah, 119–120
Water wheels, at wells, 62
Wealth
from oil, 4, 167
redistribution of, 44

Weddings, 158. *See also* Marriage
  gender segregation at,
    154–155
West. *See also* Modernization theory
  as anthropological context, 21–22
  contractual oil relationships with, 83
  feminism in, 161
  TCHSA characteristics and, 107
  view of Kingdom in, 138–139
  women's roles and, 159–160
Western region, 4
Wives, multiple, 43, 135–136
Women, 154–161
  analysis of Saudi women writers, 159–160
  attire at TCHSA, 104–105
  bedu, 64
  changing rules for, 159
  clothing of, 1–2, 128–129
  education for, 47, 52, 158
  Egyptian, 161
  face covering by, 1–3
  gender separation and, 131–132, 154–155
  hadar, 72
  leadership at TCHSA by, 106
  media treatment after 9/11, 160–161
  in Riyadh, 123
  social trends among, 156–157
  veiling of, 45
Work
  by bedu women, 64
  family responsibilities and, 136–137
Workers, gender separation and, 132
Work ethic, 79
Workforce
  foreign, 78, 80
  Saudi replacing non-Saudi, 94–95
  Saudis and expatriates in, 79
  workers for oil industry, 87
World Bank, Ease of Doing Business Index, 90
WorldCare, 100
World culture, theories about, 13
World Economic Forum, Global Competitiveness Index (GCI), 90
World system theory, 13
World Trade Organization (WTO), 15, 49, 91

Yamani, Mai, 124–125
Yemen, 36
  al-Qa'ida in, 152
Youth
  identity and change by, 124–126
  unemployment of, 169

Zagros Mountains, 30
Zakat (tax), 39